Blackout

Black

Chris Lamb

out

The Untold Story of
Jackie Robinson's
First Spring Training

University of Nebraska Press : Lincoln & London

Portions of chapter 1 originally appeared as "'I Never Want to Take Another Trip Like This One': Jackie Robinson's Journey to Integrate Baseball," in *Journal of Sport History* 24.2 (Summer 1997): 177–91. Portions of chapter 7 originally appeared as "What's Wrong with Baseball: The *Pittsburgh Courier* and the Beginning of Its Campaign to Integrate the National Pastime," in *Western Journal of Black Studies* 29 (2000): 48–50.

Library of Congress Cataloging-in-Publication Data
Lamb, Chris, 1958–
Blackout : the untold story of Jackie Robinson's first spring training / Chris Lamb.
p. cm.
Includes bibliographical references and index.
ISBN 0-8032-2956-9 (cloth : alkaline paper) –
ISBN 0-8032-0431-0 (electronic)
1. Robinson, Jackie, 1919–1972. 2. Baseball players – United States – Biography. 3. Discrimination in sports – United States. I. Title.
GV865.R6L36 2004 796.357'092–dc22 2004000614

Contents

Illustrations

Acknowledgments

I began working on this book during the late winter of 1993 when I was working as a columnist for the *Daytona Beach News-Journal* in Daytona Beach, Florida. Bill Schumann, a local radio newscaster, told me that Jackie Robinson played his first spring training in Daytona Beach. I had lived in Daytona Beach for a few years, and I thought I knew everything about baseball. Why did I not know about this story? I thought Schumann was merely passing on a sort of local legend, the kind that all towns and cities wrap themselves in. But Schumann was right and I was wrong – and I thank him for letting me know that the integration of baseball passed through Daytona Beach.

As I tried to verify the story I learned that the only thing I really knew about baseball was its statistics, and the only thing I knew about Robinson was that he broke Major League Baseball's color line when he played with the Brooklyn Dodgers in 1947. You can neither know baseball nor understand it – in any large sense, anyway – without first understanding Robinson and what he as a person and a player meant to baseball and society. The story of the integration of baseball began not in 1947 but in 1946. There has never been a more important six weeks in baseball history than the Dodgers' spring training in 1946.

Once I learned that Schumann was right, I told him I wanted to write a column describing the story. I asked Bill if he knew anyone who had been living in Daytona Beach in 1946. Schumann gave me the phone number of Billy Rowe, the retired columnist and photographer for the *Pittsburgh Courier*, which had crusaded to integrate baseball in the 1930s and 1940s. Rowe and the *Courier*'s influential sportswriter Wendell Smith had accompanied Robinson during the Dodgers' spring training in Daytona Beach. Rowe told me about the pressures faced by Robinson, his wife Rachel, and Johnny Wright, a second prospect that Dodgers' president Branch Rickey had signed for the organization's top minor league team, the Montreal Royals. Rowe told me about Robinson's courage and how Robinson struggled throughout the spring but then emerged triumphantly. I am thankful to the late Billy Rowe for the conversation we had ten years ago.

As I left journalism to work toward my doctorate at Bowling Green State University, I brought the Robinson story with me, though it stayed tucked away as I worked on my dissertation. At one point I wrote a class paper on the press coverage of Robinson's first spring training, research that required me to examine dozens of newspapers. I am indebted to the Bowling Green State University interlibrary loan staff for their assistance. In the years that followed, as I began carving out the story of Robinson's first spring training, I relied on the library staffs at Old Dominion University and the College of Charleston. I also searched through archival newspapers held at the University of Florida and the Library of Congress. These newspaper articles supplied the real story of baseball's first integrated spring training. I relied heavily on other sportswriters for the telling of this story, both for what they said and for what they did not say.

The late Billy Rowe provided the flesh and bones of this story. But I could not have given the story meaning, nor could I have enjoyed telling it as much as I have, without the cooperation of other men such as Sam Lacy, sportswriter for the *Baltimore Afro-American*, who, like Wendell Smith, was instrumental in the campaign to integrate baseball. Smith and Lacy, both of whom worked in relative anonymity for black newspapers, were good enough to work for the finest American newspapers but, like the athletes they covered, were denied the opportunity because of the color of their skin. At long last they were inducted into the National Baseball Hall of Fame for their contributions as sportswriters. Sam Lacy's contributions to this book were invaluable. I also want to mention the assistance of Shirley Povich, another Hall of Fame sportswriter, and Mel Jones, former general manager of the Montreal Royals who provided his personal insights about what happened in 1946.

I also relied on two other sportswriters, Lester Rodney and Bill Mardo, who worked for the Communist Party's *Daily Worker* and whose contributions to the integration of baseball have largely been ignored. During the 1930s the U.S. Communist Party dedicated considerable time and effort through the *Daily Worker*'s pages to the cause of integrating baseball. The *Worker*, with Rodney as sports editor, published more articles about the need to integrate baseball than any other newspaper. When Rodney was serving in the U.S. Army, Mardo acted as the *Worker*'s sports editor and covered the 1946 spring training with unmatched candor and depth. In fact, the *Worker* did better than any other newspaper in reporting the story truthfully. I appreciated the opportunity to interview both men.

Researching this book frequently brought me back to Florida, often to mine the newspaper microfilms at the University of Florida. I visited Daytona Beach and Sanford, where Robinson played for two days before being run out of town by local townspeople. Alicia Clarke, director of the Sanford Museum, provided me with information about Robinson's time in Sanford. This included clippings by the *Sanford Herald*'s former sports editor Julian Stenstrom, who wrote approvingly of Sanford's contribution to baseball, ignoring the unpleasant truth. In a very real sense, Stenstrom's denial that the city discriminated against Robinson represents a nation's denial of racism. His sin of omission is the nation's sin of omission. It is for that reason – and others – that this story needs to be told.

As I began my research, I learned that Glen Bleske, a former colleague at the *Daytona Beach News-Journal*, who had, like me, left newspaper work for academia, was also examining press treatment of Robinson. He and I collaborated on two journal articles about the integration of baseball – one for *Journalism History* and another for *Nine: A Journal of Baseball History and Social Policy Perspectives*. While attending a conference on Jackie Robinson in 1996, I met Kelly Rusinack, who wrote her master's thesis on the U.S. Communist Party's campaign to integrate baseball. Kelly and I later collaborated on an article in *Cultural Logic: An Electronic Journal of Marxist Theory and Practice* and a chapter in the book *Take Me Out to the Ballgame*. Bleske and Rusinack each contributed to my understanding of the subject and, in doing so, drew me deeper into the story.

I have also written articles on the integration of baseball for the *Western Journal of Black Studies*, *Journalism and Mass Communication Quarterly*, *The National Pastime*, and the *Journal of Sport History*. All the editors of these journals made suggestions that improved the articles I wrote for them, thus improving the content of this book. I would therefore like to acknowledge Barbara Cloud and Gerald Baldesty of *Journalism His-*

tory; Bill Kirwin of *Nine: A Journal of Baseball History and Social Policy Perspectives*; Jim Neilson of *Cultural Logic*; Lincoln James of the *Western Journal of Black Studies*; Jean Folkerts and Margaret Blanchard of *Journalism and Mass Communication Quarterly*; Mark Alvarez of *The National Pastime*; and David Wiggins of the *Journal of Sport History*.

I would like to thank the research staff at the Baseball Hall of Fame for their help. So many of us rely on the Hall of Fame, and their assistance is always first-rate. I also would like to note the financial support I received from the Communication Department at the College of Charleston and a summer grant I was awarded by the college itself, both of which helped me to work on this book.

I am indebted for the support I received from so many people in taking this manuscript from its rawest form to this book. Aside from those I've already mentioned, many friends and others also read through earlier versions and provided their feedback. I thank people like University of Tennessee professor Paul Ashdown, Drexel University professor Ron Bishop, and College of Charleston professors Vince Benigni and Greg Schmitt. I also appreciate the patience of friends who listened as I carved the book out by talking about it – people like Steve McGookin, Marc Bona, Joe Sharpnack, John Major, Ken Hornack, and Andy Abrams. And, finally, I relied mightily on the input of my parents, Bob and Jean Lamb, and my wife, Lesly, who provided her invaluable support in ways I both can and cannot express.

Blackout

PART
1234

1 2345678910

Fried Chicken and Hard-Boiled Eggs

JACKIE AND RACHEL ROBINSON arrived at Lockheed Terminal in Los Angeles in the early evening of Thursday, February 28, 1946, to board an American Airlines flight to Daytona Beach, Florida. Rachel wore a dyed three-quarter-length ermine coat that Jackie had given her for a wedding present not quite three weeks earlier, a matching black hat, and a brown alligator-skin handbag he had bought her that winter in Venezuela. Although Southern California weather hardly required a fur coat, "that piece of ermine was my certificate of respectability," she later said. "I thought that when I wore it everyone would know that I belonged on the plane, or wherever I happened to be."[1]

As Jackie's mother, Mallie, said good-bye to her son and daughter-in-law, she handed them a shoe box.

"What's this?" Jackie asked.

"It's full of fried chicken and hard-boiled eggs," his mother said.

"Aw, mamma, you shouldn't have brought this," he protested. "They serve food on the plane."

"I know," she answered. "But I just thought something might happen, and I didn't want you starving to death and getting to that baseball camp too weak to hit the ball."[2] Mallie Robinson's experiences in the South had taught her the importance of being self-sufficient. She often told her family: "God bless the child who got's his own."[3] But Jackie and Rachel did not want the shoe box. They knew the stereotype about blacks having picnics on trains and could imagine strangers' disapproving or mocking stares. They also knew, however, that they would disappoint Mallie if they did not accept her gift. So they reluctantly took the shoe box, thanked Mallie, and, in a few minutes, said good-bye.[4]

Rachel later remembered her anxiousness as she and her husband began their journey. "I did have some trepidation about entering the South for the first time," Rachel remembered. "But dressed in my wedding finery and escorted by my strong, handsome, talented husband, I couldn't foresee the need for the odorous chicken as we parted from Mallie. I was focusing my hope that whatever the circumstances, Jack would land a desperately needed job and win a place in the starting lineup."[5]

Jackie Robinson was headed to spring training, hoping to win a spot on the roster of the Montreal Royals, the Brooklyn Dodgers' AAA minor league team. When a few months earlier he had signed with the Royals, he became the first black in organized professional baseball in the twentieth century. Simultaneously, Robinson was transformed into a symbol of black America's long struggle for racial equality. After playing the 1946 season with Montreal, Robinson was promoted to the Dodgers, where the following April he broke Major League Baseball's color line. And it is there, in April 1947, that his story so often begins. Because of all Robinson accomplished from that moment on and all that he has come to represent since, the events before April 1947 have been all too easy to ignore.

But the real story of the integration of baseball had actually begun more than a year earlier, when Robinson boarded that flight to Florida deep in the Jim Crow South. For blacks, the racial climate in the South was tense, unpredictable, and violent. Discrimination was legal and enforced without regard to basic human rights. Whites reinforced Jim Crow laws through threats and physical coercion as well as by taking the law into their own hands.[6] The brunt of these attacks were borne by black war veterans, who, having bravely served in World War II, returned home believing they should be treated with the same respect as other Americans. Instead, a number were lynched "to teach them their place."

In return for fighting and dying for their country, blacks demanded nothing less than the rights guaranteed them in the U. S. Constitution – equal opportunity, equal protection under the law, abolition of public segregation, and the same treatment afforded whites.[7] In his 1945 book, *Rising Wind*, Walter White, chairman of the National Association for the Advancement of Colored People (NAACP), wrote that the war had given American blacks a sense of kinship with other oppressed people in the world. He called on the country to reject the lynchings of returning black soldiers. The United States, White wrote, "could choose between a policy of appeasement of bigots – which course she gives every indication now of following or she can live up to ideals and thereby save herself."[8]

During spring training of 1946 the inequalities and prejudices of baseball converged with those of the country they reflected. Discrimination was so institutionalized that mainstream America gave little thought to such concepts as civil rights or racial equality – especially in the South.[9] In 1944, Swedish sociologist Gunnar Myrdal had published *An American Dilemma*, a groundbreaking study of race relations. So complete was segregation in the South, Myrdal wrote, that "the white Southerner practically never sees a Negro except as his servant and in other standardized and formalized caste situations."[10] Southern newspapers enforced policies that prohibited the publication of photographs of blacks – except for those, as one black writer wrote, "who dangled at the end of ropes over limbs of trees."[11]

The story of Robinson and his first spring training thus reveals an important – and so far neglected – piece of history about the integration of baseball. In doing so, it also reveals a great deal about America as it struggled to correct its contradictory character: preaching equality for all while discriminating against millions of its own. The story of Jackie Robinson's first spring training captures America as it moved, or staggered, toward its promise of equal rights for all. In addition, the drama of baseball's first integrated spring training dramatizes the ways in which the issues of integration, segregation, and civil rights were covered by the nation's black press as well as its white mainstream press.

Both in content and context, the reporting in the mainstream press was limited by a mindset that prevented white reporters, their newspapers, and their readers from appreciating the historical significance of Jackie Robinson's 1946 spring training. To black sportswriters and their readers, however, the story clearly symbolized the hopes and the dreams of integration, not merely on a ball field but in society. Black sportswriters and their newspapers recognized this crucial juncture between the stories of baseball and civil rights and shared it with their readers.[12] Because white America learned little about civil rights from its newspapers, it failed to understand that America was changing – and thus was ill-prepared for the civil rights movement.

Baseball was one of the first institutions in postwar America to become desegregated.[13] Baseball was America's national game, and like America itself, it preached that it was a melting pot where everyone, regardless of identity or origin, could succeed, provided they had the talent or determination. The nation's mainstream sportswriters perpetuated this myth, and baseball fans accepted it, not knowing or not

7

caring that talented black ballplayers played in the shadows of white baseball, barred from the game because of an insidious "gentlemen's agreement" that had excluded blacks since the 1880s.

Though most of America did not know it, several sportswriters working for black weeklies and the Communist newspaper, the *Daily Worker*, had campaigned for integration for more than a decade before Montreal signed Robinson in October 1945.The Communists and the radical left would play a part in making the national pastime more democratic. But black and Communist sportswriters understood that they could not end segregated baseball by themselves. Like the leaders of the civil rights movement, they needed the support of white journalists, activists, and politicians. They needed someone like Branch Rickey, the president of the Brooklyn Dodgers, who had the courage, foresight, and clout to force the issue on baseball.

In late August 1945, Rickey summoned Robinson, then playing for the Kansas City Monarchs of the Negro Leagues. Rickey explained that he had been scouting black baseball for the right player and the search had led him to Robinson. Following a three-hour meeting, Rickey signed Robinson to a contract after receiving his assurances that he would have "the guts not to fight back" against racist epithets, spikings, and worse. Rickey told Robinson that if he lost his temper, it would set off race riots in stadiums or simply prove that blacks were too emotional to play in organized baseball.[14] The baseball establishment had long justified segregation by maintaining that blacks lacked the requisite ability and temperament. Rickey and Robinson kept the contract to themselves until Rickey felt the time was right to make the announcement.

On October 23, 1945, Montreal stunned the baseball world by announcing that it had signed Robinson, thus forcing integration on baseball and, by implication, American society itself. "I realize what I'm getting myself into," Robinson told reporters. "I also realize how much it means to me, my race, and baseball."[15] Intelligent and pragmatic, Robinson understood the dangers inherent in challenging segregation on its own ground in Florida. Unlike most blacks, he had been around whites – as a four-sport athlete at UCLA and then as an officer in the U.S. Army. He had faith in his ability as an athlete. He also had faith in Branch Rickey. And, finally, he believed that he was on the side of the

8

angels, that the hand of God was with him, and that he would triumphantly emerge from the challenge.[16]

Unbeknownst to the Robinsons, a few days before their flight departed from California, a race riot had erupted in the small southern town of Columbia, Tennessee. Blacks would read about it in horror over the next few weeks. A black mother and her son, Gladys and James Stevenson, recently discharged from the navy, had gone into the Castner-Knott Shop to complain that a radio she had left for repair was still not working. The repairman, a twenty-eight-year-old white man named William Fleming, resented Mrs. Stevenson's complaint, followed her and James outside, and then slapped and kicked the woman. James Stevenson then pushed Fleming through the store's plate-glass window. A number of white men, including a police officer, then attacked James. When Mrs. Stevenson intervened, the officer struck her over the eye. The Stevensons were arrested and jailed on charges of assault.[17] Fleming, however, was not arrested.

The jailing of the Stevensons did not resolve the tension. Columbia, located near Pulaski, Tennessee, the birthplace of the Ku Klux Klan, had a history of racial violence. Many of the town's three thousand black citizens still remembered the black teenager who in 1933 had been beaten, burned, and hanged by a white mob after being acquitted of raping a white girl.[18] Sheriff J. J. Underwood, hearing rumors that a white mob was forming and a rope had been acquired, called two prominent black citizens and asked for their help in smuggling the Stevensons out of town.[19]

By six o'clock, seventy-five whites had gathered in the city's public square, just a few blocks from the town's black district, known as Mink Slade. Within an hour, white men were knocking on the jail door and demanding the release of the Stevensons. Sheriff Underwood opened the door and, firing a machine gun over the men's heads, ordered the crowd to disband. He arrested two men for not dispersing and threw them in jail for public drunkenness. Hoping to defuse the situation, Underwood then ordered his men to set up a roadblock to keep blacks and whites apart.[20]

Black residents, meanwhile, fearing the worst, met in Mink Slade. A few armed men shot out the streetlights and then waited at store windows, fearful of an attack. When night came, two white police officers, without Underwood's permission, turned their engines off and rolled through the darkened Mink Slade district without identifying themselves. "Here they come!" someone yelled from his position in a store window. The air exploded with gunfire. Black townspeople, some of whom were war veterans, demonstrated that they would fight before seeing another lynching. "We fought for freedom overseas," one black shouted, "and we'll fight for it here!"[21]

Once the shooting began, the white mob ran into Mink Slade with their guns firing. In the aftermath, as blood drained into the street's gutters, the mayor of Columbia asked the governor to send state troopers and the National Guard. Early the next morning, hundreds of law enforcement officers converged on Mink Slade, forced black residents out of their houses, and confiscated their guns and even their jewelry and money. Once Mink Slade was under control, the law enforcement officers then began destroying homes and businesses, shooting out windows, tearing up furniture, burning business records, and scrawling KKK into walls.[22]

Daily Worker reporter Harry Raymond counted thirty-four bullet holes in front of a barber shop. In another shop, every jukebox was smashed and the money removed. A state patrolman's bayonet had been shoved through the music box in a refreshment store and all its beer carted off for a celebration. Raymond described the destruction done to a church: "With fiendishness, these men, sworn to uphold law and order, ripped and tore the chapel draperies. Pieces of wreckage were on top of a Bible on the pulpit."[23]

Over the next two days, dozens of blacks were arrested and charged with inciting a riot and attempted murder. According to one account by a black journalist, "The writ of habeas corpus was virtually suspended. Negroes were arrested without charges, held incommunicado, questioned without benefit of counsel, and detained on excessive bail. . . . The home of virtually every Negro in Columbia and its immediate environs was searched and all firearms taken."[24] The arrests continued throughout the week. About a hundred blacks were eventually arrested and jailed. Not a single white was arrested. While police questioned two suspects, William Gordon and James Johnson, one grabbed a weapon, and when they tried to escape, according to police, the two men were shot to death.[25]

The *Nashville Banner* and other Tennessee newspapers blamed communists and outside agitators like the NAACP for the violence. "We've always treated our niggers nice," a Columbia lawyer said, "and now they turn against us like this."[26] State politicians urged reporters to write that black folks in Columbia would not have acted so violently if it not been for "outside agitation." In an editorial, the *Columbia Daily Herald* wrote: "The white people of the South . . . will not tolerate any racial disturbances without resenting it, which means bloodshed. The Negro has not a chance of gaining supremacy over a sovereign people and the sooner the better element of the Negro race realize this, the better off the race will be."[27]

The Columbia race riot alarmed blacks. "It fulfilled predictions that mob violence would be used after the war to force the Negro back into 'his place,'" *The Crisis*, the organ of the NAACP, said. The publication added that the Columbia race riot revealed a new militancy among black Americans – that even in small communities, blacks did "not intend to sit quietly and let a mob form, threaten, and raid their neighborhoods."[28] Walter White immediately contacted Washington DC and asked the Justice Department to "safeguard the constitutional rights of Negroes against state violation of these rights," a strategy that would become central to the civil rights movement in the 1960s.[29]

NAACP attorney Thurgood Marshall, who later argued *Brown v. Board of Education* in front of the U.S. Supreme Court and then became America's first black Supreme Court justice, agreed to represent the suspects. When he contracted pneumonia, however, he turned the case over to fellow attorneys Alexander Looby, Maurice Weaver, and Leon Ransom. The judge moved the case to nearby Lawrence County, where an all-white jury acquitted twenty-three of the twenty-five suspects charged in the riot. Black newspapers praised the stunning decision. "America justice has triumphed over the klan," White told reporters. In November, Marshall, now recuperated, represented the two suspects who were charged with attempted murder. After a four-day trial, the all-white jury in a neighboring town found one suspect not guilty but the other guilty. Marshall's life in danger, he, like the Stevensons, had to be smuggled out of town for fear he would be lynched.[30]

Unaware of what was unfolding in Columbia, the Robinsons flew over the western deserts, their thoughts focused on what awaited them

in Florida.[31] They had been married on February 10 in a simple cere-
mony at the Independent Church in Los Angeles. After the reception,
they checked into their hotel room on Central Avenue, and, as Rachel
put it, "closed the door on the outer world, all of my fears and doubts
vanished. It was a precious moment filled with feelings of complete-
ness."[32]

For Rachel, spending the spring in Dixie was not the honeymoon
she had dreamed of. She had heard the stories of lynchings but tried to
hide her concern from Jackie. "I was worried because I had heard so
many stories about the treatment of Negroes in the Deep South," she
later said. "I knew how quickly Jack's temper could flare up in the face
of a racial insult." If that were to happen, she did not know whether
they both might be "harmed, or killed, or, at best, we might jeopardize
this opportunity to wipe out segregation in baseball."[33]

Jackie could indeed be fiercely stubborn and temperamental. In August 1943, Robinson, then a lieutenant in the army, was arrested and
then court-martialed for refusing to go to the back of a bus near Fort
Hood, Texas. Black newspapers, such as the *Pittsburgh Courier*, publicized the incident about the onetime college star athlete. Because of his
athletic fame, Robinson had advantages not afforded other blacks facing punishment in the armed services. In fact, given the frequency of
violence against impudent black soldiers, if he had been Joseph Robinson or James Robinson, Jackie might not have survived to face a court-
martial.

Instead, as Jackie Robinson, he was cleared of charges and spared a
sentence in a military jail. During his arrest he had been called a "nigger" by a superior officer and was forced to sit in chains throughout his
trial. In November 1943, he was discharged from the army a changed
man. "He was far more deeply interested now in a personal commit-
ment to the ideal of social justice, especially for blacks," Arnold
Rampersad wrote in his biography of Robinson. "But he had paid a
stiff price in the process."[34] Without any clear direction in his life, he
joined the Kansas City Monarchs in the Negro Leagues the next spring.
If Robinson had not been court-martialed for challenging Jim Crow
laws, he would have remained in the army and would thus have been in
the service, and probably in Europe, when Rickey instructed his scouts

to search for the right man to integrate baseball. Someone else's name would have been typed on that Montreal contract.

About 7 a.m. on Friday, March 1, Jackie and Rachel arrived at the New Orleans airport, having flown through the night from California. After a scheduled four-hour layover, they would fly on to Pensacola in the Florida panhandle for another stop, before going on to Daytona Beach. When Rachel went to find a bathroom, she saw something she had never seen in California: signs that said "White Woman" and "Colored Woman." More indignant than embarrassed, she refused to sacrifice her self-respect and rushed head down into the white ladies' room with such determination that nobody said anything.[35]

When the Robinsons lined up to board the plane, an American Airlines employee instructed them that they had been bumped for military reasons, though the war had been over for six months. The Robinsons decided to get a bite to eat in the airport's restaurant and wait for the next available flight. But they were prohibited from entering the restaurant. They could buy sandwiches, they were told, but they would have to eat them elsewhere. The Robinsons bristled at the suggestion. Now they understood why blacks took food with them when traveling – and why Jackie's mother had given them the shoe box.[36]

After a few hours, the Robinsons, impatient and tired, decided to find a hotel room and wait there for word on their flight. A cab driver took them to a nearby hotel, but when they found that it prohibited blacks he deposited them at a blacks-only hotel. The room was small and cramped, and it reeked. It left a lasting impression on Rachel. "I was almost nauseated. It was a dirty, dreadful place, and they had plastic mattress papers. Lying on the bed was like trying to sleep on newspapers," she remembered.[37] Finally, the Robinsons returned to the airport, where they waited several more hours before boarding their plane.[38]

When the American Airlines plane landed to refuel in Pensacola, a flight attendant asked three passengers – the Robinsons and a Mexican – to exit. In explanation, another employee told them that to counter the weight of additional fuel needed in case of an expected storm, three passengers had to be removed. As the Robinsons listened, Jackie saw three white passengers get on the plane.[39] Frustrated, he felt a mounting rage in the pit of his stomach, but remembering what Rickey had told him – he would have to have "the guts not to fight back" – the ballplayer choked back his anger.[40] The airline told the Robinsons that there would be another plane to Daytona Beach the next day but could not guarantee them seats.[41] Ironically, only a week earlier, American Airlines had apologetically characterized as "clumsy and unusually stupid" an airline advertisement showing a black messenger carrying a tray and speaking in dialect.[42]

Already late for spring training, Jackie did not have the luxury of waiting for an airplane that might, or might not, allow him to board. When he called Rickey's office in Florida, he learned that Rickey was displeased that Robinson was not yet in camp. Rickey's frustrations were passed on to Robinson. Rickey also was frustrated – partly because he did not know what to expect and partly because he did. Rickey, a devout Methodist who refused to attend games on Sundays, believed, like Robinson, that God was with him – though he knew that a lot of mortals were not.

Rickey's success in baseball had a lot to do with his ability to leave as little as possible to chance. "Luck," as he observed, "was the residue of design." As unpredictable as things were in the South, he could make the proverbial playing field slightly more level for Robinson. Rickey sent his top assistant, Bob Finch, on a tolerance campaign to Florida. Knowing that Robinson was going to be the loneliest man in Florida, Rickey considered signing several other blacks but in the end signed only one – Johnny Wright, a pitcher. He also hired Wendell Smith, the crusading sports editor of the *Pittsburgh Courier*, to find accommodations for his two black players and keep an eye on them.

Wright, like his teammate, had problems getting from his home in New Orleans to training camp. After his car broke down, Wright was forced to take the train, where he met Cleveland Indians catcher Dutch Meyer. When Wright identified himself, Meyer told him that Montreal Royals manager Clay Hopper, who was traveling from his home in Mississippi, was sitting in the same car. During a stop, Meyer then introduced Wright to Hopper. Wright remembered a cordial exchange. "He was very nice," Wright told Wendell Smith. "He seemed pleased to meet me."[43] Wright arrived in Sanford, Florida, where the Montreal team began spring training, on Saturday, March 2. But Rickey sent him to Daytona Beach to wait for Robinson. According to the

Chicago Defender, Wright was "hustled away" from reporters and taken to Bethune-Cookman College in Daytona Beach.[44] The *New York Times* reported that both Robinson and Wright were to be secluded from the press until Monday, March 4.[45]

Spring training began Thursday, February 28 – the day the Robinsons left California. When reporters inquired about the absence of Robinson, Rickey – though he knew the real reason – explained that the ballplayer had been detained by bad weather.[46] Sportswriters may have suspected something else but did not investigate. After the third day of practice, Rickey changed his story, saying that Robinson had been bumped from two planes and was now traveling by bus.

Mainstream dailies, for the most part, provided no details about Robinson's travel difficulties. However, the *New York Daily News*, which had long feuded with Rickey and seized opportunities to embarrass him, expressed its suspicions: "There was considerable mystery about [Robinson's] traveling difficulties since he apparently has twice been 'bumped' off his plane . . . at a time when travel priorities have been so relaxed as to preclude such 'bumping.'"[47]

Black newspapers were more detailed. The *Chicago Defender*, which had a national circulation and whose readership and influence surpassed all other black newspapers except the *Pittsburgh Courier*, reported that Robinson and two other passengers had been bumped from an airplane in Pensacola "because the plane could not refuel with the weight of three people aboard."[48] Wendell Smith wrote in the *Pittsburgh Courier* that the Robinsons had twice been bumped. When the Robinsons could not find a train to Daytona Beach, Smith wrote sarcastically that "they reluctantly got on a bus and made the rest of the journey riding 'comfortably' on the back seat in accordance with the jim-crow laws in Dear Ole Dixie."[49]

Meanwhile, having been bumped from two planes, the Robinsons looked for a hotel room in Pensacola to spend the night but could not find one. A bellboy at a whites-only hotel mentioned a black family that might have room for them. The family opened its doors to the Robinsons, but they had no room either. "Their willingness to share made us forget about being sorry for ourselves," Jackie remembered. "Realistically, though, there was just no room for us. We thanked them, telling

15

them we couldn't dream of inconveniencing them and got a ride to the Greyhound bus terminal."[50]

When the Robinsons boarded the Greyhound bus in Pensacola late Friday night, it was nearly empty. They relaxed in reclining seats toward the front of the bus and fell asleep. When additional passengers boarded at the first stop, the driver walked back to Rachel and Jackie, woke them up, and calling Jackie "boy," brusquely ordered them to the back of the bus.[51] Jackie, who had been court-martialed for refusing to comply with the same injunction, begrudgingly obeyed the driver's wishes. "Rae and I had said to each other during the months we had tried to prepare ourselves for exactly this kind of ordeal," he later said. "We had agreed that I had no right to lose my temper and jeopardize the chances of all the blacks who would follow me if I could break down the barriers. So we moved."[52]

For hour after hour, the Robinsons bounced around in the uncomfortable seats in the back of the bus, trying to ignore the nauseating engine fumes wafting through the window. At daybreak, working men in dirty overalls going off to fields and rock quarries crowded into two or three rows at the back of the bus. Everyone was equal at the back of the bus – and nobody recognized Jackie. "Nobody knew who Jack was. Nobody knew anything about it," Rachel recalled. "I was all dressed up, and some of the others were in farm clothes, and we looked different, but no one could identify him."[53]

At some point, Rachel looked at the ermine coat her husband had saved for years to buy her. It was now stained from being pushed against mens' dirty overalls.[54] She began crying – not for herself but for her husband. "She felt badly because she knew I felt helpless," Jackie said. "She hoped I realized that she knew how much strength it took to take these injustices and not strike back."[55] It took the better part of a day to cross the state to Jacksonville, where they waited for hours inside a bus station that Rachel later described as a "wretched hell hole." The segregated section was full of flies and crammed with people. "We waited there for what seemed like an eternity," she said. "As long as I live I think I shall never have a good thought about that place."[56]

Greyhound's racial practices would be questioned by black newspapers at least twice in the days after the Robinsons' trip. One reported that a white bus driver, with the help of two white military police of-

16

ficers, ordered two black noncommissioned officers at the Aberdeen Proving Ground in Aberdeen, Maryland, to move to the back of the bus. When questioned about the incident, a Greyhound official said the bus driver lacked the authority to supercede military law.[57]

In the other, a Greyhound driver in Palmetto, Georgia, ordered two black veterans to give up their seats in the bus's segregated section so two whites could sit rather than stand. A Greyhound official said the driver had shown "bad judgment."[58]

Ninety miles away, Wendell Smith and *Courier* photographer Billy Rowe waited in Daytona Beach. For Smith, the road to integration had been a long and a personal one. His intense feelings about segregated baseball had their roots on a ball field in Detroit, Michigan. As a teenager, Smith pitched his integrated American Legion team to a 1–0 victory in a championship game. After the game, a professional scout signed the losing pitcher and Smith's catcher Mike Tresh, who later played twelve years in the big leagues. "I wish I could sign you too, but I can't," he told Smith. "That broke me up," Smith remembered. "It was then I made a vow that I would dedicate myself and do something on behalf of the Negro ballplayers. That was one of the reasons I became a sportswriter."[59]

After graduating from West Virginia State College, Smith began working for the *Courier*, which was the right newspaper for a journalist interested in racial equality. Smith – first as assistant sports editor and then as sports editor – acted as the newspaper's point man on its baseball crusade. Using his "Sports Beat" column as a pulpit to preach the gospel of integration, he told readers that baseball could never be the national pastime until it allowed blacks to play. If black players were given the opportunity, he said, it would improve the game.

Black sportswriters, however, like black ballplayers, faced their own color line. They were denied press cards, which meant they were prohibited from Major League baseball fields, dugouts, and locker rooms. Undeterred, Smith sought out players and managers in their hotel lobbies. He sent telegrams to league executives and owners and went to their offices, pleading his case over and over. In February 1939, Smith went to see National League president Ford Frick. Frick told Smith that baseball was interested in signing blacks, but this would not happen until white players and managers would accept blacks. Smith then interviewed about fifty big league players and managers. According to Smith, 75 percent supported integration. "Most of the ballplayers said if a Negro had the skills to play in the big leagues," Smith said, "it was okay with them."[60]

In May 1945, Rickey asked Smith to recommend a ballplayer for a Brooklyn team in a new black league, which Rickey had announced would be more credible than black baseball, as it then existed. Smith suggested Robinson. In a subsequent conversation, Smith recalled that Rickey told him: "This may be more extensive than you visualize. I don't know how this is going to turn out."[61] Smith learned that Rickey had signed Robinson long before Montreal made the news public. He remained closer to the story than any other journalist.

During the 1945–1946 off-season, Smith and Rickey corresponded. In one letter, Rickey said that he was keenly aware of the dangers entailed by challenging Jim Crow in the Deep South.[62] In his reply, Smith pledged his cooperation.[63] Smith and *Courier* photographer Billy Rowe thus became the two black ballplayers' constant companions during spring training, sharing the roles of father confessor, chauffeur, and guardian angel. "We were told to take care of them and keep them out of trouble," Rowe said.[64] As a result, Smith and Rowe got closer to the spring-training story than any other journalist, and it was in their columns and photos that the story was best told.

Robinson's arrival in Daytona Beach on Saturday afternoon, March 2, drew little attention from the press in Daytona Beach. Indeed, Smith and Rowe were the only reporters at the bus station. This was not lost on Smith, who wrote: "Although his arrival by bus lacked the usual glamour and sensationalism tendered outstanding sports personalities, Robinson's presence at the station was soon discovered."[65] Word quickly spread. A white man noticed the large crowd and asked a black porter what all the excitement was about. "Don't you know?" the porter said excitedly, "Jackie Robinson is coming in."[66]

Nearly thirty-six hours after they left Los Angeles, the Robinsons, hungry, tired, and angry, ended their journey from one end of the South to the other. They had been bumped from planes, barred from restaurants and hotels, and banished to the back of a bus. As they got off that bus, they saw the friendly faces of Smith and Rowe, but their long journey wore heavily on them. "Well, I finally made it," Robinson snapped, "but I never want another trip like this one."[67]

Rowe, who did not know what the Robinsons had been through, smiled and said, "I'm your chauffeur." Robinson stared at Rowe and then looked at his car and snapped: "I've had better chauffeurs and I've had better cars."[68] As Rowe remembered, "Jackie was very angry about the bus business, but he didn't say anything to anyone" – at least in front of his wife. After Rachel went to bed, he unloaded on Smith and Rowe. "He told Wendell and me, flat out, 'Get me out of here.' . . . We told him, 'You can't do that.' But he was in no mood to listen. He wanted out and that was that. We told him if he did that, he'd blow the whole thing, and he said, 'Just get me out of here!'"[69]

Robinson bitterly recounted, into the early hours of the morning, what he and his wife had been through. "He was very annoyed and hurt," Rowe remembered. "He had been called a 'boy.' This man had become a 'boy.'"[70] Robinson said he did not think he could get a fair tryout in Florida and that he wanted to quit and return to the Negro Leagues. Smith and Rowe talked with him through the night, explaining – as Rickey had – that it was important for him to suffer certain indignities so other blacks could follow him into baseball.

"We talked all night. That calmed him down," Rowe said. "We tried to tell him what the whole thing meant, that it was something he had to do." When the sun came up the next day, Robinson was a different person. His frustrations had subsided, for the moment anyway, but it would not be the last time he considered quitting.[71] He understood, either consciously or not, that he simply could not quit. He spent Sunday, March 3, in Daytona Beach, preparing to begin his spring training tryout the following day in Sanford.

12345678910

Jim Crow Baseball Must End

O
N FEBRUARY 5, 1933, the grand ballroom of New York City's Commodore Hotel crackled with laughter during an evening of songs, skits, and speeches at the tenth annual New York Baseball Writers Association dinner. Sportswriters took turns spoofing everyone from the guest of honor, retired New York Giants manager John McGraw, to the New York Yankees, who had defeated the Chicago Cubs in the World Series the previous October. In addition, the journalists performed their annual minstrel show in front of the all-white crowd of six hundred owners, managers, players, journalists, other dignitaries, and guests. According to *New York Times* sportswriter John Drebinger, the minstrel show was the most entertaining part of the evening.[1]

The Sporting News reported how judges, financiers, industrialists, and men of less lofty position joined with owners, ballplayers, and writers "in the glorification of baseball." In its February 16 issue, *Sporting News* correspondent Dan Daniel, the chapter president of the Baseball Writers Association, reported that a humbled McGraw waxed sentimental about his long career. Other speakers included Branch Rickey, the vice president of the St. Louis Cardinals; toastmaster Bugsy Baer; Philadelphia comic Joe Cunningham; and *New York World-Telegram* sportswriter Heywood Broun, author of the popular column "It Seems to Me."[2]

In his speech, the outspoken Broun responded to a recent editorial in the *New York Daily News*, headlined "What's Wrong with Baseball," that bemoaned the fact that good black players were not eligible for the national pastime.[3] Broun asked his audience why there were no blacks in baseball, though they were allowed in college athletics and professional football: "I can see no reason why Negroes should not come into the National and American Leagues."[4] If former Rutgers University star Paul Robeson was good enough to be named to the team of the greatest college football players ever and Eddie Tolan could represent America at the 1932 Olympic Games, Broun said, then blacks were good enough for the big leagues.[5]

When Broun was told that baseball had no rule or policy prohibiting blacks, he told the story of how McGraw had once tried to sign

Charlie Grant.⁶ A few days before the 1901 season, McGraw, who was then managing Baltimore, tried to finesse his way around baseball's color line by disguising light-skinned second baseman Charlie Grant as a Cherokee Indian by the name of Chief Tokohama. Before Grant could play his first game, however, Chicago White Sox owner Charles Comiskey objected. "I'm not going to stand for McGraw bringing in an Indian on the Baltimore team," he said, calling the ballplayer a "Negro . . . fixed up with war paint and a bunch of feathers." Once exposed, McGraw dropped the idea, and though he kept a list of blacks that he wanted to sign for the Giants, he never pushed the issue again.⁷

During the 1870s and 1880s, a few dozen blacks played in organized baseball. Among them were Moses Fleetwood Walker and his brother, Welday, both of whom played for the Toledo Blue Stockings of the American Association, which was briefly considered one of baseball's major leagues. In the mid-1880s, the baseball establishment came to a so-called gentlemen's agreement to forbid the signing of further black players, thus creating the color line. Segregation in baseball coincided with the implementation of segregation in America.⁸ Jim Crow turned segregation's frustration into unrestrained fury, dismantling Reconstruction reforms and leaving southern blacks vulnerable to mobs and Klan justice. By the end of the century, the U.S. Supreme Court had upheld legal segregation in *Plessy v. Ferguson.*

After Broun's speech, *Daily News* columnist Jimmy Powers asked several league and team officials if they objected to blacks in baseball. National League president John Heydler, New York Yankees owner Jacob Ruppert, Philadelphia Phillies president Gary Nugent, and ballplayers such as Lou Gehrig, Herb Pennock, and Frankie Frisch all told him they did not. Only McGraw objected on the record.⁹ On February 8, 1933, Powers wrote that he was pleased by the response to his query, calling it a sign of progress in race relations. It contrasted markedly with the prejudice of ballplayers of the past, he said, who wandered into the ballparks straight from southern swamplands. "The bulk of the players then came from the other side of the Mason Dixon line. They brought the [Jim Crow] . . . ideas into the North with them." Powers wrote that it was only a matter of time before blacks were admitted into the big leagues.¹⁰

On February 11 *Pittsburgh Courier* sportswriter Alvin Moses congratulated the *Daily News* for what it called its "editorial on fair play."[11] In a page one story on February 18, the *Courier* quoted Broun's remarks and reprinted much of Powers's column.[12] In the same issue, sports editor Ches Washington praised Broun and Powers for their courageous stand on the color line.[13] On February 25, Washington announced the beginning of the *Courier's* symposium on baseball. Over the next several weeks, he would publish the views of big league owners, managers, ballplayers, and sportswriters on why there were no blacks in baseball.[14]

In the first installment of the series, Heydler told the newspaper that the only requirements for the major leagues were good athletic ability and good character. He said: "I do not recall one instance where baseball has allowed either race, creed, or color to enter into the question of the selection of its players."[15] Commissioner Kenesaw Mountain Landis did not respond directly to the survey – though Leslie O'Connor, the secretary-treasurer of organized baseball, echoed his boss's words when he told the *Courier* that no rule kept black players out of baseball. He added that any decision to sign blacks would have to come from team owners and not the commissioner's office.[16] White Sox owner Charles Comiskey said that he, too, had no objections but was prevented from signing blacks because baseball had a rule against it. He insisted that he would never reject a player based on his skin color; in reality, he had prevented McGraw from signing Grant.[17]

Thus began the *Courier's* campaign to end segregated baseball. The newspaper's crusade to change baseball was part of its larger crusade to effect social change in America. For example, it demanded anti-lynching legislation, advocated the integration of the armed services, and touted its Double v program during World War II – one "v" stood for victory in Europe and Asia, the other for the victory of civil rights in America. Between 1933 and 1946, the *Courier's* circulation rose from 46,000 to more than 260,000 – or 100,000 more than its nearest rival. Not coincidentally, these years coincided with its campaign to integrate baseball.[18]

Beginning in the early 1930s, a growing number of black journalists began calling for the end of segregated baseball, including sportswriters like Washington, Wendell Smith, Rollo Wilson, Fay Young, Ed Harris, Sam Lacy, and Joe Bostic. In 1934, Wilson, the *Courier's* assistant sports editor, wrote in the NAACP's *The Crisis* that it was racism and not something else that "precluded the possibility of blacks playing in the major leagues."[19] Ed Harris of the *Philadelphia Tribune* said that the arguments for denying blacks in baseball were invalid, adding that, in essence, baseball had nothing to fear but fear itself. "Some day, someone will surprise the baseball world and sign a couple colored players," he said. "And the baseball world will be surprised to find out that after the initial interest and excitement, that the Negro will be accepted . . . and the world will go its way."[20]

Baseball could – and did – turn a deaf ear to the criticisms of the color ban in the black press. But it could not ignore the intemperate remarks of a little-known, big league ballplayer named Jake Powell. In late July 1938, the New York Yankees outfielder was asked what he did during the off-season in a pregame interview with WGN radio in Chicago. Powell replied that he was a police officer in Dayton, Ohio. When he was asked how he kept in shape, he replied that he beat "niggers over the head with my blackjack."[21]

The next morning, a delegation of blacks, including executives with the Chicago Urban League and *Defender* sports editor Fay Young, took their protests over the remark to White Sox owner Charles Comiskey.[22] Before the game, another delegation presented umpires with a resolution demanding that Powell apologize and be suspended from baseball for life.[23] Commissioner Kenesaw Mountain Landis suspended the ballplayer for ten days, making him the first Major League player to be suspended for making a racist remark, *The Sporting News* reported.[24]

In his official statement announcing the suspension, Landis said that Powell had made "an uncomplimentary reference to a portion of the population." Although he believed the remark was "due more to carelessness than intent," he said he had nevertheless decided to suspend Powell.[25] Using practically the same language as Landis, *The Sporting News* also characterized Powell's comment as "careless" and not intentional. Columnist Dan Daniel claimed that the controversy would quickly fade, with no lasting impact on the ballplayer: "Powell could have been more careful. But he is a hustling player, aggressive, and always getting into a jam."[26] To Daniel, talk of cracking blacks over the head with a nightstick was equivalent to boldly taking an extra base.

The Associated Press characterized the comments as "slighting re-marks" against blacks.[27] The *New York Times* described it as "a flippant remark that was taken to be offensive" to Chicago's black population.[28] The *Washington Post* reported that Powell had made an "uncomplimen-tary remark about a portion of the population."[29] In his column, Shir-ley Povich quipped that blacks in Dayton had little to worry about if Powell "is no more effective with a police club that he is with his bat."[30] In truth, Powell never worked as a policeman, whether in Dayton or anywhere else. He talked frequently of wanting to join the Dayton po-lice department. He used to joke to friends that if he were ever a cop he would use his nightstick on blacks.[31]

Powell's slur ignited black sportswriters' considerable and long-standing indignation. On August 6, the *Chicago Defender* published a letter across the top of its front page demanding apologies from brewer Jacob Ruppert, the owner of the Yankees, and Old Gold cigarettes, the tobacco company that sponsored the broadcast of the interview.[32] WGN aired a number of apologies immediately after the interview. Two weeks later, a front-page editorial urged blacks to boycott Ruppert's beer and Old Gold cigarettes until they apologized.[33] In his *Defender* column, Fay Young told readers to continue to pressure Landis and the Yankees to keep Powell out of baseball.[34]

In New York City, the *Amsterdam News* reported that thousands of names appeared on a petition to ban Powell from the game.[35] Hun-dreds of people mailed letters of protest to the team and others pick-eted outside Yankee Stadium.[36] The *Philadelphia Afro-American* reported that blacks were staying away from Yankee Stadium.[37] Ed Harris wrote that Powell's remark could cost the Yankees: "The Yankees and the players on other teams have got a good lesson in just what decency and a sense of non-prejudice is worth. By the hard way – the cash box."[38] "L'affaire Powell," as *The Nation* called it, made it harder, though obvi-ously not impossible, for baseball to ignore the issue of race. The main-stream press reported the suspension, then let the story fade. This itself reflected two prevailing realities affecting coverage of black issues. One was that nothing important happened in black communities. The other was that the white press was subservient to commissioner Landis and the baseball establishment.[39]

Three weeks after Powell's interview, tens of thousands of spectators packed Comiskey Park for the Negro League's annual East-West All-Star Game. Young wrote that it might be a turning point for black baseball because the crowd included white journalists and baseball executives. He quoted *Chicago Daily News* sports editor Lloyd Lewis that it was "inevitable" that blacks would one day play in the major leagues. But that would require at least one owner to raise the issue, and none was willing to do so. "It is inevitable," he said. "Just how soon no one can tell, but it is sure to come."[40]

It may be difficult for us today to understand both the vastness of American racism or the rising popularity of communism in the 1930s. Yet the two converged in the story of the integration of white baseball.[41] The U.S. Communist Party and its newspaper, the *Daily Worker*, seized upon the issue of segregation in baseball because it represented one of the more obvious evidences of discrimination. The *Worker*'s journalists understood that ending the game's discrimination could make a truly revolutionary change in American society. For the Communist Party, baseball represented all that was wrong with American capitalism.[42] Although it was certainly interested in using sports to advance its political philosophy, in this, the Party's most effective effort to influence American society, it emphasized democracy, not communism. Ironically, the Party's involvement made it easy for the baseball establishment to dismiss integration as a communist front.

When Lester Rodney became the *Daily Worker*'s sports editor in early August 1936, he immediately turned his attention to baseball's color ban. If he wanted to cover it, it was his by default – none of the other white dailies in New York City were interested.[43] "We were the only non-black newspaper for a long time to write on the issue," Rodney later recalled.[44] On Sunday, August 16, the *Worker* published a banner headline that read, "Fans Ask End of Jim Crow Baseball," over a story that bluntly began: "Jim Crow baseball must end."[45]

A week later, the newspaper published an interview with National League president Ford Frick, who denied that baseball had a color line. Like John Heydler, his predecessor, Frick maintained that the only requirements for the major leagues were "ability" and "good character."[46] When the *Worker*'s journalists put the same question to Commissioner Landis, they were given the same line. To the *Worker* if there was no "gentlemen's agreement" prohibiting blacks, there was certainly a conspiracy in which no one took responsibility for the ban – not the commissioner, league presidents, or team executives.

Over the next decade, the *Worker* published hundreds of articles calling for integration. *Worker* sportswriters openly and brashly challenged baseball's establishment to permit black players; condemned white owners and managers for perpetuating the color ban; publicized the exploits of Negro League stars; distributed antidiscrimination pamphlets outside ballparks; and organized petition drives. The petitions read in part: "Our country guarantees the rights of life, liberty, and the pursuit of happiness to all, regardless of race, creed, or color. Yet in our national sport we find discrimination against outstanding Negro baseball players who are equal to or surpass in skill many of the greatest players in the National and American League." Tens of thousands of signatures went ignored by the baseball establishment.[47]

In March 1942, the Chicago White Sox, who were in Pasadena, California, for spring training, played an exhibition game against a local team that included a twenty-three-year-old Jackie Robinson. After his second hit, he easily stole second base off catcher Mike Tresh. An inning later, he made a tremendous defensive play, turning a hit into a double play. "If that kid was white, I'd sign him right now," Chicago manager Jimmy Dykes remarked.[48] The *Worker* published a story with the headline: "'Get After Landis, We'd Welcome You,' Sox Manager Tells Negro Stars."[49] The *Worker* was the only newspaper to cover the game.[50]

In mid-July, the *Worker* reprinted Wendell Smith's column that said a number of big league ballplayers supported integration. The article quoted Brooklyn Dodgers manager Leo Durocher as saying he would be happy to sign blacks if only he could. "I'll play the colored boys on my team if the big shots give the OK," he said, adding: "Hell, I've seen a million good ones." He added that there was a "grapevine understanding or subterranean rule" that barred blacks. On July 15, 1942, an incensed Landis ordered Durocher to Chicago for a closed-door meeting. When Durocher left the meeting, he said he had been misquoted.[51]

Landis told reporters that blacks had not been barred from baseball during his twenty-one years as commissioner. "There is no rule, formal or informal, no understanding, subterranean or otherwise" against hiring blacks, he said. "If Durocher, or any other manager, or all of them, want to sign one, or twenty-five, Negro players," he said, "it's all right with me."[52] The *Worker*'s Bill Mardo expressed its skepticism. He called Landis's comments "baloney."[53] The paper's Lester Rodney later added: "Landis was a blatant liar when he said there was no rule forbidding black players in baseball."[54]

In an interview with *Worker* journalist Conrad Komorowski, Landis answered most of the questions with a "no comment." When Komorowski asked him why he refused to comment, Landis snapped: "You fellows say I'm responsible." To another question Landis indicated that team owners were responsible for the color line, asking: "Why don't you put them on the spot?"[55] The communist journalists then pressured William Benswanger, owner of the hapless Pittsburgh Pirates, into giving a tryout to Negro League catcher Roy Campanella, pitcher Dave Barnhill, and second baseman Sammy T. Hughes on August 4, 1942. But Benswanger canceled it. On July 30, he told Nat Low of the *Worker* that the tryout had been canceled because of "unnamed pressures."[56] According to Rodney, the pressure came from "the baseball establishment."[57]

Brooklyn president Larry MacPhail actually confronted Landis after thinking the commissioner had grown soft on segregation. MacPhail told reporters that there were no blacks in baseball for five reasons. First, there was no demand for black players. Second, there were no blacks who could make it in the big leagues. Third, integration would ruin black baseball. Fourth, blacks did not want to play in the big leagues. And finally, MacPhail said, baseball had an agreement forbidding the signing of blacks.[58]

On August 6, *Sporting News* editor J. G. Taylor Spink defended segregation in an editorial called "No Good from Raising Race Issue." In it, he said that no rule was needed to keep blacks out of organized baseball because it was in everyone's interest to keep the races separate. Integration would ruin the Negro Leagues, he said, and without the Negro Leagues, blacks would have nowhere to gain the training to play in either the major or the minor leagues. Spink blamed communists for stirring up trouble, referring to them as "agitators" who used the issue for their own benefit.[59]

Unlike the communists, who liked confrontation, black sportswriters like Wendell Smith and Sam Lacy preferred to work within the existing system, cautiously approaching team executives and league officials. For years Smith told Benswanger, the Pirates' owner, that he could make his team a pennant contender if he signed top players from either of the city's Negro League teams – the Pittsburgh Crawfords or the Homestead Grays.[60] Smith once even reported that Grays' owner Cumberland "Cum" Posey had agreed to sell two of his stars, Josh Gibson and Buck Leonard, but Benswanger rejected the offer.[61] Later Benswanger would claim that he had tried to obtain Gibson from the Crawfords but that Posey said no. Smith scoffed at Benswanger's revisionism as "unmitigated story-tell[ing]."[62]

Americans accepted baseball's policy of racial exclusion because the baseball establishment denied the existence of a color line. The mainstream press accepted those denials. In other words, baseball could not have maintained the color line as long as it did without the aid and comfort of the country's white mainstream sportswriters. Together, they participated in what Joe Bostic of Harlem's *People's Voice* and other black sportswriters called a "conspiracy of silence."[63] This conspiracy was, in part, a reflection of what was happening in American society at large, where racism was viewed as the South's problem. Sportswriters, like other journalists, remained quiet because doing so was the path of least resistance or because they believed in segregation. As *Washington Post* sportswriter Shirley Povich put it: "I'm afraid the sportswriters were like the club owners. They thought separate was better."[64]

Mainstream sportswriters perpetuated the myth that the national pastime was a melting pot and all were equal on the ball field, regardless of ethnic background. But the reality was something else. The truth was that baseball writers, like league executives, team owners, managers, and players, believed that baseball, like the rest of society, should be segregated. Most sportswriters were conservative in their politics yet evangelical in their belief that baseball represented the American dream because everyone was equal on the playing field. As a result, according to one historian, they "wrote fantasies about the great American pastime . . . and were generally apathetic about baseball's color line."[65]

The Sporting News's J. G. Taylor Spink, for example, was a staunch defender of segregation and an unabashed supporter of the myth that all were equal on a baseball diamond. "No matter how humble the home from which an American youth may come," he wrote in an editorial, "an opportunity to rise above his environment is open to him, if he has the necessary energy and talent." He continued: "That is the American way, and baseball, as America's national pastime, offers an easy entry into the field of opportunity."[66] Yet, in another editorial Spink wrote that it was not appropriate to comment on the unwritten rule excluding blacks.[67] And in still another, he said that "no good" would come in even discussing the race issue because the color line was in the best interests of both blacks and whites.[68]

Sportswriters like Spink protected segregation in baseball by ignoring it as long as they could. In doing so, they conspired with league executives and team owners to keep blacks out of baseball. Simultaneously, black and communist sportswriters were crusading for integration, black athletes were proving their ability both in baseball and in other sports, and World War II was illustrating the irony of a country fighting against racism abroad while allowing it to exist on its home soil.

Above all, it was World War II that forced Americans to reconsider their views on discrimination. Nowhere was the hypocrisy of America's antiracist rhetoric during the war years more evident than in the armed services. While accepting blacks, the army and navy relegated most to the lower rungs of service. Black soldiers grew impatient with the discrimination they faced, whether it was in the inequity in military ranks or the treatment they endured on military bases. They were relegated to the backs of military buses and denied water from whites-only drinking fountains – though German prisoners of war could drink from those same fountains. Blacks who questioned these conditions were often jailed, beaten, or killed.

As the war dragged on, black activists increased their demands for racial equality. In 1942, black labor leader A. Phillip Randolph threatened to march on Washington to protest federal job discrimination. He successfully pressured President Roosevelt to create the Fair Employment Practices Commission to investigate antidiscriminatory hiring practices.[69] To satisfy Randolph, Roosevelt signed an executive order forbidding job discrimination in plants with war contracts. But the federal government did little to enforce these decisions, which exacerbated racial tensions and led to bloody race riots in cities like Detroit and Philadelphia.[70]

Some cities and states acted on their own to address racial inequality. The New York legislature passed the Quinn-Ives Act, for example, which banned discrimination in hiring and created a commission to investigate complaints. In some cases, progressive politicians attacked baseball in particular. Democratic state senator Charles Perry introduced a resolution into the New York legislature criticizing organized professional baseball for its unwritten law barring "certain people because of their race."[71] Brooklyn's communist councilman Peter Cacchione and black New York City councilman Benjamin Davis each called for the integration of baseball.[72]

Shortly after the 1944 baseball season, Landis suffered a fatal heart attack. The following March, Lacy wrote owners suggesting that a committee be created to consider bringing blacks into baseball. Leslie O'Connor, who chaired the search for Landis's replacement, invited Lacy to address the owners at their next meeting at the end of April 1945.[73] After Lacy presented his proposal to the owners, they agreed to form a committee on integrating the major leagues. The committee included Lacy, Branch Rickey, and MacPhail, who was then president of the New York Yankees.[74] MacPhail, however, refused to commit to any of the proposed meetings. Rickey remarked to Lacy: "Well, Sam, maybe we'll forget about Mr. MacPhail. Maybe we'll just give up on him and let nature take its course."[75]

On April 6, 1945, however, Nat Low of the *Worker*, Joe Bostic of the *People's Voice*, and Jimmy Smith of the *Pittsburgh Courier* arrived unannounced at the Dodgers' wartime spring-training camp in Bear Mountain, New York. Their purpose was to demand a tryout for two aging Negro League ballplayers, Terris McDuffie and Dave "Showboat" Thomas.[76] Rickey did not like being put on the spot. If he allowed the tryout, both the journalists and the ballplayers would make a name for themselves. If Rickey rejected the tryout, he would be vilified in the *Worker*, in the black press, and possibly in the anti-Rickey mainstream dailies. Rickey begrudgingly consented. At the end of a brief workout the next day, the ballplayers were dismissed.[77]

New York City sportswriter Bill Roeder said that the presence of

35

Low and a *Worker* photographer added "a sickening Red tinge ... to the invasion of the Brooklyn training camp at Bear Mountain." The mainstream press considered the tryout no more than a publicity stunt.[78] According to Bostic, it was a publicity stunt, but it was more than that. "It was the psychological breaking of the conspiracy of silence," Bostic said. "The real problem was that the press ignored [the issue of integration]."[79]

Shortly after the Bear Mountain incident, Boston city councilman Isadore Muchnick, who had friends on the radical left, pressured the city's Major League teams – the Red Sox and the Braves – to sign blacks or he would reject their permit for Sunday baseball. Red Sox general manager Eddie Collins wrote a letter to the councilman asserting that his team had never practiced discrimination during his twelve years in Boston. Blacks were simply not interested in organized professional baseball. "It is beyond my understanding," Collins said, "how anyone can insinuate or believe that all ballplayers, regardless of race, color, or creed, have not been treated in the American way as far as having an equal opportunity to play for the Red Sox." When Muchnick made Collins's letter public, *Boston Record* columnist Dave Egan reminded Collins that he was "living in anno domini 1945 and not the dust covered year 1865" and "residing in Boston, Massachusetts, and not Mobile, Alabama."[80]

In early April 1945, Wendell Smith contacted Muchnick and told him that he would find ballplayers for a tryout in Boston. Smith then selected three ballplayers on the basis of their youth and their 1944 statistics – Jackie Robinson, Sam Jethroe, and Marvin Williams. At the *Courier*'s expense, Smith brought the three to Boston. To Muchnick's frustration, neither the Red Sox nor Braves approved the tryout. Smith reported that Robinson, Jethroe, and Williams had vowed to stay in Boston until they got their tryout. "We can consider ourselves pioneers," Robinson told Smith in words that became prescient. "Even if they don't accept us, we are at least making the way easier for those who follow. Some day some Negro player or players will get a break. We want to help make that day a reality."[81]

Under mounting pressure, the Red Sox finally allowed Robinson, Jethroe, and Williams to try out at Fenway Park. On April 16, the ballplayers arrived at the ballpark, and coaches Hugh Duffy and Larry

Woodall put them through an hour-and-a-half workout in the near-empty stadium. Collins, manager George Cronin, and a number of reporters watched from the stands. Clif Keane, then a sportswriter for the *Boston Globe*, later recalled: "I can distinctly remember during the workout somebody yelling 'get those niggers off the field.' I can't recall who yelled it. People used to say it was Collins."[82]

The Red Sox obviously were not serious about the tryout: high school prospects pitched batting practice. Smith called it demeaning to throw the Negro League stars in with a bunch of kids. Robinson agreed. "It would be difficult to call it a tryout because they had these kid pitchers throwing,"[83] he said. "I sort of laughed within myself at what I felt was the uselessness of the venture. I didn't feel anything would come of it."[84] None of the ballplayers ever heard back from the Red Sox. Smith had hoped that the story would be played up in the papers. It was not, further frustrating black sportswriters.[85]

A month after Rickey begrudgingly permitted the spring-training workout of two blacks at Bear Mountain, he called a press conference. He announced that he would own a team, the Brooklyn Brown Dodgers, in the newly created United States Baseball League. He called the league a "legitimate Negro League" that might eventually become a part of organized baseball. At the same press conference, he condemned the communists as agitators who used integration to further their own cause, while also denouncing the shaky and shoddy organization of black baseball.[86] The Negro Leagues, Rickey asserted, were "the poorest excuse for the word 'league.'"[87]

Black sportswriters walked out of the press conference in protest. Ludlow Werner, editor of the *New York Age*, responded: "My aching back! Did you ever hear such double talk from a big pompous ass in your life? I predict that'll be a cold day in hell when that big windbag puts a Negro in a Brooklyn uniform."[88] The *Defender*'s Fay Young questioned Rickey for trying to "assume the role of Abraham Lincoln."[89] He added that "we want Negroes in the major leagues if they have to crawl to get there . . . but we won't have any major-league owners running any segregated leagues for us."[90]

Having effectively created a smokescreen, Rickey sent his three best scouts – George Sisler, Clyde Sukeforth, and Wid Matthews – to search for players ostensibly for the Brown Dodgers. In reality, and unbe-

37

knownst to his three scouts, Rickey's intentions were more ambitious: integration. From the beginning of his search, all roads seemed to lead to Robinson. During a meeting with Rickey, for example, Wendell Smith recommended Robinson for the Brown Dodgers.[91] In a pre-season article, Lacy named several Negro League players who could succeed in the majors, but singled out Robinson as the ideal man for the experiment.[92]

However, Rickey's investigation of Robinson revealed the young player's temper. Since he had been a young boy in Southern California, Robinson had scuffled with those who called him "nigger" and other racial epithets. He fought with whites who treated blacks as second-class citizens and sneered at blacks who accepted second-class treatment. Because of his sensitivity to racial slights, Robinson earned the reputation as a troublemaker. His court-martial did nothing to alter that image. During his year in the Negro Leagues, Robinson struck many as a hothead, and someone who needed little provocation to argue with umpires, opponents, or even his own teammates.

When Rickey's scouts mentioned Robinson's temper, Rickey repeated their concerns to Smith. Smith well knew about Robinson's temper. "I didn't want to tell Mr. Rickey, 'Yes, he's tough to get along with.' A lot of us knew that." At the same time, Smith informed Robinson that Rickey was scouting him for the Brown Dodgers and that he should "watch himself, . . . watch his conduct. Everything he did, on and off the field, would get back to Rickey." In one conversation Smith asked Rickey if there was any chance that Robinson might play for the Brooklyn Dodgers – rather than the Brooklyn Brown Dodgers. "He was evasive," Smith recalled. "He didn't say yes and he didn't say no. But I had the definite impression there was more behind it than the Brown Dodgers."[93]

Quietly, Rickey's program for integrating baseball began to unfold. During the summer of 1945, he met with New York University sociologist Dan Dodson, who was the executive director of the Mayor's Committee on Unity, formed to investigate violations of Quinn-Ives. Realizing that Dodson could force his hand, Rickey persuaded him to organize a committee – the Mayor's Committee to Integrate Baseball – to study the possibility of integrating baseball. This bought the Brooklyn executive additional time.[94]

Finally, on August 28, 1945, Rickey summoned Robinson and explained that he had been scouting black baseball for the right player, and the search had led to Robinson. After a long and intense meeting, Rickey signed Robinson in exchange for the athlete's assurances that for the next three years he would have "the guts not to fight back." Though Rickey and Robinson intended to keep the contract to themselves, Smith at some point learned of it but – at Rickey's behest – agreed to keep the news to himself. The journalist later said that he would do whatever Rickey asked if it led to the integration of the game – and that included suppressing the biggest story of his career.[95]

Like the Berlin Wall, the collapse of baseball's color barrier came as a complete shock to casual observers. But to those who had been paying attention, the writing had been on the wall for some time. Invisible to most of America, activists like Wendell Smith and Sam Lacy had worked for more than a decade to end segregated baseball before Rickey signed Robinson. The breaking of baseball's color barrier was part of a long struggle – a chip here, a chip there. When it finally collapsed it did so for reasons that had everything to do with Rickey and Robinson, and for reasons that had nothing to do with them.

12**3**45678910

Rickey and Robinson Challenge Segregated Baseball

I N THE EARLY AFTERNOON of Tuesday, October 23, 1945, Hector Racine, the president of the Montreal Royals, the Brooklyn Dodgers' AAA team, informed reporters he would be making a big announcement at 5 p.m. at the team's offices at Delormier Downs in Montreal. He said nothing else, leaving reporters wondering and rumors flying. The *Montreal Star* speculated that the city would get a Major League team.[1] According to another story, the Royals would fire manager Bruno Betzel and replace him with retired Yankees slugger Babe Ruth.[2]

About two dozen sportswriters, newscasters, and photographers were waiting when Racine entered the room as scheduled accompanied by Romeo Gavreau, the team's vice president; Branch Rickey Jr., director of Brooklyn's farm system and the son of the organization's president; and a broad-shouldered black man, who was introduced as Jackie Robinson, formerly of the Kansas City Monarchs of the Negro Leagues. Branch Rickey Sr. remained in Brooklyn.

Racine announced that his International League team had signed Robinson, thus erasing professional baseball's seemingly impenetrable color line. In just a few words, Racine forever changed baseball and American society. Stunned silence followed. Then chaos erupted as camera bulbs flashed and reporters surged forward with questions while others rushed to phones to alert their newspapers and radio stations.

When order was restored, Racine explained that the team had signed Robinson because he was "a good ballplayer." But, he added, the Royals has also signed Robinson because it was a "point of fairness." According to Racine, blacks earned their right to play alongside whites by serving their country during World War II. The team would support Robinson, but, Racine noted, there were no guarantees. Like any other player, Robinson would have to earn his uniform the following March at spring training in Daytona Beach, Florida.[3] When reporters asked Robinson how he felt, he described himself as "a guinea pig in baseball's racial experiment."[4]

A popular and still prevailing misperception gives Rickey most, if not all, the credit for signing Robinson. This myth began taking shape in the hours, perhaps even the moments, after Montreal signed Robinson. Rickey co-opted the story and shaped it in his own image, ignoring the contributions of others. The mainstream press, for the most part, made little or no attempt to interpret or dig beneath the information Rickey or his associates fed it. This left readers with no reason to believe other than that it had been Rickey and only Rickey who deserved the credit for integrating baseball. Only in the black and communist press would readers get a sense of the story's context. And only in that alternative press would readers get a sense of what the story meant to America.

In his initial account of the press conference, filed within hours of Montreal's announcement, Sid Fedor of the Associated Press reported that Robinson was the first black to be admitted into organized baseball. He mentioned Robinson's athletic success at UCLA and stated that Robinson had been signed by Rickey Sr. after a three-year, twenty-five-thousand-dollar search to find the right ballplayer. He also included remarks made at the conference by Racine, Robinson, and Rickey Jr.[5] Branch Jr. had remarked that his father knew he had "the alligator by the tail" and was prepared for whatever might come. "The Twig" also predicted that his father would be severely criticized "in some sections of the country where racial prejudice is rampant." He also said that the Dodger organization was prepared for the possibility that a number of southern players might quit in protest. "Even if some players quit," he said, "they'll be back after a year or two in a cotton mill."[6]

Rickey Jr.'s comments angered Southerners, including Billy Werber, a onetime Major League third basemen who had grown up in Maryland. Werber wrote Rickey Sr. that his son's reference to "ballplayers from the South is a definite insult to every Southern boy." It was wrong, Werber said, to expect southern ballplayers to accept blacks on the ball field or anywhere else. Philadelphia Athletics pitcher Bobo Newsom of Hartsville, South Carolina, made the following jab at the tightfisted Rickeys: "A ball player would make more money in a cotton mill if young Rickey pays the same kind of dough his father [does]."[7]

Other southerners criticized the signing of Robinson as well. The United Press reported that Rogers Hornsby, a Texan who had retired after a Hall of Fame career as a player, had asserted that integration would never work. Baseball players lived and traveled together, Hornsby said, and it was unfair for Rickey to force the mixing of races on southern ballplayers. George Digby, a scout with the Boston Red Sox, was no less sanguine: "I think it's the worst thing that can happen to organized baseball," he said. "I don't think anyone should go in and start a lot of trouble." Dick Callahan of New Orleans, an eighteen-year-old pitching prospect just signed by Digby, agreed that integration was not a good idea.[8]

Cincinnati Reds catcher Johnny Riddle of Clinton, South Carolina, and Pittsburgh Pirates coach Spud Davis, of Birmingham, Alabama, offered that integration was "all right as long as [blacks] are with some other team." Dixie Walker, the popular Alabama-born Brooklyn outfielder, also said he did not object as long as Robinson played for Montreal and not Brooklyn.[9] In *The Sporting News*, W. G. Bramham, the president of the minor leagues and a resident of Durham, North Carolina, declared that the mixing of whites and blacks would never work in baseball. "It is my opinion that if the Negro is left alone and aided by his unselfish friends of the white race, he will work out his own salvation in all lines of endeavor," he said. "It is those of the carpet-bagger stripe of the white race, under the guise of helping, but in truth using the Negro for their own selfish interests, who retard the race."[10]

The black newspaper *Chicago Defender* called Bramham "stupid" for saying that gullible blacks had to be protected from "carpetbaggers" like Rickey. In an editorial, the *Defender* characterized the opinions of Walker, Hornsby, and Digby as "prejudiced."[11] Writing in the *Baltimore Afro-American*, Sam Lacy reported that the wire services and mainstream newspapers had only sought the reactions of southern ballplayers, which gave the impression that all, or at least most, ballplayers were opposed to integration.[12] In the *Daily Worker*, Nat Low also criticized the wire services for quoting only southern ballplayers.[13]

Newspapers also sought the reactions of baseball officials and team owners, but, for the most part, they said nothing. Commissioner Happy Chandler, National League president Ford Frick, and American League president Will Harridge were all "unavailable for comment." Philadelphia Athletics owner and manager Connie Mack, Cincinnati Reds owner Powell Crosley, and Detroit Tigers general manager Jack Zeller also had no comment. Cleveland Indians owner Alva Bradley and Boston Red Sox general manager Eddie Collins denied that there had ever been a color line. Collins said that the Red Sox had given Robinson a tryout but had not been interested in signing him.[14] New York Giants president Horace Stoneham told reporters that baseball's primary responsibility was to returning GIS – and not black players. New York Yankees president Larry MacPhail criticized Rickey for taking players from the Negro Leagues without compensating the teams.[15]

The Associated Press filed several articles related to the Robinson signing in the days that followed. None of them included an interview with Robinson nor anything substantive on the social or historical significance of the story. Writing from New York the day after the announcement, Jack Hand corrected Fedor's comment that Robinson was the first black in organized baseball. According to Hand's dispatch, a black named George Stovey had pitched in the minor leagues in 1887. In fact, as noted earlier, dozens of blacks had played in organized baseball in the 1870s and 1880s, including two in the big leagues: Moses Fleetwood Walker and his brother Welday. The Associated Press also quoted Rickey's response to charges that he had signed Robinson without informing the Kansas City Monarchs of the Negro Leagues. The Negro Leagues, he pointed out, were not in fact a formal league, and thus had no legally binding contract with Robinson.[16]

Hand asked Rickey if political pressures had coerced him into signing Robinson. Rickey said he took into account only Robinson and the Brooklyn organization when he signed the ballplayer. "No pressure groups had anything to do with it," he said. "In fact, I signed him in spite of such groups rather than because of them." To reporter Gayle Talbot, Rickey elaborated that he had given a lot of thought to racial discrimination since his days coaching baseball at Ohio Wesleyan in the early 1900s. Rickey recalled that during a road trip one of his black ballplayers, Charlie Thomas, was denied a room at a hotel. Rickey said he asked the hotel clerk if he would allow the ballplayer to sleep on a cot in Rickey's room. The clerk obliged. Later that evening, Rickey said he looked over at Thomas and saw that he was intently rubbing his skin, saying, "Black skin. Black skin. If only I could make them white."[17] In the days, months, and years to come, Rickey told the Charlie Thomas story so often that it became a parable, guiding the Brooklyn executive's efforts to do what was fair and right for all God's people. However, no one in the press questioned why, if Charlie Thomas had had such a profound impact on Rickey, it had taken Rickey forty years to integrate baseball.

To the black press and its readers, Montreal's announcement signaled the beginning of what was hoped to be a new day for fairness and equality. Unlike mainstream newspapers, which said little after the initial coverage of the signing, black newspapers played up the story on their front pages and sports sections for weeks.[18] In addition to commenting on the story in articles, editorials, and columns, they also published interviews with and photographs of Robinson. While hyperbolically praising Rickey as another Abraham Lincoln the black press also recognized that there was more to the story than Rickey and Charlie Thomas.

When black America learned that the Brooklyn organization had signed Robinson, the world as it had been stopped for a moment, and the things denied for so long began to seem possible. In Harlem, the *Amsterdam News* called the news "a drop of water in the drought that keeps faith alive in American institutions." Roy Wilkins, who would become executive director of the NAACP, asserted that the signing of Robinson meant that blacks "should have their own rights, should have jobs, decent homes and education, freedom from insult, and equality of opportunity to achieve."[19] According to black congressman Adam Clayton Powell, the signing was "a step that will bring cheer to all real Americans; . . . this is a definite step toward winning the peace, and now that this gentlemen is in the International League, the other leagues will not be able to furnish any alibis."[20]

In an editorial, the *Chicago Defender* wrote that the signing of Robinson was more than just an opportunity for the ballplayer. It was an opportunity for all blacks.[21] Sports editor Fay Young called the news "a step toward a broader spirit of democracy in baseball and will do much to promote a friendlier feeling between the races."[22] Striking a less hopeful note, Ludlow Werner, editor of the *New York Age*, wrote that many Americans were hoping Robinson would fail. "Knowing that he will have to be Superman will bring out the best in him; and the best in him should prove sufficient to break up another myth that Negroes do not belong in white baseball."[23] Werner added that Robinson "would be haunted by the expectations of his race. . . . Unlike white players, he can never afford an off day or off night. His private life will be watched,

47

too, because white America will judge the Negro race by everything he does. And Lord help him with his fellow Negroes if he should fail them."[24]

Pittsburgh Courier sports editor Wendell Smith called the Robinson signing "the most American and democratic step baseball has made in 25 years."[25] For Smith and the *Courier*, the news had been a long time coming. The paper packed its next issue with ten stories (two covering much of page one) and three photographs on the integration of baseball. In one of the page-one stories, Rickey insisted that this was only the beginning of a movement in support of fairer play in baseball. "This is a movement that cannot be stopped by anyone," he said. "They may be able to detain it for a while, but not for too long. The world is moving on and they will move with it, whether they like it or not."[26] The other page-one story appeared under Jackie Robinson's own byline though it was, in all likelihood, ghostwritten by Smith. In it, the ballplayer admitted he had initially doubted Rickey's sincerity, but had concluded after their August meeting that he was not being signed simply as a "gesture." He was going to be given a chance to make an impact. "If I make the team," Robinson wrote, "I will not forget that I am representing a whole race of people who are pulling for me." He pledged that if he was about to become a guinea pig, he would be "the best guinea pig that ever lived, both on the field and off."[27]

In a front-page story in the *Baltimore Afro-American*, Robinson told reporter Michael Carter that he understood that the eyes of millions of blacks would be on him. "I don't guess anybody really understands exactly how I feel about being signed up," he said. "I feel sort of as if everyone was looking at me. I feel that if I flop, or conduct myself badly – on or off the field – that I'll set the advancement back a hundred years. Why, I feel that all the little colored kids playing sandlot baseball have their professional futures wrapped up somehow in me."[28]

Robinson told Carter that he owed a debt of gratitude to blacks who had pressured baseball for years. "I owe this to the colored people who helped make it possible, and I hope I shall always have their good will." Robinson also recognized the contributions of black journalists. "It's a press victory, you might say," he said.[29] Writing in the same issue, Sam Lacy mentioned his long involvement in the effort to end segregated baseball.[30] The *Courier*, too, reminded its readers that it had long fought for the inclusion of blacks in organized baseball. In November the newspaper published a letter that Robinson had written Wendell Smith: "I want to thank you and the paper for all you have done and are doing in my behalf. As you know I am not worried about what the white press or people think as long as I continue to get the best wishes of my people."[31]

The *Daily Worker* also reported that it had linked arms with blacks to end segregation. On October 25, for example, *Worker* sportswriter Mike Gold reminded readers of the newspaper's ten-year campaign against baseball's color line. The newspaper would fight on against discrimination in America, it said, until Jim Crow was "ruined, finished, destroyed in every dirty root and fibre."[32] In the same issue, the newspaper quoted Walter White of the NAACP and New York City councilman Benjamin Davis Jr., who praised baseball for its progress in race relations. Brooklyn city councilman Peter Cacchione added that the people of his city were happy that Robinson had signed with Montreal but would be happier "when he is playing for the Dodgers in Ebbets Field."[33]

The October 25 *Daily Worker* also featured a column by Nat Low, in which he praised Davis and Cacchione for introducing resolutions to end Jim Crow in baseball in their respective city councils. Low also called for the creation of Jackie Robinson fan clubs to fight the reactionaries in baseball, in politics, and in the press, who wanted Brooklyn and Montreal to stop what they had started.[34] Likewise, *Worker* sportswriter Phil Gordon criticized the New York dailies for their reporting of the Robinson story. The *Times*'s account, he said, was "cold and antagonistic."[35] An unbylined story buried in the sports section, it included nothing of substance beyond the basic details of the press conference.[36]

New York Times columnist Arthur Daley, who often represented baseball's management, praised Rickey for his moral courage but wondered if he were not "rushing things too rapidly" given that there were so many southern ballplayers and several southern minor leagues.[37] Other mainstream papers were equally unenthusiastic. Neither John Drebinger of the *Times* nor Red Smith of the *Herald-Tribune* had anything initially to say about the Robinson signing. When interviewed about Robinson's chances, Smith responded with the following platitude:

49

"There is more democracy in the locker room than on the street."[38] *New York World-Telegram* columnists Joe Williams and Dan Daniel and *New York Daily News* columnist Jimmy Powers criticized the announcement.[39] Williams suspected that Rickey had signed Robinson because of politics and not because of the ballplayer's ability. He warned against the involvement of "pressure groups, social frauds and political demagogues." Williams quoted the *Baltimore Afro-American*'s Sam Lacy as saying that no blacks were ready for the Major Leagues.[40] According to Lacy, he meant that black ballplayers might first require socializing with whites in the minor leagues before playing in the big leagues. MacPhail, Williams, and others tossed around that quotation, Lacy complained, "whenever it served their purpose."[41]

Powers had long called for the end of segregated baseball. Yet when the moment arrived, he characterized Robinson's chances of making it in organized ball as "a one-thousand-to-one shot." Like Powers, Dan Parker of the *New York Daily Mirror* had also called for integration in his columns. When Montreal announced it had signed Robinson, however, Parker wrote that he had never understood why blacks had been kept out of professional baseball when they had succeeded so well in college athletics: "Why a good respectable Negro athlete shouldn't fit just as well into organized baseball as he does into college football, basketball, boxing, or cricket," he said, "is something I have never been able to figure out."[42]

In his October 26, 1945, column in the *Daily Worker*, Phil Gordon wrote that unlike the city's other sportswriters, Al Laney of the *Herald-Tribune* and Joe Cummiskey of the liberal *P.M.* wrote "stirringly sympathetic" articles.[43] Laney's columns had noted that for months there had been a lot of discussion about bringing blacks into baseball, and everyone thought that Rickey was against it. In addition, Laney quoted *Crisis* editor Roy Wilkins, who said that Robinson would forge a greater respect between the races. Similarly, Laney quoted a black baseball fan, Jimmie Odoms, who said that Robinson would have to face the ugliness that came his way, beginning at spring training in Florida. "This boy Robinson [has] got to take it," Odoms declared. "I hate to think what he got to take. They'll find plenty [of] ways to give it to him [at] Daytona Beach [during spring training]. And he['s] got to take it. Otherwise, it don't make no sense signing him."[44] Laney then added his own conclusion: "Without further preliminaries it may be said that, if there are baseball players who will refuse to play with or against this personable, intelligent, sensitive man, they must, indeed, be blinded by prejudice."[45]

National magazines – such as *Time, Newsweek, Life, Look,* and *Opportunity* – also reported Robinson's signing with Montreal but failed to examine what it meant beyond baseball.[46] The *Saturday Review*, by contrast, praised the announcement and quoted Laney at length. Integration, it wrote, "is absolutely inevitable if America is going to live up to its high protestations of democracy. And there is no better place to begin it than on a baseball diamond."[47] *The Sporting News* published several related stories in its first issue after the Montreal signing, but they tended to be shallow and one-sided. In the second paragraph of its main story, for example, correspondent Al Parsley provided this profound description of the ballplayer: "Robinson is definitely dark. His color is the hue of ebony. By no means can he ever be called a brown bomber or a chocolate soldier."[48]

In the same issue, *The Sporting News*'s editor J. G. Taylor Spink wrote that the signing of Robinson "touched off a powder keg in the South, unstinted praise in Negro circles, and a northern conviction that the racial problem in baseball is as far from a satisfactory solution as ever." For two decades, in fact, Spink had opposed integration – and the reality of integration did little to change his mind. Spink dismissed the news by writing that if Robinson were white and six years younger, he might make Brooklyn's AA team in Newport News, Virginia. He called the press coverage "out of proportion to the actual vitality of the story."[49]

In his *Sporting News* column, Daniel agreed with his editor that the story "had received far more attention than it was worth." Daniel, the longtime president of the New York chapter of the Baseball Writers Association, echoed organized baseball's party line by saying that ability and nothing else had excluded blacks. The signing of Robinson was "unquestionably" an effort by Rickey to comply with the state's anti-discrimination law. Robinson, Daniel assured his readers, did not have the talent to succeed in baseball now that the best players had returned from the war: "The dope is that he will not make the grade."[50]

In a separate article in the same issue, Daniel suggested that politics

51

had motivated Rickey's decision. On July 1 New York's Quinn-Ives legislation had gone into effect, which banned discrimination in hiring and created a commission to investigate complaints. In an interview with Rickey, Daniel asked the Brooklyn president why he had failed to sign any black players when he ran the St. Louis Cardinals and allowed Sportsman's Park to remain segregated. Rickey replied that he regretted not doing more to end the ballpark's racist policy but that he had not thought much about integration until he moved to Brooklyn and began watching Negro League teams play at Ebbets Field. This same issue of *The Sporting News* reprinted Joe Williams's column from the *World-Telegram* that criticized the signing of Robinson.[51]

Rickey's failure to pay the Monarchs for Robinson left the Brooklyn executive vulnerable to criticism. Within a day of the announcement, the wire services shifted the story from reporting that baseball's color line had been broken to Rickey's supposed transgression of taking a ballplayer from the Negro Leagues. The Negro League owners were caught in the middle. If they supported Rickey, they knew they would be signing their own death warrants, as their best stars would jump to organized professional baseball. If the owners sued Rickey, they would be accused of obstructing integration. *The Sporting News* quoted Negro League president A. B. Martin as saying: "I admire Branch Rickey for his courage, but the method of signing Robinson raises some problems."[52] The Monarchs, which did have an agreement – however informal – with Robinson, found themselves squeezed both by Rickey and the black press. Tom Baird, the team's owner, briefly considered filing a lawsuit blocking Robinson's contract with Montreal. In a patronizing column on this fact, Tommy Holmes of the *Brooklyn Eagle* claimed that it was blacks and not whites who stood in the way of integration.[53]

After being criticized in the black press, Baird changed his mind, however. He began urging the national pastime to sign blacks and avowed he would not challenge any player's contract with a team in organized baseball. Weighing in on the controversy, Wendell Smith of the *Pittsburgh Courier* said it would not have approved of Brooklyn's raiding of black players if the circumstances had not been extraordinary. Baird may have had a legal and moral justification for challenging Rickey, Smith noted, but he should nevertheless drop the matter. The signing of Robinson, Smith said, "transcended everything else at this particular time."[54]

For their part, mainstream sportswriters realized they could not come right out and criticize integration or they would appear as obstructionists. They believed, however, that it was fair game to criticize Rickey's method in signing Robinson or to raise doubts about Robinson's ability to make it to the Major Leagues – even though he had been signed by a minor league team. As far as these sportswriters were concerned, if others were willing to question Robinson's ability, so much the better. The United Press, for example, quoted one of Robinson's former coaches as saying that Robinson was better in football, basketball, and track than baseball. "Jackie didn't try too hard at baseball," he said.[55]

When Cleveland Indians pitcher Bob Feller – who had fronted exhibition games between black and white all-stars – was asked about Robinson, he too expressed doubts. Both Satchel Paige and Josh Gibson, he said, were good enough for the big leagues, but not Robinson. Robinson had "football shoulders" and could not hit an inside pitch. Feller added: "If he were a white man, I doubt if they would consider him big-league material. . . . I hope he makes good. But I don't think he will."[56] Feller later defended his comments by saying that when he had faced Robinson, he had held him hitless.[57]

But a few weeks before Montreal's announcement, Robinson had a double in two at bats against Feller. Robinson told *New York Post* columnist Jimmy Cannon that he had played two games against Feller but doubted if Feller knew who he was. "If you lined up ten of us," he said, "I'll bet he couldn't pick me out of the bunch."[58] In a letter to Wendell Smith, Robinson said he respected Feller but wondered what he had meant by "football shoulders." Robinson, for his part, admitted that he had doubts about his fielding but not his hitting. "The few times I faced Feller has made me confident that the pitching I faced in the Negro American League was as tough as any I will have to face if I make it at Montreal."[59]

For a decade, Satchel Paige had been America's best-known black ballplayer and had been Feller's counterpart in a number of white-versus-black all-star games. It was always Paige who was mentioned whenever someone talked of integration. As the reigning clown prince of black baseball, Paige was deemed acceptable to white America. He too believed he would be the one who would break the color line. But when sportswriters asked Paige if Rickey had erred in choosing Robinson, the pitcher, while greatly disappointed, praised Robinson. "They didn't make a mistake in signing Robinson," he said. "They couldn't have picked a better man."[60]

Yet Hy Turkin, writing in *Negro Digest*, agreed with many other black players that Robinson – who after all had played just one season in the Negro Leagues – was not the best available black player. Robinson was, however, according to Turkin, "the greatest prospect" for making it in organized baseball. There would be no conspiracy against Robinson, he added, and the ballplayer would have the support of baseball fans. "No matter what the prejudices of club owners has been," Turkin said, "the sports fan always tends to lean toward the underdog."[61]

Robinson could win over the hearts of baseball fans if he proved himself. However, changing the minds of those with deep-seated prejudices who were opposed to giving blacks any measure of equal opportunity was a far more daunting task. A day after the Montreal announcement, Tommy Holmes of the *Brooklyn Eagle* wrote that Robinson's first challenge would come during spring training in Daytona Beach. "Anyone who has ever traveled that far South can't help but wonder just how things can be arranged. Fundamental things such as where he will sleep and where he will eat," Holmes said. "Not to mention what traveling accommodations they'll let him have in deepest Dixie."[62]

In Daytona Beach, where the Brooklyn organization would go for spring training, the *Daytona Beach Evening News* published wire service stories about the Robinson signing. However, it provided no local reaction beyond reporting that Rickey would be arriving in town soon to discuss his spring training plans.[63] Twenty miles to the west, the *Deland Sun News* published a United Press account that Daytona Beach city officials were surprised to learn that Robinson would join the rest of the Brooklyn organization during spring training.[64] As the *Sun News* sports editor told the *Chicago Defender*: "Opinion here is divided on whether it will work or not."[65] But the same editor had no comment on the matter in his own newspaper. Newspapers in nearby Florida cities – such as Jacksonville, Sanford, and Orlando – likewise suppressed the news. The *Miami Herald*, however, ran the story of the signing of Robinson across the front page of its sports section and also included an Associated Press photograph of Robinson signing his contract.[66]

Newspapers, whether in Florida or elsewhere in the South, gave the story either minor play or ignored it. They relied almost exclusively for their information on wire-service stories. Columns or editorials let it pass unremarked. Rare exceptions included the *Louisville Courier-Journal* and *Charlotte Observer*, which ran the photos of Robinson and referred to Robinson in columns. An unbylined column in the *Courier-Journal* expressed approval of the signing of black ballplayers in theory but not if they already were under contract to another team.[67] In the *Observer*, sports columnist Jake Wade took issue with Rickey Jr. for saying that the announcement would be criticized in the South where "racial prejudice is rampant." Times had changed, Wade said, and so had southern views about blacks. He expected no negative reaction to the announcement.[68] *Atlanta Journal* sports columnist Ed Danforth applauded the signing of Robinson but said that liberal newspapers could ruin Robinson's chances, writing: "Robinson probably will have a minimum of trouble getting along with his teammates until the red-eyed press begins to challenge the official scorers on unfairness in giving base hits."[69]

Elsewhere, in metropolitan newspapers, the story received more prominent – though only marginally more local – reaction. The stories, for the most part, came from wire service accounts. In an unbylined column, for example, the *Detroit News* blamed the persistence of the color line not on prejudice but on tradition. The columnist suggested that Robinson would be a "credit to his race."[70] The *Washington Post*, unlike most other mainstream newspapers, understood that the story transcended baseball. Robinson would stand as a test of whether "the recent laws and rulings aimed at the end of racial discrimination really reflect a change of popular feeling."[71] *Post* columnist Shirley Povich, who on at least one occasion had suggested that owners sign blacks, praised both Rickey and Robinson.[72]

Unlike the big league baseball establishment, which reserved comment on the signing of Robinson, Frank Shaughnessy, the president of the International League (which included the Montreal Royals), welcomed the news. "It depends entirely on the individual player. . . . If he's the right type [of ballplayer], there's no reason in the world why he shouldn't find a place in organized baseball. I think Jackie Robinson is definitely the right type."[73] Stories in the mainstream press, with Rickey's assistance, portrayed Robinson as someone who would not stir up racial issues. They did not mention that the baseball establishment had kept blacks out of the national pastime for decades. The stories said nothing about the campaign to integrate baseball or that the signing of Robinson had ramifications that transcended baseball and impacted the rest of American society. Nor did reporters seek reactions from either the black or white activists who had crusaded for greater civil liberties.

When Hector Racine announced that his team had signed Robinson, he told reporters that Jackie had been assigned to Montreal because the city, being the northernmost in professional baseball, would give Robinson a sanctuary relatively free of the discrimination he would find in America.[74] Indeed, in Montreal, a city unburdened by centuries of institutionalized bigotry, the signing of Robinson was met with unqualified praise. The *Daily Star* called the story "one of the most revolutionary moves in baseball since Abner Doubleday started this pastime."[75] The *Herald* added: "Those who were good enough to fight and die by the side of whites are plenty good enough to play by the side of whites."[76]

The *Montreal Gazette* included a profusion of staff-reported stories, wire-service stories, and columns. In his column, Dink Carroll wrote that Japanese propaganda had stressed that blacks were discriminated against in America. The war had forced America to question its color line: "It is a social problem that has been facing the American people," he wrote, "and the signing of young Jack Robinson to a Royal contract here yesterday is bound to have an effect upon it."[77] In his column the next day, Carroll noted that Montreal fans did not seem to appreciate the story's significance because they did not have the same history of racial discrimination. "This reaction surely proves the absolute absence here of an anti-Negro sentiment among sports fans," Carroll wrote, "which is what Mr. Rickey doubtless had in mind when he chose Montreal as the locale for his history-making experiment."[78]

To quell the less favorable welcome Rickey anticipated for Robinson in Florida, Rickey sent his trusted assistant Bob Finch to organize a tolerance program in central Florida. In an odd twist, before leaving for

Florida Finch learned for himself what it meant to be restricted because of his skin color. When Robinson returned to New York from Montreal, Finch went to the ballplayer's Harlem hotel. He tried to go upstairs to Robinson's room, but the clerk prevented him because he was white. A porter was then sent to Robinson's room, and Robinson and Finch met outside the hotel.[79]

1234**4**5678910

Robinson and Wright Take Their Game to Sanford

O N OCTOBER 11, two weeks before Montreal announced it had signed Robinson, a black teenager named Jesse Payne was lynched in Madison, Florida. Payne had spent several weeks in custody at a state prison in Raiford near Tallahassee for allegedly attacking the five-year-old niece of a Florida sheriff, Lonnie Davis. Payne was subsequently transferred back to Madison for arraignment and trial, where he was left in an unguarded and unlocked jail. In the middle of the night, a mob of white men dragged Payne from the shack, shot him to death, and left his body on a highway seven miles away.[1]

According to news stories, Davis, who lived next to the jail, stood in a window watching the mob as it removed Payne. Florida's attorney general called for Davis's suspension because he had conspired with the lynch mob, but two Madison County grand juries refused to indict him. The state's governor, Millard Caldwell, took no action against Davis. In both *Time* and *Collier's* magazines Caldwell was quoted as saying that he did not consider Payne's killing a lynching because it had saved the courts the cost and trouble of a trial. In *Collier's*, Governor Caldwell asserted that the ordeal of having Davis's niece testify in open court would be as great an injury as the crime itself. Payne's killing was therefore justified because it prevented the girl from reliving her horror. "This fact probably accounts for a number of killings which might otherwise be avoided," the governor said.

When Caldwell was asked why he had not removed Davis from office for permitting the mob to reach Payne, he said that there had been no evidence to link the sheriff with the mob. Davis, according to Caldwell, was "a dumb public servant" but was not guilty of a crime and could not therefore simply be dismissed.[2]

Two weeks before Payne was murdered, a sixty-year-old black man living near Live Oak, Florida, was taken from his car, pistol-whipped, lynched, and then dumped into the Suwanee River. The suspects, including a local police chief, were not indicted.

The murder of Jesse Payne made front-page headlines in black newspapers because it chillingly illustrated not just the brutality of racism but the lengths that white southerners, whether acting on their own or as part of the Ku Klux Klan, would go to protect their way of life. After crosses were burned outside the homes of five black families in a sub-division near Miami in the fall of 1945, Thurgood Marshall, the chief counsel of the NAACP, asked the U.S. attorney general to investigate. "This method of intimidation by the recently rejuvenated Ku Klux Klan and kindred organizations most certainly deserves the immediate attention of the Department of Justice," Marshall said. "This is especially true in the light of the recent lynching [of Jesse Payne] in Florida."[3]

The months between the signing of Robinson and the beginning of spring training saw an escalation of violence against blacks – much of it directed against war veterans. Black newspapers regularly ran first-page accounts of these incidents. On November 17, for example, St. Claire Pressley, a war veteran, got off a bus in Johnsonville, South Carolina, and was immediately arrested for a minor disturbance that had occurred several days before, long before he had even arrived in town. As he walked down the street toward the jail, a police officer shot and killed him. In December, when a white police officer in Union Springs, Alabama, overheard blacks discussing racial equality, he open fired, killing two and injuring a third.[4]

On February 5, 1946, a white police officer shot and killed Private First Class Charles Ferguson and his brother, Alphonzo, and injured a third brother, Seaman Third Class Joseph Ferguson, after the men objected to being denied service at a café in Long Island, New York. Four days later, when a group of black prisoners at the U.S. Disciplinary Barracks in Granville, Wisconsin, complained that meat had been omitted from their lunch, a white guard responded by firing his machine gun, killing Private National Jackson.

On February 12, Isaac Woodard, who had just been discharged after serving four years in the army, was traveling by public bus to his home in North Carolina. When his bus stopped in Batesburg, South Carolina, Woodard, still wearing his army uniform, asked the driver if he had time to use the restroom. The bus driver swore at Woodard, who swore back. The bus driver called the police and told them Woodard had created a disturbance. The town's police chief then savagely beat and blinded Woodard. A local jury acquitted the chief, who had also been accused of beating other black veterans.[5]

Only five days later, a veteran named Timothy Hood was shot five times by a streetcar conductor after taking down a Jim Crow sign in Bessemer, Alabama. The town's police chief then followed Hood home and emptied his pistol into the mortally injured man's head. On February 25, three police officers beat war veteran Kenny Long, his brother, and a cousin outside a filling station near El Campo, Texas. One of the officers – a deputy sheriff – then said, "Don't you know I hate a god-damn nigger," and shot Long to death.[6] A day earlier, Columbia, Tennessee, became the site of the first race riot in postwar America.

Despite these incidents, as blacks stood firm against prejudice, more and more whites in the North as well as the South stood with them, and the pace of stinging attacks on southern customs like Jim Crow mounted. To sociologist Howard Odum, the South and the North now faced their greatest conflict since Reconstruction. Other Americans appeared to agree. "A small group of Negro agitators and another small group of white rabble-rousers are pushing this country closer and closer to an interracial explosion," one Southern newspaper editor said. "Unless saner counsels prevail, we may have the worst internal clashes since Reconstruction, with hundreds, if not thousands, killed and amicable race relations set back for decades."[7] Branch Rickey's signing of Jackie Robinson had thrust baseball into the middle of what Gunnar Myrdal called the "Negro problem in America."

For baseball, the end of the war meant that teams could once again train in Florida. Like other Florida coastal cities that relied on tourism economically, Daytona Beach had struggled during the war. Gas rationing limited travel, and few Americans thought about taking a trip to the beach when their sons were fighting and even dying. With the end of the war people could once again begin taking vacations. Daytona Beach in particular understood the advantages of having a big league team train in their city. Being a team's spring-training home would mean an infusion of money into the local economy, as ballplayers, managers, their families, and other visitors – their wallets and purses in tow – stayed in Daytona Beach hotels, ate in its restaurants, drank in its bars, and shopped in its stores.

Other organizations trained further south in Florida because more teams were based there and the weather was generally warmer. But Rickey was also interested in the racial climate of prospective spring-training sites – and he liked what he heard about Daytona Beach.

Sportswriter Bill Roeder, who lived in Daytona Beach part of the year, had recommended the city to Rickey. Because Daytona Beach lacked the resources for an organization as large as Brooklyn's, however, Rickey had to find a nearby town to accommodate the overflow. Rickey, who listened carefully to the advice of people he trusted, chose Sanford at the suggestion of Brooklyn announcer Red Barber, who had grown up there.

In September, Rickey visited Daytona Beach and saw for himself that the city was unlike other southern cities. Daytona Beach offered advantages rarely seen in the South, such as black bus drivers, a black middle class, and a black political presence. It was also the home of a black college, Bethune-Cookman, whose founder and president was Mary McLeod Bethune, one of the more influential blacks in America. While going over the contract with Daytona Beach officials, Rickey was pleased to hear that one of the possible practice fields – Kelly Field – was in the city's black section.

Given Rickey's penchant for secrecy, he probably excluded Robinson from his discussions with Mayor William Perry, City Manager James Titus, and other city leaders, such as Herbert Davidson, the progressive publisher and editor of the *Evening News* and the *Morning Journal* and member of the city's inner circle. On October 24, the *Sun News* in Deland, twenty miles from Daytona Beach, published a United Press article in which Titus declared his surprise that Robinson would join the rest of the Brooklyn organization during spring training. "This matter will certainly be discussed with [Rickey]," Titus said.[8] Titus added, however, that he was not concerned about Robinson's presence in Daytona Beach. "We have a very good situation between the races here because we give the Negroes everything we give the whites," he said. "There is no discrimination, but there is segregation."[9]

Titus later told Wendell Smith that the city knew about Robinson long before it signed a contract with Rickey. "If we were going to voice an objection," he said, "we would have raised it then. We would have torn up the contract and forgotten about the whole thing. The people of Daytona Beach are not the kind of citizens who would object to any young athlete training here."[10]

On October 25, the *Daytona Beach Evening News* reported that Branch Rickey was expected to arrive in a few days.[11] Upon Rickey's arrival, the *Evening News* and *Morning Journal* hailed him as the city's "foster father of baseball."[12] In a follow-up story, the *Evening News* reported that Rickey had inspected City Island Ball Park, where Brooklyn practiced, and Kelly Field, where Montreal would practice. When asked about Robinson, Rickey replied: "I really think the press can have a lot to do with the outcome of this thing by not overplaying Robinson," adding: "It is important to avoid the appearance of difficulties and not to invite them."[13]

Rickey understood that he needed to win over the people of Daytona Beach and surrounding towns. To do this, he relied on his immense public relations skills. In a series of interviews, Rickey stressed time and again that his intent was not to challenge segregation laws in Florida but to give all ballplayers the same opportunity. Rickey told reporters that Robinson would have to adjust to Florida's laws – not vice versa. "I can't go to the Florida Legislature and say: 'Look here, now, you've got to change your laws because Montreal has a colored player.'"[14]

Rickey then returned to Brooklyn. He left behind Bob Finch, who preached racial equality while trying to assure townspeople and the business community that the Dodger organization would respect local ordinances. Finch repeated his boss's words that the club was not interested in overturning decades of segregation, only in giving black baseball players the same opportunities as white ballplayers. Finch also acted as a liaison between Rickey and the black community, telling blacks it was important that they behave appropriately and refrain, for the moment, from demanding greater civil rights. He spread the gospel of Rickey throughout Daytona Beach and into nearby cities and towns. He told a Deland Rotary Club, for example, that Robinson represented what all Americans wanted: equal opportunity for everyone. "Perhaps I delved too deeply into a subject that is more or less taboo in the South," Finch later told Smith, "but much to my surprise, it was accepted enthusiastically and without a single rebuff."[15]

Meanwhile from his Brooklyn office, Rickey consumed himself with the business of running the organization, which included monitoring the tolerance campaign and organizing the February camp in Sanford. Rickey also faced the task of hiring a new general manager and a new manager for the Montreal Royals. In both cases, he selected loyal men within the Dodger organization: naming Mel Jones the team's general manager and Clay Hopper its manager. Coincidentally, both men came from former slave states – Jones from Missouri and Hopper from Mississippi.

Beginning in January 1943, Jones had worked briefly as a publicist for the Dodgers, before serving as an officer in the navy during the war. He learned about Robinson after his discharge in November 1945. After visiting his parents in St. Louis, Jones traveled to Brooklyn, where he spent the next week discussing strategy with Rickey. "We talked about Robinson and how we were going to handle it," Jones remembered. Rickey expressed his concerns about southern white bigots and militant northern blacks. He confided in Jones, "the only thing we had to fear was the ignorant whites in the South and the ignorant Negroes in the North."[16]

In early December Rickey announced that Montreal's new manager would be Hopper, who worked as a Mississippi cotton broker in the off-season. The *Baltimore Afro-American* reacted to the news with suspicion. "Uh oh," it said. Indeed, Hopper seemed like an odd choice. But Rickey trusted and respected Hopper, who had worked for him in the St. Louis and Brooklyn organizations, managing several teams to league championships. If Hopper, a southerner with Deep South beliefs, accepted Robinson, Rickey hoped, then maybe the rest of the team would, too.[17]

When Rickey informed Hopper that the Montreal team would have at least one black, the manager pleaded with his boss to assign Robinson to another team. "Please don't do this to me," he said. "I'm white and I've lived in Mississippi all my life. If you're going to do this, you're going to force me to move my family and home out of Mississippi."[18] Rickey told Hopper that if he wanted to manage Montreal he would have to accept Robinson. "We signed Robinson before we signed Hopper, so he must have been forewarned," Montreal vice president Branch Rickey Jr. commented.[19] In fact, Rickey Sr. bluntly addressed the issue with Hopper: "You manage this fellow the way I want him managed, and you figure out the way I wanted him managed." Hopper replied: "Yes, Mr. Rickey."[20]

A few days after Robinson reported, sportswriter Maury Allen asked Hopper how his family reacted to the news. "My father is dead," Hopper said. "If he were alive he would probably kill me for managing a black player." Allen did not use the quote. "I never wrote anything like that because Clay was a nice man, and we all expected he would judge Robinson on his baseball ability," Allen said. "I think he did."[21] Hopper, to his credit, did not – at least openly – let his prejudice as a man affect his judgment as a manager. Robinson later said he was treated fairly by Hopper.

Robinson and Hopper had little in common; however, each man struggled with his own demons that spring. With so much at stake, Robinson rode an emotional roller coaster that left him exhausted and often at the brink of defeat. Hopper, for his part, felt like he was being untrue to all that he had been taught to believe. During one game, he watched Robinson make a good play, and then turned to his boss and asked, "Mr. Rickey, do you really think a nigger's a human being?"[22] Rickey's first impulse was to laugh – not because he thought the question particularly funny but to relieve the tension. He wondered whether Hopper would make it through the spring without having a nervous breakdown.[23]

So much depended on Robinson and Hopper. But at least as much depended on Rickey, who, at sixty-four, was placing himself under pressures unlike anything he had experienced in his long baseball career. For six months, Rickey worked day and night, moving forward his secret plan to integrate baseball while simultaneously trying to wrest financial control from the Dodgers. From July to September 1945, he maneuvered to acquire 25 percent of the team, which left him weary and heavily in debt. During the fall, he began experiencing dizzy spells and his eyesight worsened. One afternoon, he had a seizure and collapsed on a Brooklyn street, resting briefly on a cot in a haberdasher's shop. Once he felt better, he resumed his frantic schedule, neither seeing a doctor nor letting his health problems become public.[24]

In early December, Rickey attended minor league meetings in Columbus, Ohio, where he bickered and cajoled with other executives trying to assert their influence and gain advantages. From these meetings, he went straight to Chicago for the annual meeting of Major League executives. Again, Rickey worked from the early morning until late at night, haggling over new rules and possible trades.[25] During a break in the meetings, Rickey, days away from his sixty-fifth birthday, turned to

67

one of his fellow owners, William DeWitt, and said: "William, I'm in terrible trouble. The room is going around. You're going around." DeWitt quietly checked Rickey into a hospital. Doctors could not diagnose his health problems but agreed he needed rest. On the train from Chicago to New York, Rickey suffered a more serious attack. He was rushed to the Jewish Hospital in Brooklyn, where he registered as "John Doe."[26]

After two weeks of tests, Rickey was diagnosed with Ménière's disease, a disorder of the inner ear characterized by dizziness, deafness, and vertigo. His doctors told him to pursue a more peaceful life or risk other attacks. Rickey ignored the advice.[27] For the next several weeks from his hospital bed, he plotted and schemed in hopes of winning the Dodgers their first pennant since 1920 and juggled the myriad variables of training camp. Rickey remained in the hospital until the Dodgers moved to Florida at the end of January.

Shortly after the New Year, Robinson returned to the United States from his tour with other Negro Leaguers in Venezuela. Flying into Miami, he boarded a train to New York City, where Rachel was working as a nurse, and presented his fiancée with an alligator-skin handbag and a wooden jewelry chest. While in New York, Robinson also visited Rickey in the hospital, where Rickey again stressed the need for Robinson to hold his temper in check. Robinson then returned to California to make final preparations for his wedding.[28] Rickey and Robinson would not be in direct contact with one another until spring training.

On December 19, Wendell Smith wrote Rickey, suggesting that he sign Kenny Washington, Robinson's backfield teammate at UCLA and the son of a former Negro League star. Smith described Washington as an even better baseball player than Robinson. Smith told Rickey that he would be covering Montreal's spring training for the *Courier* and would be available if Rickey needed him.[29] In his January 8 reply, Rickey asked Smith if he would go to Florida before spring training to find room and board for Robinson and another black player, whom he identified as a pitcher named Wright. Rickey also asked Smith if he would watch over the two ballplayers in Sanford and Daytona Beach "because much harm could come if either of these boys were to do or say something or other out of turn."[30]

On January 14, Smith wrote Rickey that he was pleased that the

Dodger president intended to sign other black players. He also said he was happy to know that Rickey was relying on the *Courier* and Smith himself "in trying to accomplish this great move for practical Democracy in the most amiable and diplomatic manner possible." Smith added that he knew a family in Sanford who might have room for Robinson and Wright. He also suggested that the two ballplayers could avoid possible travel difficulties if Smith acted as their chauffeur.[31] In return for his services, Rickey paid Smith fifty dollars a week, which equaled his salary with the *Courier*.[32]

On January 29, Montreal announced the signing of twenty-seven-year-old Johnny Wright, a right-hander with the Homestead Grays of the Negro Leagues. In 1943, Wright went 31–5 and pitched two shutouts in the Negro League world series. While serving in the navy, he pitched for both the Great Lakes Naval Station and Floyd Bennett Air Field teams. According to news stories, he assembled a 15–4 record and had the lowest earned run average of any pitcher in armed forces baseball.

The *Daily Worker*, which had named Wright as a possible Montreal prospect in mid-November, noted that the pitcher had thrown well against the Dodgers in an exhibition game in 1945. Later that summer, he pitched brilliantly in the Negro League all-star game at Ebbets Field in Brooklyn. Wright, the *Worker* reported, was "the owner of a blazing fast ball and a sharp-breaking curve and plenty of control." In an interview, Wright told the newspaper that he was delighted with the opportunity. "I just can't wait to get a baseball in my hands. This is great," Wright said. The newspaper reported that Rickey intended to sign three or four more blacks before May 15.[33]

In his *Worker* column, Bill Mardo looked ahead to spring training. "Within a month the eyes of America will be focused on the playing field at Daytona Beach," he wrote. "As Jackie Robinson turns in those spectacular plays of his at shortstop; as John Wright blazes across his fast ball underneath the hot Florida sun – at that precise moment will the hypocrisy and stupidity of jim crow be mirrored across America in letters big enough for even the most narrow-minded to understand?" In the next day's issue Mardo chided the New York press for its silence on the signing of Wright. "Why in hell didn't the other papers play it up big? I ain't never seen no Negroes playin' big-league ball. Sure this is news. Big news," Mardo noted sarcastically. "You sure this guy Wright ain't a Communist."[34]

Writing in the *Baltimore Afro-American*'s March 16 issue, Sam Lacy acknowledged that Wright lacked the college education of Robinson, but declared that he possessed "something equally as valuable – a level head and the knack of seeing things objectively. He's a realist in a role which demands divorce from sentimentality."[35] Wright, he said, had the talent to make it with Montreal. Wright himself claimed he was aware of what lay ahead for him: "I am a Southerner. I have always lived in the South, so I know what is coming. I have been black for 27 years and I will remain like that for a long time."[36]

Lacy also reported that Grays owner Cum Posey became enraged when told that he had lost his best pitcher. "That's a damn dirty trick, Sam, that's all I can say!" Posey reportedly said in an obscenity-filled tirade. Lacy was not sympathetic. He had begged the Negro Leagues to adapt more formal rules so they might be recognized by organized professional baseball, but they never did.[37] On page fourteen of its February 7 issue, *The Sporting News* reported that Posey had filed a complaint with Commissioner Happy Chandler over the Dodgers' acquisition of Wright. Posey argued that Rickey should be required to purchase players from the Negro Leagues just as he did from the minor leagues. On page 18 it ran a brief article on Wright, summarizing the highlights of his career. *The Sporting News* reported that the real reason for Wright's signing was to keep the highly publicized Robinson company in Florida.[38]

Hundreds of veterans, fresh from a victorious war but uncertain about their postmilitary futures, had collected their gloves and bats and descended on Florida. Southern highways were full of the hopes and the dreams of these men, some so desperate they hitchhiked hundreds of miles. Competition was so stiff that men who had been stars in 1945 found themselves out of baseball the following year. Of the top five leading hitters in the American League in 1945, only Stuffy Stirnweiss of the Yankees played regularly in 1946, and his batting average fell by fifty-eight points from 1945.

There were other big stories that spring. In early February, Mexican businessman Jorge Pasquel and his brothers began recruiting big league ballplayers for a six-team summer league. Pasquel called American organized baseball "a slave market" because its reserve clause bound ballplayers to their teams. While organized baseball did not treat the Pasquel brothers seriously at first, that changed after a number of players, including hard-hitting Brooklyn outfielder Luis Olmo, left their teams for more money in Mexico.[39] Commissioner Chandler condemned the Mexican League as an "outlaw" league and vowed he would punish any ballplayer who tried to return to the Major Leagues after a Mexican stint.[40] Rickey, who was particularly susceptible to the Pasquels' scheme since he paid his players poor salaries, denounced the Mexican League's player raids. *The Sporting News* published a cartoon that showed Rickey yelling, "Help, police! Outlaws!" only to be rebuffed by a police officer, who says: "Quit yelling, you did practically the same thing when you snatched Jackie Robinson from the Kansas City Monarchs!"[41]

In early February, the Brooklyn organization began its monthlong, pre-spring training camp. Almost two hundred returning servicemen and other ballplayers gathered at Sanford Memorial Athletic Field and other nearby makeshift fields. The sheer number of ballplayers exceeded the organization's resources. Players had to wear the same uniforms day after day and were offered only celery to snack on, a plentiful commodity in the city known as the "celery city." Mel Jones remembered sitting in the bleachers and typing contracts. As soon as one player signed his contract, he called out another name. This continued for the first few days.[42]

Shortly after arriving in Sanford, Branch Rickey, wearing a baggy brown suit and a brown felt hat and chewing an unlit cigar, walked into the newsroom of the local newspaper and asked to see the sports editor. When Julian Stenstrom identified himself, Rickey asked if there was somewhere the two could go for a private conversation. As they shared a bench next to Troughton's drugstore, Rickey asked Stenstrom if he would have any objections to Robinson and Wright training in Sanford.[43] Stenstrom said he would not. Rickey asked if his editor would have any problems with it. Stenstrom told him that the editor did not care one way or another about baseball. And then Rickey asked Stenstrom how the town would react to Robinson and Wright. "Mr. Rickey," he said, "I can't answer that question. However, my gut feeling is that the Brooklyn organization is much too big for anyone in this town to question anything it wants to do." Stenstrom then promised Rickey he would cover the story fairly.[44] As it turned out, Stenstrom wrote a number of stories on the Brooklyn organization – none of them mentioned Robinson or Wright.

Before sportswriters left en masse for spring training, the New York chapter of the Baseball Writers Association held its annual meeting.[45] Twelve hundred journalists, owners, managers, players, politicians, and other dignitaries attended the twenty-third annual event at the Waldorf-Astoria Hotel. Affirming the greatness of baseball, the speeches produced loud, solemn applause. But as it always had, the annual evening was also measured in terms of laughter, as sportswriters took turns spoofing the national pastime in song, skit, and minstrel show.

Dan Daniel, the emcee of the 1946 show, called it the best one yet.[46] Arthur Daley wrote in the *New York Times* that "the burlesque was so broad that the scribes were able to risk bringing into the cast of characters as delicate a subject as Jackie Robinson. But it was all such lampoonery that no one's feelings really were hurt."[47] To make his point, Daley included the dialogue of a skit that had opened at a mansion in which a butler – or, as the columnist described him, "a darky" – appears in satin knee breeches and wearing a Montreal uniform. Before the thinly disguised Robinson character exits the stage, he refers to his boss, Commissioner Chandler: "Looks lak de massa will be late dis ebning." The Chandler character (played by sportswriter James Kahn) then enters with four other colonels (among them *The Sporting News*'s Tom Spink). Chandler claps his hands and calls out: "Robbie! Robbie!"[48] The butler enters, saying: "Yassuh, Massa. Here Ah is." Chandler then replies: "Ah, there you are, Jackie. Jackie, you ole woolly headed rascal. How long yo' been in the family?" Robinson replied: "Long time, Kunl, marty long time. Ebber since Massa Rickey done bots me from da Kansas City Monarchs." And then Chandler replies: "To be sure, Jackie, to be sure. How could ah forget that Colonel Rickey brought you to our house? (Aside) Rickey – that no good carpetbagger! What could he be thinking of."[49]

Another skit was written by Arthur Mann, a sportswriter and publicity assistant to Branch Rickey who wrote many skits and parodied his boss at every Baseball Writers Association show. This year, he noted the Robinson signing with the anthem "Glory Massa Rickey." When Rickey, who was in Florida, heard about the digs directed at Robinson and himself, he snapped: "That's nonsense."[50]

Wendell Smith also saw nothing funny about the parodies of Robinson and Rickey at the Waldorf-Astoria. He reprinted the skit with Robinson as a butler and then unleashed his anger upon New York sportswriters. "They are not for equality in sports and they gave vent to their feelings in this vicious manner," he said. "They weren't courageous or brave enough to express their feelings in their respective newspapers (that might affect circulation), so they put on this dastardly act behind closed doors." He added: "The parts were played by well known writers of the New York chapter of the association, but their names were not made public for fear of being reprimanded. Therefore, the entire blame for that 'Nazi Opera' must be heaped upon the entire body."[51]

While the parody was perhaps extreme, racist stereotypes were not unusual in the sports pages of the period. "This brand of racism, rarely given a second thought," Jules Tygiel wrote, "spoke for an age in which as 'invisible men,' blacks could feel no pain and well-intentioned whites had little sense of the harm they inflicted." Syndicated columnist Westbrook Pegler, who got his start as a sportswriter, referred in print to black sprinters as "African savages" and called boxer Joe Louis "the colored boy."[52] Similarly, in his biography of sportswriter Grantland Rice, Charles Fountain noted that Rice described boxer Jack Johnson as "the Chocolate Champ," characterized Jesse Owens's performance at the Berlin Olympics as "a wild Zulu running amuck," and in conversation referred to Owens and Robinson as "niggers."[53] A number of authors have charged that southern-born *New York World-Telegram* columnist Joe Williams was a racist. However, his son, Peter, defended his father's views, saying he was no different from his colleagues. "Most (if not all) of these men," he said, "were closet racists."[54] By today's standards, Fountain claimed, Rice was a bigot, but he was not unusual by the standards of his day and must be judged by them. Such journalists represented mainstream America and mainstream American journalism. "As such," Fountain concluded, "it can be served by no apologies or defenses, and deserves damnation less than it demands understanding."[55]

In early February, Rickey opened up the Dodgers' pre-training camp in Sanford, transforming the site into a baseball college – or "Rickey University," as it was called. He lectured ballplayers like a college professor, preaching morality off the field and stressing fundamentals on the field. The days began at 7 a.m. and went until 9 p.m. Every morning, the ballplayers tumbled out of their bunks, ate breakfast, and then went to Mayfair Hotel ballroom for the first lecture of the day, which was given by either Rickey or one of his thirty coaches. Rickey had given up any attempt to follow his doctor's orders to take things easy. He awoke each morning at six, then drove the forty miles from Daytona Beach to Sanford and, according to Dan Daniel, was the first one in the hotel ballroom each morning. "[Rickey] is a marvel at operating a major league organization, a master trader, a dynamic figure, absolutely unsparing of himself, until he leaves for Daytona around 10 at night," Daniel said.[56]

In Sanford, Rickey introduced the first automatic pitching machine, which used electric power to propel a baseball accurately to home plate. "The thing can throw 25 hundred baseballs a day," Rickey enthused to reporters. "This equals 20 pitchers working nine innings. And it takes only one man, who doesn't have to be a pitcher, to operate it."[57] The *Sanford Herald* reported that Rickey was pleased with the ballpark and its facilities and was interested in making Sanford a permanent part of the Dodgers' spring-training plans.[58] The presence of so many reporters meant good publicity for the city. The *Herald* noted the presence of several New York beat writers.[59]

Wendell Smith and *Courier* photographer Billy Rowe arrived in Sanford in mid-February to find accommodations for Robinson and Wright. Smith had attended college with a woman from Sanford whose last name was Brock. He hoped that her family could put up either the Robinsons or Wright. "I had to tell her what was happening and I said, 'Can we stay with your family?' And, of course, she said yes. They were well-to-do, had a beautiful home, a mansion," Smith said.[60] If Rickey had known that Mr. Brock made money in a numbers game called Bolita, the devout Methodist might not have approved, as Smith later noted.[61] As a lawyer, however, Rickey knew that you never ask a question unless you know the answer, and as a result he did not to ask too many questions. Upon inspecting the Brock's home himself, he gave it his approval. "This is a fine home," he said. "If we can't put them in hotels, then they should stay some place that represents something."[62] Thus, Smith, Rowe, and the Robinsons stayed with David and Viola Brock at 612 Sanford Avenue. Wright stayed across the street with Mr. A. L. Jones.[63]

In his March 2 *Courier* column, Smith praised Rickey's tolerance program, which he referred to as a "a map to prepare the baseball world" for integration. Smith tried to assure his readers that, while Robinson and Wright were betting against the house, the game was not rigged and that minds were open to integration in Sanford. He noted that he had taken Wright into a men's clothing store and introduced him as a pitcher in the Dodgers' organization. "Well, if you're a pitcher," the man said cheerfully, "you're in a good spot to get into the majors. Brooklyn certainly needs good pitchers." From this, Smith concluded that Sanford was "one of the most hospitable cities in the South" and that "a 'New Day's a-Coming' in the beautiful and picturesque Southland!"[64]

Bill Mardo provided a different picture of the town in his *Daily Worker* column. "Sanford's got the smell," he wrote. "The Smell of the South, the silent, lazy and ominous smell of a million lynchings that weren't good enough for the pretty palms. Strange Fruit Hangin' on the Poplar Trees." If you walked away from the nice houses on the clean streets with the pretty palms, Mardo wrote, you found yourself in the black section of town. "Here's where the Negroes live," he continued. "Here's where every street is a shanty-town. Here's where you walk by and the Negroes look up at you quickly and then away again. Here's where they live and die. . . . Some sooner than others."[65]

Sanford, like many small southern towns, had a strong Ku Klux Klan tradition. John Daniels, a black who later ran a successful home-fuel-oil business, remembered that the Klan used to meet across the street from Sanford Municipal Park. "My friend Walter Ware and I used to spy on those fellows," Daniels said. "We'd get us a quiet spot and watch them mount their horses and go off intimidating whomever they could. . . . There was no doubt about this being a Southern town. No doubt at all."[66] A lot of things could go wrong for Robinson and Wright in Sanford, perhaps even violently wrong. Rickey understood this when he refused to answer reporters' questions about where Robinson and Wright would be staying. The *Afro-American*'s Sam Lacy also admitted he never felt comfortable in Sanford. "I didn't feel safe," he said simply.[67]

When training camp officially opened on February 28, neither Hopper, Robinson, and Wright nor many of the hopeful ex-servicemen were there. But a few hundred ballplayers had arrived and were now under contract, each assigned to Brooklyn or one of the seventeen teams in its organization.[68] All but two of the teams had moved from Sanford to Daytona Beach, leaving behind only the organization's AAA teams – Montreal of the International League and St. Paul of the American Association – and a handful of writers to cover the beginning of integrated baseball. The Sanford press corps included sportswriters from the *New York Times*, *New York Daily News*, *New York Daily Mirror*, and *Brooklyn Eagle*; the *Daily Worker*; the black weeklies, such as the *Pittsburgh Courier*, *Baltimore Afro-American*, *Norfolk Journal and Guide*, and the *People's Weekly*; and wire services such as the Associated Press, United Press, and the American Negro Press Association.

Between 150 and 170 Montreal and St. Paul ballplayers and coaches crammed onto several makeshift ball fields. After the first day of practice, Rickey lectured the Montreal players on subjects such as religion, morals, and the sensitive issue of integration. He urged them to act like gentlemen and to treat Robinson and Wright as they would any teammate. "Be natural. Be yourself. Impose no restrictions on yourself," Rickey said, "and I'm sure we'll all work together harmoniously."[69] After Rickey finished talking to the players, he reiterated to reporters that he had signed the black ballplayers because he wanted a winning team – and not because of "political pressure." While this was not entirely true, it was Rickey's story and he was sticking to it. "If an elephant could play center field better than any man I have," he said, "I would play the elephant."[70] Rickey also told reporters he was not concerned about how Robinson and Wright would be treated in Sanford and Daytona Beach. "In fact, I'm not worried about anything except that I want to be sure nothing hampers the progress of those two players," he said. "I want the doors left wide open so that they will be free to think baseball as well as play it."[71]

But Rickey, in truth, had real concerns. He did not know how Montreal's white players would react to Robinson and Wright. There was some talk of a strike to protest the signing of the two ballplayers, though nothing came out of it.[72] Rickey also did not know whether the two men would be allowed to take the field for any of that spring's games. And if they were allowed to, he did not know if their lives would be in danger. Moreover, Rickey was concerned for their safety off the field. As the *Brooklyn Eagle* conceded, there was only so much Rickey or anyone else could do to protect the ballplayers from "hoodlums in the bleachers" – or bigots outside the ballpark.[73]

Unlike other attempts to integrate baseball, Rickey seemed determined to make this one succeed. But there was only so much he or anyone else could do. As *Eagle* sportswriter Harold Burr put it: "The future of the Negro in baseball is all bound up in Jackie Robinson's destiny." Given the fierce competition for positions and Robinson's limited baseball experience, Burr suggested that there was substantial doubt whether Robinson was even good enough for AAA baseball.[74] The Associated Press reported that experienced observers declared that Robinson would have to play exceptionally just to make the Montreal team.[75]

Chicago Defender sports editor Fay Young cautioned readers not to expect too much too quickly from Robinson and Wright. It would be unrealistic for either of the ballplayers to make it to the big leagues that summer. "In the meantime," he wrote, "everybody will watch both Robinson and Wright – those wanting to see both men make good will do a heap of praying and hoping."[76] According to Wendell Smith, Montreal's spring training would answer such questions as: Do Robinson and Wright have the ability to make the team? Will they be accepted by their teammates and by baseball fans? And will they withstand the insults and worse from opponents and teammates?[77]

While Rickey had broken baseball's color barrier, black sportswriters did not want him to stop at one or two ballplayers. When Lacy asked Rickey how soon it would be before he signed other blacks, he initially refused to answer. Then Rickey, being Rickey, began chattering about such stars as Roy Campanella, Monty Irvin, Verdel Mathis, Piper Davis, Sam Jethroe, and others. While Rickey made no promises, the implication was clear: If Robinson or Wright succeeded, he would sign other blacks.[78] If Robinson or Wright proved to be "good guinea pigs," Smith concurred, it would only be a matter of time before other blacks played in the national pastime.[79]

When Robinson and Wright arrived for their first day of training camp on Monday, March 4, Rickey was in Fulton, Missouri, attending British prime minister Winston Churchill's address at Westminster College. On March 5, Churchill delivered his "iron curtain" speech, which warned the Soviet Union that America and England would prevent their wartime ally from spreading communism. The fear of communism in the United States would eventually result in the Red Scare and the suppression of such publications as the *Daily Worker*. The world, as Rickey had noted more than four months earlier, was changing. In late October, he referred to his critics and detractors by saying simply: "The world is moving on and they will move with it, whether they like it or not."

1234**5**678910

Robinson and Wright Flee Sanford by Sundown

I N THE LATE MORNING of Monday, March 4, 1946, Jackie Robinson, Johnny Wright, Wendell Smith, and Billy Rowe arrived at the Sanford training camp at Memorial Athletic Field. Robinson and Wright, standing in their street clothes, paused and looked out over the practice field, where Montreal and St. Paul ballplayers were taking batting practice, shagging fly balls, playing catch, or running the bases. Seeing them, the ballplayers stopped what they were doing and stared back at them. "It seemed that every one of these men stopped suddenly in his tracks and that four hundred eyes were trained on Wright and me," Robinson recalled.[1]

It was an unsettling moment. Once Robinson and Wright crossed the imaginary line that separated them from the other players, they could not go back again. Each man probably wondered for a moment what he had gotten himself into. Bob Finch then emerged to shake their hands. Finch motioned Robinson and Wright toward the dressing room where they were to change into their uniforms. The dressing room was empty, except for the clubhouse man, Babe Hamburger. "Well, fellows," he said, "I'm not exactly what you'd call a part of this great experiment, but I'm gonna give you some advice anyway. Just go out there and do your best. Don't get tense. Just be yourselves."[2]

Robinson and Wright both knew it would be difficult to relax under the circumstances. Robinson nevertheless appreciated the man's words and later said he never forgot his smile. After Robinson and Wright put on their uniforms, the two players joined their teammates across the street from the ballpark in an empty lot, described by *Brooklyn Eagle* columnist Tommy Holmes as "a huge, vacant lot, as bumpy as a cow pasture."[3] There were seven spectators and maybe a dozen or so sportswriters and photographers in attendance. As Robinson walked past the sportswriters, he uttered a few words to Finch that would be repeated in newspapers throughout the country: "Well, this is it." Finch patted Robinson on the back and said the same thing.[4]

History came quietly. Robinson's first day of practice consisted of calisthenics, running, and some batting practice. If reporters and spectators expected a burning bush or at least a lightning bolt, they were disappointed. "It could be readily seen that Cecil B. DeMille had noth-

83

ing to do with the setting for the debut of Jackie Roosevelt Robinson," Holmes wrote. "There was no fanfare and no curious, milling crowd."[5]

In his story for the *Baltimore Afro-American*, Sam Lacy included such mundane details as Wright jogging twice around the field alone because the other pitchers had already finished their calisthenics. When Wright finished, he joined a pepper game, fielding bunts with four other pitchers.[6] The *Norfolk Journal and Guide* reported that Robinson and Wright went through practice drills that "aroused less excitement than a bally-hooed freshmen–senior class contest."[7] The Associated Press also reported that the workout failed to create much excitement or interest.[8]

Recalling the day years later, *Daily Worker* sports editor Bill Mardo laughed at the low-key descriptions. To him, if you looked beyond the pepper games and batting practice, you could see that this first day was a good day for racial equality, bringing with it progress and hope for even better days. "It was a thrilling day," he remembered. "The day belonged to decent-minded people who understood that discrimination against a man because of his skin hurt the nation as a whole."[9]

In his column on March 8, Mardo took Florida newspapers to task for not being at the Sanford ballpark. Under the headline "Florida Papers 'Forgot' Negro Workouts," he wrote: "I suppose some people and some papers would need an atom bomb bursting about their heads before admitting that this world of ours does move on."[10] Mardo was right: there were no reporters from Florida newspapers in Sanford. The *Sanford Herald* said nothing, and the *Daytona Beach Morning Journal* published an Associated Press story.[11] The *Deland Sun News* published a one-paragraph account from the United Press that referred to Wright by the name "White."[12]

New York City newspapers, having the luxury of distance – both geographical and emotional – reported that history was indeed made that day. As Robinson walked onto the field in an unlettered uniform, the *Times*'s Roscoe McGowen wrote that he "promptly sounded the keynote of the difficult symphony he will attempt to lead for his race."[13] Jack Smith of the *Daily News* noted the historical significance of Robinson as "the first Negro ballplayer to sign in organized baseball."[14] In the *Eagle*, Harold Burr, using slightly different wording, called Robinson "the first boy of his race in about 50 years to enter professional baseball."[15]

84

Robinson had rarely been on an athletic field where he felt self-conscious, wondering if he belonged. But he acknowledged that day feeling alone and pierced by the glare of so many unfriendly eyes. At one point, while waiting in line for batting practice, Robinson recognized Bob Daley, whom he had once played with in the same California league. To Roscoe McGowen of the *Times* Daley had described Robinson warmly as "very fast" and "a pretty good hitter."[16] And to Bob Cooke of the *Herald Tribune* he had characterized Robinson as "one of the best base runners I've ever seen. Of course I haven't played with him in three years, but I think he's got the stuff to make it."

As Robinson and Daley conversed, a number of other players introduced themselves to him and Wright.[17] After his brief conversation with Daley, Robinson then stepped in for his first swings against one of Rickey's new pitching machines – or "Iron Mike" as it was called. What happened next is subject to interpretation. Mardo wrote in his column the next day that Robinson grounded two pitches into the dirt and then sent the next two pitches into deep left, the second barely missing a cow grazing in the grass. According to Mardo, one of the players joked: "You almost got yourself a quart of milk with that poke, Jackie."[18]

In contrast, Lacy wrote that Robinson lined the first pitch into left field and that his second swing produced a weak roller down the first base line. And, in Lacy's account, Robinson's third at bat yielded an unimpressive fly to center field.[19] According to Holmes of the *Eagle*, however, Robinson bunted twice and swung at three or four others in his first appearance, making little or no contact with the ball.[20] *The Sporting News*, for its part, reported that Robinson "took several turns against the mechanical pitcher, smacking a number of pitches squarely."[21] Robinson remembered hitting a couple of long flies and impressing his teammates. "I felt as happy as a youngster showing off in front of some other boys," he said.[22]

Robinson's first day of practice was interrupted so he could talk to reporters and pose for photographers. The next day's stories included biographical information, such as his athletic successes at UCLA, his military background, his statistics in the Negro Leagues, his winter tour in Venezuela, and his recent marriage. Sportswriters, as they had in late October 1945, praised him for his courage, poise, intelligence,

85

physical appearance, athletic ability, and sense of humor. For instance, Robinson told reporters he weighed about 195 pounds but wanted to get down to 180, his college football weight. When someone remarked that the extra weight did not show, he grinned and said, "It's in my feet."[23]

When Robinson was asked to compare the Negro Leagues with the International League, he acknowledged that organized baseball was superior in terms of training and conditioning. He said he thought he could benefit from the coaching in organized baseball: "I think my biggest trouble is lack of any teacher," he told the *Herald Tribune*. "Nobody ever told me anything about the correct way to do things in baseball."[24] Arch Murray of the *Post* quoted Robinson as saying: "You fellows who have been around the big leagues all the time don't appreciate what good coaching and teaching means. Fellows like us on the sandlots just have to learn the best we know how. But maybe, it'll be different. I hope so."[25]

Robinson came to camp a few days late, several pounds overweight, and slightly out of shape. However, within a few days he had worked himself back into shape. But Montreal already had six shortstops, including Stan Breard, a popular Canadian, who had started at the position the year before. Brooklyn coach Clyde Sukeforth told Sam Lacy that it would be difficult for Robinson to make the team at shortstop. "Maybe he can be shifted to another slot," Sukeforth said.[26] When asked if he thought he could make the team as a shortstop, Robinson said he was not sure. He would not be disappointed if he did not play shortstop for Montreal, he said, or even if he did not make the team. "Certainly I would be willing to go to a lower class league," he said, "but I want to make this club."[27]

In his autobiography, *My Own Story*, published in 1948, Robinson remembered a relatively cordial exchange with the press, which he affirmed in *Wait Till Next Year*, published in 1960. But in *I Never Had It Made*, written with Alfred Duckett and published shortly before his death in 1972, Robinson described the first day's interview with reporters as contentious. When a reporter asked him what he would do if someone threw at his head, Robinson answered that he would duck. When another reporter asked him if he thought he could "make it with

these white boys," he replied that he had never had any trouble com-
peting with whites before.[28]

In Robinson's recollection the press had suggested to him that he
was trying to oust the popular Pee Wee Reese as Brooklyn's shortstop. He replied that he was trying to make the Montreal team, not the
Brooklyn team. "This confrontation with the press was just a taste of
what was to come," he wrote. "They frequently stirred up trouble by
baiting me or jumping into any situation I was involved in without
completely checking the facts."[29]

In fact, sportswriters rarely, if ever, treated Robinson with outright
hostility. Rather, they ignored him. After that first day in Sanford,
Robinson was rarely quoted again. The press appeared to see him as
little more than a curiosity or a novelty – like a one-armed player or a
thirty-five-year-old rookie. Wright, by comparison, was characterized as little more than Robinson's shadow, ignored entirely, or incor-
rectly identified. Burr wrote that Montreal had signed Wright prima-
rily to keep Robinson from "becoming homesick with none of his race
around."[30] In *The Sporting News*, Burr repeated the indignity: Wright
was signed "to keep Robinson from becoming too lonely and homesick."[31] While it was true that Robinson was the feature attraction,
black journalists reported the truth, that Wright was a talented pitcher
in his own right, not merely an appendage to Robinson and his story.

Robinson and Wright faced no overt racial problems during their
first two days of practice. No objections were voiced as the two ballplayers hit, ran, and pitched with their teammates. At lunchtime, the
whites ate all the celery they wanted, and Robinson and Wright went
back to the Brocks, where Mrs. Brock prepared their meals. When practice ended, most of the Montreal team went back to the Mayfair Hotel
on Lake Monroe. Robinson and Wright returned to the black section
of town, where they were viewed in equal measure as celebrities and
heroes.

Blacks in Sanford had rarely experienced anything like this before.
To be sure, writer Zora Neale Hurston had been raised in the nearby
town of Eatonville. Moving to Harlem, she had given wings to the spo-
ken fables and stories she had heard as a young girl. But Hurston belonged to Eatonville. Robinson and Wright, however briefly, belonged
to the blacks living in the Georgetown area of Sanford. Many knew

87

where Robinson and Wright were staying, and some approached the Brocks' house hoping to speak to the ballplayers. Others watched from a safer distance, reaching out with their prayers and shyly waving at the ballplayers when they sat on the Brocks' front porch.

Though he was barred from the press box, Wendell Smith assured his readers that Sanford was indeed "one of the most hospitable cities in the South."[32] But his optimism was short-lived. While much of Sanford had no qualms about the ballplayers' presence in their town, others certainly did. After the second day of practice, Smith and Billy Rowe were sitting on the Brocks' porch when a white man approached. Without identifying himself, he said he had been sent from a gathering of a hundred townspeople to deliver a message: "We want you to get the niggers out of town."[33] There would be trouble unless, he said, Robinson and Wright were "out of town by nightfall."[34]

Smith called Rickey in Daytona Beach, who ordered the journalist to bring Wright and the Robinsons to Daytona Beach immediately. Smith and Rowe instructed the ballplayers to pack their bags but did not explain why. At first, Robinson thought that Rickey was sending the ballplayer home and canceling the tryout. Devastated, he concluded he had come across the country for nothing. As the group headed out of Sanford, Robinson did not say a word; he had risked everything and lost. When their car stopped at a traffic light, according to *My Own Story*, they saw several whites milling about.

"How can people like that call themselves Americans!" Rowe snapped bitterly.

"They're as rotten as they come," Smith said.

"Now just a minute," Robinson objected. "They haven't done anything to us. They're nice people as far as I'm concerned."

"They sure are," Wright agreed. "As far as I can tell, they liked us."

"Sure, they liked you. They were in love with you," Rowe responded bitterly. "That's why we're leaving."

"What do you mean?" Robinson asked.

"I don't get it," Wright said.

"You will," Rowe said. "You will."

"We didn't want to tell you guys because we didn't want to upset you. We want you to make the ball club," Smith said. "But we're leaving this town because we've been told to get out. They won't stand for Negro players on the same field with whites."[35]

While Robinson was relieved that Rickey was not canceling his try-out, the truth was every bit as unsettling: his life had been in danger. The incident left Robinson shaken. And if he known what was occurring in other southern towns like Columbia, Tennessee, he would have had even more reason to worry. For the second time since leaving California, he considered quitting. "What hope was there that I would not be kicked out of Daytona Beach just as I had in Sanford," he wrote in *My Own Story*. "I was sure as soon as I walked out on the field, an objection would be raised."[36]

Though already tired of being a martyr, Robinson could not quit, not after what he had seen and heard in Sanford. During his two days of practice, he had noticed black spectators, though there were only a few of them, who cheered him with little reason – when he fielded a ground ball or when he bent down to tie the laces of his spikes. "I understood that my being on the field was a symbol of the Negro's emerging self-respect," he later remembered, "of a deep belief that somehow we had begun a magnificent era of Negro progress."[37]

Rickey kept the Sanford fiasco to himself. He told only those people who had to know – and no one else. He had his reasons for not telling reporters. This sort of publicity would play into the hands of those who believed that the mixing of races was wrong for baseball and society. It also would encourage other towns to act similarly. Montreal's white ballplayers did not know why Robinson and Wright failed to return for a third day in Sanford. "The next day he was gone," outfielder George Shuba said, "and we didn't see him again until we got back to Daytona Beach."[38] Ballplayers and sportswriters may have had their suspicions, but, on the other hand, the team was scheduled to return to Daytona Beach in a few days.

Rickey and Finch had given their fairness speech to Sanford city officials and civic groups, but obviously not everyone had gotten the word. Many in Sanford believed what they believed and that was that blacks and whites did not belong together. To this day, many people in Sanford believe that the man who had gone to the Brocks' with a warning was acting alone. If so, his bluff was an effective one, so great was the fear of racial violence.

Wendell Smith, disappointed by the Sanford incident, did not mention it in his column. Despite the reality, he wanted to convince his *Courier* readers that all was well in Florida.[39] In the March 7 issue Julian Stenstrom noted that the Royals had moved their training camp to Daytona Beach, but he also made no reference to Robinson or Wright or their reasons for leaving Sanford.[40] Years later, Red Barber explained what had happened in Sanford: "They ordered the Brooklyn Dodgers to get the Robinsons out of Sanford in twenty-four hours," he said. "When you made Branch Rickey make a move like . . . it was serious. It had to be!"[41]

John Daniels, who lived near the ballpark, remembered the tense racial climate in postwar Sanford. The city had vagrancy laws for blacks, which meant they could be arrested during the day if they were not working. Because Daniels had to work, he missed the opportunity to go to the ballpark to see Robinson. The threats against Robinson, in Daniels's estimation, were indeed serious. "Word got around quickly about his staying at D. C. Brock's place, and that the civic leaders weren't pleased," Daniels said. "Two nights later, Robinson and the other black player were gone. They took them to Daytona Beach. There wasn't all that fuss over there at all. Blacks and whites came to see Jackie play in Daytona."[42]

Things would be different in Daytona Beach because Daytona Beach was different. When spring training began, Mayor William Perry said the city had no objections to Robinson and Wright training there. "City officials and the population in general simply regard them as two more ball players conditioning themselves here," he said. "We welcome them and wish them the best of luck." According to Wendell Smith, this dispelled fears that Robinson and Wright would find themselves in "hostile territory."[43]

Rickey's interview with Daytona Beach City Manager James Titus was arranged by local real estate operator and politician Joe Harris, known as "the Negro mayor of Daytona Beach." To Harris, Smith raised his concerns about the racial problems that might develop because of Robinson and Wright's presence. Titus said he did not expect any problems because black entertainers had come to the city in the past without incident. "No one gets excited when Cab Calloway comes here, nor do they get excited over the many other outstanding Negro entertainers who come here," he said. "[Robinson and Wright] are artists and their ability is appreciated. Robinson and Wright are artists in their own field of entertainment and we will look upon them in that light."[44]

Smith, echoing Rickey, wrote in the *Courier* that the two ballplayers did not come to Daytona Beach to challenge the city's segregation ordinance but to play baseball. "If they are successful in that highly skilled field, however, they will leave an impression and establish a precedent unequaled in the turbulent, stormy history of the South," Smith wrote.[45] The American Negro Press Association reported that the ballplayers would not be confronted with hostility as long as they obeyed segregation laws.[46]

Daytona Beach was clearly unlike other southern towns and cities. Blacks lived a second-class existence there versus the third-class existence they lived elsewhere in the South. They could mingle downtown without being hassled. They could even shop in some of the stores. Joe Harris served an important link between the black community and the city's white power structure by, for example, registering black voters but not inciting them to question segregation. Likewise, his wife, Duff, wrote a newspaper column for the edition of the Daytona Beach newspaper that was circulated in the black parts of town.

As we've seen, the city was also the home of educator Mary McLeod Bethune, founder of Bethune-Cookman College and one of America's most influential blacks. Bethune, who was almost seventy-one years old, had served as vice president of the National Urban League and the NAACP. During the administration of Franklin Delano Roosevelt, she was part of the so-called Black Cabinet, black New Dealers who influenced government policy. One historian called Bethune "one of the few, perhaps the only black adviser who actually administered programs directly to black Americans."[47] She had the ear of both President Roosevelt and the first lady, Eleanor.

Eleanor Roosevelt had even appeared at several benefits for Bethune-Cookman College, including one in 1941 that drew twenty thousand people from all over Florida. "The sight of these many thousands of Southerners, white and black, mingling freely and democratically on the campus of a Negro college in Florida," Bethune once wrote, "was an unforgettable experience." During the war, Bethune joined Walter

White and other black leaders in pressing the president to address the grievances of black soldiers.[48]

Bethune, whose views on race were moderate and unthreatening, had relatively good relations with the city's white power structure. Even in her advanced years, she represented a powerful voice in black America. In November 1946, for example, she was one of the main speakers at the Southern Conference for Human Welfare in New Orleans, which attracted twelve hundred blacks and whites. "The share-croppers, the common, neglected and oppressed people of the South, white and black alike," she declared, "appeal through the Southern Conference for Human Welfare for the elimination of hate and the stimulation of love, for the annihilation of segregation and discrimination, for the abolition of the poll tax and mob violence. Today the cry is for freedom, to do and to have, regardless of race, color or creed."[49]

Daytona Beach officials had a measure of respect for Bethune – in part because she was a moderate who scorned violence in favor of working within the system. For blacks, having Bethune living in their town gave them a sense of pride. According to one resident, even the "bums" stood up straight with their heads high when they saw her on the street.[50] *Courier* photographer Billy Rowe later recalled that black and white people behaved well toward him in Daytona Beach and attributed this to Bethune's presence. "Her reputation had a lot to do with the way we were treated," he said.[51]

For all that, Daytona Beach was still unmistakably a southern city. The city council established separate residential limits or districts for white and black residences "in order to promote the public peace, welfare, harmony, and good order." Blacks lived in two areas of town. One stretched north from Volusia Avenue – or Highway 17 – to North Street; the other went south from Volusia Avenue to Shady Place. The Florida East Coast Railway tracks and Canal Road, now known as Nova Road, outlined the black neighborhoods on the east and west.[52]

Montreal practiced at Kelly Field, at the corner of Cypress and Keech streets, not far from Bethune-Cookman College. The Dodgers worked out a couple miles away at City Island Ballpark, on the banks of the Halifax River, in downtown Daytona Beach. Most of the players in the organization lived a few miles to the north at the comfortable Riviera Hotel. The Robinsons lived with Joe and Duff Harris. Wright stayed with Vernon Smith, a retired real estate operator. Wendell Smith and Rowe stayed nearby as guests of Bethune-Cookman College. Sam Lacy, like the Robinsons and Wright, stayed with a black family.

Each morning, a bus transported the white ballplayers from the Riviera Hotel to Kelly Field. Robinson and Wright dressed at their respective homes and then walked the short distance to Kelly Field. The Kelly Field community center was the hub of the surrounding neighborhoods' social life. It included a swimming pool, tennis courts, horseshoe pits, a baseball diamond, and a band shell, where there were talent shows and beauty pageants. But no such activities could compare with the impact of Robinson during the spring of 1946. "I was just a kid, and I was awed by it all, and I prayed for him," said Ed Charles, who grew up across the street from Kelly Field. "I would say, 'Please, God, let him show the whites what we can do and that we can excel like they can.'"[53]

Rachel Robinson and her "journalist friends," as she called Smith and Rowe, would spend their days watching baseball and keeping an eye on what was happening outside the foul lines. They were not alone in the makeshift bleachers. Among the spectators were kids playing hooky from school to catch a glimpse of Robinson, some of whom would hang over the outfield fences just for a chance to see him. "We would hang over the fence," Charles recalled, "and say, 'Let him be successful.'"[54]

Montreal opened camp on Wednesday, March 6. Robinson played four innings at shortstop during a seven-inning scrimmage against Brooklyn's substitutes. He failed to get a hit in two plate appearances.[55] If the contest, merely a scrimmage before a few nonpaying spectators, had any significance, hardly anyone noticed. Sam Lacy did, however, telling his *Afro-American* readers: "It marked the first time in history that a colored player had competed in a game representing a team in modern organized baseball."[56]

Lacy's column, which was published in the other newspapers in the *Afro-American*'s chain, served the important function of letting readers know that there was a story merely because Robinson had played that day, regardless of the game's official unimportance and thin crowd. Lacy saw that progress was being made. With so much at stake, victories, however small, were still worth noting.

In a game against Brooklyn's second team the next day, Robinson

93

played errorless ball in the field, shifting between shortstop and second base. He again went hitless at the plate. Clay Hopper did not seem disappointed. "He hasn't started to hit yet. The pitchers have been feeding him curve balls. He has fanned on curves, but he didn't look bad going after them," Hopper told *The Sporting News*. He also critiqued Robinson's defense: "He hasn't got a very good arm, but he gets to the ball very fast. He covers a lot of ground and has a good pair of hands."[57]

Wendell Smith meanwhile reported that Wright's arm had looked strong during a twenty-minute stint of batting practice. Instead of throwing flat pitches, Wright decided to throw a few fastballs. This brought Hopper to the mound to warn his pitcher that he risked hurting his arm if he threw too hard too early in spring training. "I just don't want him to get a sore arm. Pitchers with sore arms can't help us one bit," Hopper said. Smith said Wright was determined to make the Montreal team and then be promoted to Brooklyn, which had a weak pitching staff.[58]

Robinson was well aware that his arm was considered weak for a shortstop. He therefore tried to impress Hopper and his coaches by throwing the ball as hard as he could to first base. Clyde Sukeforth, a Brooklyn coach who had scouted Robinson the summer before, cautioned Jackie to relax or he would hurt his arm. Robinson ignored the advice.[59] After the second scrimmage, Robinson told Jack Smith of the *New York Daily News*: "My arm is pretty sore now, though it seems to be just a muscle soreness and nothing serious."[60] But when he returned to the Harrises that night, his arm hurt and he could barely lift it. He tossed and turned all night.

At practice the next morning, Robinson could not throw the ball across the infield. Hopper told him to rest his arm for a few days. Robinson spent extra time on his hitting, but this did not give him any comfort. He was so anxious he could not hit.[61] "I couldn't throw," Robinson later wrote. "On top of that, I couldn't hit. The harder I tried, the more I popped up or pounded the ball into the dirt. . . . The more I tried, the more tense I became." At night, Rachel massaged his arm, but the soreness persisted. "She and I realized later that there is virtually nothing you can do about a sore arm except to let time work it out," Robinson said.[62]

After Rickey learned that Robinson was sitting out fielding practice, he left the Dodgers' camp at City Island and went to Kelly Field. He ordered the ballplayer to practice, sore arm and all. "Under ordinary circumstances, it would be all right, but you're not here under ordinary circumstances," Rickey told him. "You can't afford to miss a single day. They'll say you're dogging it, that you are pretending your arm is sore."[63]

If Robinson could not play short – and that now seemed likely – he said he would play second or go wherever he was needed. "If the manager wants me at second base, that's where I'll play. I'm here to make good," he told Wendell Smith, who predicted Robinson would finish the spring as the team's second baseman.[64] But Robinson's arm was so sore he could not make the relatively short toss from second to first base. Montreal then tried Robinson at first, where a strong throwing arm was not necessary. Having never played the position, he struggled making the adjustment, missing easy throws and bobbling easy grounders.[65]

Rickey himself tutored Robinson at the position. Brooklyn coach George Sisler, a Hall of Fame first baseman, also worked with him.[66] Rickey also worked with him on his base running, yelling encouragement: "Be more daring" or "Gamble. Take a bigger lead."[67] Meanwhile, batting coach Paul Chervinko continued to tutor him at the plate. Sukeforth also spent a lot of time with Robinson, repeatedly telling him to relax and be himself, or, as Robinson put it, "massaging my morale."

This did not sit well with either Montreal players or with sportswriters who considered it special treatment. With so many war veterans in training camps, competition was stiff at every position. Ballplayers grumbled to one another that Robinson was receiving preferential treatment. At least one white sportswriter expressed this in print: "It's do-gooders like Rickey that hurt the Negro because they try to force inferior Negroes on whites and then everybody loses," he wrote. "Take this guy Robinson. If he was white, they'd booted him out of this camp long ago."[68]

Robinson no doubt felt his worlds closing in – both the one he was living in and the one he was playing for. He depended heavily on his wife for emotional support. But she, too, was a stranger in a strange land, a few thousand miles away from her family and friends in California. She, too, could feel the tension in the air as she watched her husband struggle day after day at Kelly Field. Though this could have put a strain on the newlyweds, it brought them closer.[69] Jackie began to refer to himself not as "I" but as "we." As Rachel explained later: "We began to see ourselves in terms of a social and historical problem, to know that the issue wasn't simply baseball but life and death, freedom and bondage, for an awful lot of people."[70]

In his *Afro-American* column, Sam Lacy asserted that he thought both Robinson and Wright would make the team. "I'll tell you what. I think our cause is in good hands."[71] Lacy himself was also squirming under the Florida sun. In his "Looking 'Em Over" column on March 11, Lacy called Robinson "a man in a goldfish bowl. . . . It is easy to see why I felt a lump in my throat each time a ball was hit in his direction those first few days; why I experienced a sort of emptiness in the bottom of my stomach whenever he took a swing in batting practice," he wrote. "I was constantly in fear of his muffing an easy roller under the stress of things. And I uttered a silent prayer of thanks as, with closed eyes, I heard the solid whack of Robinson's bat against the ball."[72] Lacy later said that he became personally involved in the story that spring. "It came from my heart," he said. "I did feel it. I was emotionally involved in everything."[73]

Like his friend Wendell Smith, Lacy had recognized the injustice of segregated baseball since his boyhood. Growing up a few blocks from Griffith Stadium in Washington DC, Lacy often accompanied his father to ball games, where he would root for the Senators from the Jim Crow bleachers. While he was in his teens, he worked at the ballpark during Major League and Negro League games – running errands for players, chasing batting practice balls, selling concessions, and operating the scoreboard. He saw for himself that a number of blacks were good enough for the Major Leagues. "I would watch both sides," Lacy said. "It struck me as unfair that the ballplayers I observed were more capable that those who played in the major leagues. There was something wrong with this picture."[74]

After attending Howard University, Lacy worked as a sportscaster before taking a job at the *Washington Tribune* in 1934. There, he began questioning why there were no blacks on the Senators or any other big league team. In 1937, he walked two and a half blocks from his desk at the *Tribune* to Griffith Stadium to discuss integration with Senators owner Clark Griffith. Griffith told him "the climate wasn't right." Lacy replied that the climate would never be right if it was not tested. He said that black stars such as Josh Gibson, Buck Leonard, and Cool Papa Bell belonged in the Major Leagues. Griffith disagreed. He said integration would destroy the Negro Leagues. "Griffith didn't budge," he said. "He didn't even entertain my thought."[75]

After Lacy left Washington to become national editor of the *Chicago Defender* in 1940, he began contacting Commissioner Kenesaw Mountain Landis, whose office also was in Chicago. Landis rebuffed Lacy's attempts to discuss integration. "Judge Landis did everything possible to avoid meeting with me or anyone to talk about the segregation issue," Lacy said, adding: "I sent him a note that said I would meet with him any hour of any day, any day of any week, any week of any year. I got no response."[76]

During the fall of 1943, Lacy again asked Landis if he could make the case for integration in front of team owners at their next meeting. Landis resisted the idea at first, then gave his approval that a delegation could address owners in a closed-door session. The speakers included *Defender* publisher John Sengstacke and *Courier* editor Ira Lewis. Lacy, much to his dismay, was replaced by internationally known singer and actor Paul Robeson because the rest of the delegation believed that Robeson would have a bigger impact.[77] Robeson spoke eloquently about how he had been accepted by his white teammates when he played football at Rutgers University. He added that he had been well received by white cast members during his recent success as *Othello* on Broadway. When Robeson finished, there were no questions, Landis thanked the group for its thoughts – and that was the end of that.[78]

Lacy believed Landis had suggested Robeson, a Communist, to taint the campaign to integrate baseball as a Communist front. Lacy also felt betrayed by the *Defender* for forsaking him. He quit the newspaper in protest and returned to his hometown of Washington DC, where he began working for the *Baltimore Afro-American*, part of a chain of several influential weekly newspapers in metropolitan cities in the East.[79]

In his first "Looking 'Em Over" column in the *Afro-American*, he said that Landis reminded him of a cartoon he had seen of a man extending his right hand in a gesture of friendship while clenching a long knife in a left hand, which was concealed behind his back. According to Lacy, Landis "told the gullible colored folks" that he was going to give them a fair chance, then, in private, told owners that there was "a Communist influence along with the torchbearers."[80] The meeting between owners and black representatives did not go for naught, however. As Brooklyn president Branch Rickey listened to Robeson and the others interested in integrating baseball, he jotted down notes weighing the advantages and disadvantages of integration. Secretly, he had already begun searching for the right player to integrate baseball. After replacing his onetime law school classmate Larry MacPhail in Brooklyn, in early 1943 Rickey brought up the issue of signing blacks during a meeting with the Dodgers' board of directors. George V. McLaughlin, president of the Brooklyn Trust Company, the team's majority shareholder, replied: "Get the right ball player and the thing is a success."[81]

Lacy believed that baseball would never be integrated as long as Landis was commissioner. And he was right. When Landis died, he was succeeded by U.S. Senator A. B. "Happy" Chandler of Kentucky, a onetime segregation state. Lacy responded to the selection as follows: "It appears that his choice was the most logical one to suit the bigoted major league operators, of which there is a heavy majority on hand."[82]

After Chandler assumed office in spring 1945, New York Yankees owner Larry MacPhail wrote Chandler and described the race issue as "increasingly serious and acute." He warned the commissioner that "we can't stick our heads in the sand and ignore the problem. If we do, we will have colored players in the minor leagues in 1945 and in the major leagues shortly thereafter."[83] *Sporting News* editor J. G. Taylor Spink sent Chandler a copy of his own 1942 editorial, "No Good from Raising Race Issue," obliquely noting that it had "taken care of the situation."[84] But Chandler stunned baseball by saying: "If a black boy can make it on Okinawa and Guadalcanal, hell, he can make it in baseball." He then added that he could be taken at his word. "I don't believe in barring Negroes from baseball just because they are Negroes."[85]

Spink fumed that baseball was moving toward integration. His publication expressed reservations about whether Robinson would be accepted in the International League, which had teams in southern cities like Baltimore and Louisville. It noted that the ballplayers would not have to suffer the indignities of segregation in Montreal. Harold Burr's story in the same issue included this curious insight into the racial attitudes of French Canadians: "There are 10,000 Negroes in Montreal. The population of the city is 75 percent French, who are without race prejudice."[86]

According to the mainstream press, International League teams were worried that their attendance would drop when they played Montreal because white spectators did not want to mix with black spectators or watch blacks and whites compete against each other on a ball field. The *Norfolk Journal and Guide* and other black newspapers countered, however, by predicting that Montreal would draw big crowds at home and throughout the International League, particularly in cities with large black populations, such as Newark and Baltimore.[87] The *Atlanta Daily World* asserted that blacks in Montreal were looking forward to seeing Robinson and Wright and the team's front office was rubbing its hands gleefully in anticipation of the attendance boost.[88]

But the regular season still lay ahead. For now, Rickey had to contend with Florida's Jim Crow laws, which forbade blacks and whites from playing together on a ball field or sitting together in the bleachers. Indeed, in many parks blacks were simply not allowed, period. Before Brooklyn left for a series of games in south Florida, the city of Miami, mistakenly believing the Dodgers would bring Robinson and Wright, announced that the team would have to leave behind its black players because its ballpark was restricted. "I don't want to embarrass any ball club," a city official told the New York Giants' Louisiana-born player-manager Mel Ott. "But if they come here they can't play and that's flat."[89]

Paul Waner, a hitting star of the Pittsburgh Pirates in the 1920s and 1930s and now a part-owner and manager of Miami's minor league team, was indignant when he read that the city's ballpark lacked segregated bleachers. Instead of acquiescing to Miami's segregation ordinance, he announced that he would challenge it and find a way for blacks to attend ball games. "I don't care if I have to build [bleachers] and pay for them myself," he said, "but I'm going to have special stands built here."[90]

But another of baseball's grand old names was not as progressive minded. When sportswriters asked Connie Mack, the revered owner and manager of the Philadelphia Athletics, what would happen if

Brooklyn brought Robinson to West Palm Beach to play the Athletics, Mack answered sharply: "I wouldn't play him. I used to have respect for Rickey. I don't any more." Mack later took the comments "off the record" and the incident received no publicity.[91] Red Smith, who was present at the interview, remembered Mack's tirade. "You wouldn't want that in the paper, would you, Connie?" asked Stan Baumgartner of the *Philadelphia Inquirer*. "I don't give a goddamn what you write," he replied. "Yes, publish it." Don Donaghey of the *Philadelphia Bulletin* recognized the explosive ramifications of the comments, however, and convinced Mack to take them off the record. Smith did not mention anything about the incident in print, though he later said: "I decided that I'd forgive old Connie for his ignorance."[92]

The Mack anecdote provides an example of how sportswriters suppressed sensitive information on the integration story. Ira Berkow wrote in his biography of Red Smith that the columnist was sympathetic to breaking the color line but did not think it should be challenged in print. When Smith was asked later how he felt about the story of baseball's first integrated spring training, he answered, "I don't remember feeling any way except having a very lively interest in a good story."[93] If he indeed had such a lively interest in the story, why did he not write anything about it?

Montreal began its spring schedule with four games against its organization rival, the St. Paul Saints of the American Association. It then had 22 games left in its schedule – 11 at home and 11 on the road. Montreal rested Robinson during the first 4 games to allow his arm to heal. Despite Rachel's nightly massages, however, he could feel no relief when he tried to throw. He continued to take extra batting practice, hoping that he would find his hitting stroke. But this, too, did not help – and only enforced the white stereotype that black athletes could not play hurt. So much rested on Robinson, and he knew it. Even if Robinson were in top form, Rickey did not know what would happen when he took the field for his first game. Rickey waited patiently for the right opportunity to unveil Robinson before the baseball world.

Jackie Robinson Memorial
Stadium in Daytona Beach.
Photo courtesy of Bob Lamb.

Left: J. G. Taylor Spink. Photo courtesy of National Baseball Hall of Fame Library, Cooperstown NY.

Above: Jackie Robinson. Photo courtesy of National Baseball Hall of Fame Library, Cooperstown NY.

Left: Jackie Robinson tags sliding
Brooklyn Dodgers runner during
spring training game. Photo courtesy of National Baseball Hall of
Fame Library, Cooperstown NY.

Above: Jackie Robinson talks with
Bob Finch, assistant to Branch
Rickey, on first day of spring training, March 4, 1946. Photo courtesy
of AP/Wide World Photos.

Jackie Robinson signs contract with
Montreal Royals, October 23, 1945. *From
left:* Royals president Hector Racine,
Branch Rickey, Robinson, and Royals vice
president Romeo Gauvreau. Photo courtesy of AP/Wide World Photos.

Branch Rickey. Dodger boss Rickey said he realized a lifelong ambition when he broke baseball's color line by signing Jackie Robinson. Behind Rickey is a picture of Abe Lincoln. "I cannot face my God much longer knowing that His black creatures are held separate and distinct from His white creatures in the game that has given me all that I can call my own." Photo courtesy of Library of Congress, Prints and Photographs Division, LC-USZ62-119888. Originally published in *Look* magazine, vol. 10, no. 6 (March 19, 1946): 70.

Sam Lacy. Lacy fought for the integration
of baseball for more than a decade. The National
Baseball Writers Association once banned him
from the organization. Later, it named him to
the Baseball Hall of Fame. Photo courtesy of
the *Afro-American* Newspapers Archives and Research Center, Baltimore MD.

1234**5**6**7**8910

Robinson Takes the Field

O N SUNDAY MORNING, March 17, Jackie Robinson was penciled into the Montreal starting lineup for an afternoon game against Brooklyn at City Island Ballpark in downtown Daytona Beach. Writing in the *Brooklyn Eagle* Harold Burr declared that "Tradition will be shattered when Robinson starts at second base, marking the first time a Negro has ever played against a big league team in the South."[1] Roscoe McGowen of the *New York Times* added that Robinson would break "Southern tradition and precedent. . . . Never before in this state, or any other Southern state, has a Negro played with whites."[2]

While it was true that no blacks had played with or against whites in the South, Burr and McGowen allowed their readers to infer, erroneously, that blacks had been free to play in organized professional baseball in the North. By projecting a sense of regional superiority to their readers, such sportswriters, purposely or not, obscured the uncomfortable truth that baseball's color line crossed the Mason-Dixon Line. In fact, there was much more at stake than southern tradition. When Robinson took the field, he would become the first black to wear the uniform of an organized professional baseball team since the 1880s.

Robinson himself was keenly aware of what the March 17 game meant for black America and for him personally. "All you have to do is make a good showing against the Dodgers," a teammate told him, "and you'll be sure of staying with Montreal."[3] Burr wrote that Robinson had hit the ball well in a practice game at Kelly Field the day before, but his arm was still weak and he could not throw. The pain in his right arm constricted both his throwing and his confidence, and he had still not found his hitting stroke.[4]

There were other things to worry about, too. Robinson could not help turning over in his mind all the things that could go wrong, including the possibility that his life might be in danger. What might white spectators yell at him, throw at him – or worse? As the March 17 game approached, Robinson imagined a torrent of racial abuse. But neither he nor his inner circle knew whether Montreal would put him in the lineup, and if it did, whether Daytona Beach would even allow the game to be played. For several days, Robinson and the others wondered if the city would enforce its segregation ordinance and prohibit the ballplayer from taking the field. In the *Daytona Beach Sunday News-Journal*, Bernard Kahn quoted Montreal manager Clay Hopper as saying: "I don't know if Robinson will play or not. But he'll accompany the Montreal squad."[5] Rickey also was uncertain: "If there's an issue," he said, "we'll face it."[6]

Robinson had little control over the game. He had no choice but to trust Rickey and hope he could make things work – just as the next generation of black activists would depend on influential whites to create and enforce civil rights legislation. Rumors flew that city officials were putting pressure on Rickey to remove Robinson from the lineup.[7] As Robinson later learned, the reverse was true. Rickey secured the promises of city officials that Robinson and Wright would be permitted to play, not just in practices but in games. "He had done a fantastic job of persuading, bullying, lecturing, and pulling strings behind the scenes," Robinson recalled later.[8]

But what if Daytona Beach changed its mind? What if a minority of reactionaries forced the city to cancel the game in the interests of public harmony? It had been relatively easy to keep the Sanford incident out of the papers. If something happened on this day, it would be harder – even impossible – to suppress it. This time the press would include Wendell Smith and Billy Rowe of the *Courier*, Joe Johnson of the *People's Weekly*, *Daily Worker* sportswriter Bill Mardo, several New York City sportswriters and correspondents, and wire service reporters.

The weather was threatening in the morning of the game, but it cleared up in plenty of time for the 3 p.m. game. Long before the first pitch, it became clear that the Jim Crow section of City Island Ballpark would not be big enough to accommodate all the black spectators who wanted to attend. The March air crackled with optimism. As blacks sat in church that morning, they prayed for Robinson and heard sermons about him. Robinson dominated conversations that morning and early afternoon. Blacks by the hundreds walked in a parade to the stadium in their Sunday dress clothes. Mothers and fathers held the hands of small children, others clutched the arms of the frail, and young boys hurried ahead excitedly ahead of their families.[9]

As was the custom that postwar spring, the Dodgers announced that military men would be admitted to the game without charge. A large number of soldiers, many black, many white, came to the game from the nearby U.S. Army Welch Convalescent Center. Some were bandaged, and others were walking with crutches.[10] Decades after the game, the Daytona Beach newspapers often reported that the ballpark had relaxed its Jim Crow rules for Robinson's first game and that blacks and whites sat intermingled throughout the stadium. According to these stories, black and white soldiers began sitting together, and stadium officials, out of respect for the servicemen, allowed it to continue. Other blacks supposedly saw this and moved from the segregated section, so that on this day, blacks and whites watched the game together in harmony.[11]

This scenario is unlikely, however. Certainly no reporter mentioned it at the time. In any event, the park's segregated section was packed beyond capacity. Two hundred or so blacks stood beyond the right-field foul line. Smith, who often cautioned blacks to behave themselves at ball games, kept an eye on things, hoping nothing would happen that might embarrass Robinson. There were rumors that Commissioner Happy Chandler would attend the game. He was, in fact, in Daytona Beach but did not attend the game. Rickey himself also decided not to make an exception to his rule against attending Sunday games.[12] Thus, the Brooklyn executive had not been present for Robinson's signing, for his first day of spring training, and now for his first game.

During batting practice, sportswriters and photographers joined the players and coaches on the field or in the teams' dugouts. Black journalists, however, denied press cards, were restricted to the cramped segregated section down the right-field line, more than a hundred feet away from home plate. Rowe, so close to history and yet too far to take a decent photo, squinted hard for an image of Robinson for the *Courier*'s readers across America.

At one point, Brooklyn manager Leo Durocher spotted Rowe and motioned him to the field. "You can't get any pictures from way back there!" he said. "Come into the dugout!" As Rowe remembered later, he began to walk across the field when someone in the bleachers yelled, "Get that nigger out of there!" Rowe froze. He did not know whether to continue or go back to the segregated stands. Durocher motioned him to keep walking. According to Rowe, Durocher then went to ballpark officials and demanded the removal of the spectator who called Rowe a "nigger." In a few minutes, a man was escorted from the ballpark. "I don't know if it was the right guy or not, but they made somebody leave," Rowe remembered with a laugh.[13]

A standing-room-only crowd of four thousand, including three thousand whites, packed City Island Ballpark. For years owners and sportswriters had warned that integration would chase away white spectators. But that was hardly the case on this day. According to Roscoe McGowen, Montreal could predict how Robinson would be treated throughout the coming summer from the reaction he received that afternoon. The crowd would include many northern tourists, who would be sympathetic, McGowen felt, but native southerners might cause problems.[14]

Montreal failed to score in the top of the first inning. In the bottom of the inning, Brooklyn's Dixie Walker hit a bases-loaded triple. After one inning, Brooklyn led 4–0.[15] When Robinson came to bat in the second inning, he steeled himself for the jeers. Nothing in his long and successful athletic career had prepared him for this moment, and he expected the worst. "This is where you're going to get it," he told himself as he walked to the plate. Instead, to his surprise, he heard applause – loud raucous applause from the distant right-field bleachers but also applause from the whites. He remembered hearing one drawling southern voice say: "Come on, black boy! You can make the grade!" He heard someone else yell: "They're giving you a chance – now come on and do something about it!"[16]

In his first at bat, facing Ed Chandler, Robinson chased a curve ball and fouled out weakly to Brooklyn third baseman Billy Herman. He played five- and-a-half innings before being removed to rest his arm. In three at bats, he went hitless, fouling out twice. In the sixth inning, Robinson put the ball in play for the only time all game and reached base on a fielder's choice. He then stole second and scored, running "like a scared rabbit" between second and home, the *Daytona Beach Evening News* reported.[17]

Brooklyn won the game, 7–2. But Robinson won the day by becoming, as Jack Smith of the *New York Daily News* noted, the first black to play against a Major League team in a regularly scheduled spring training game.[18] The *New York Daily Mirror*'s Gus Steiger used slightly different wording, saying that it was the first time in fifty years in organized baseball that a black had played in a game involving two teams.[19] The *Times* reported that, however historic, the game was "seemingly taken in stride by a majority of the 4,000 spectators," nearly a quarter of whom were black.[20]

The *New York Post* agreed, describing Robinson as "just another ball player trying for a job. . . . There were a few cheers here and one or two muffled boos there, but for the most part the crowd accepted him."[21] In the *Eagle*, Burr wrote that Robinson was on the spot "when he shuffled out to cover second base for the Montreal Royals." Robinson, he claimed, was booed mildly during his at bats.[22] Moreover, *The Sporting News* – no doubt reflecting its editor's disdain for integration – buried Burr's three-paragraph account toward the back of the issue.[23] None of New York City's high-profile columnists – Red Smith, Grantland Rice, Joe Williams, Jimmy Powers, Dan Parker – attended the game, or if they did had anything to say about it.

In terms of the local press, *Daytona Beach Evening News* sports editor Bernard Kahn covered the game, though he did not mention Robinson until the fourth paragraph of his article. Plainly, Kahn did not consider the game particularly important. In later years, the newspaper would trumpet the story as one of the most significant sports events in the city's history, but this is not how it saw the game when it happened. The Montreal-Brooklyn game shared the page with longer stories, including one on the city's class-D minor league team and another on a pair of Swedish long-distance runners.[24] The *Morning Journal* said nothing about the game; the Sanford and Deland papers also ignored it. Other Florida dailies either published brief wire service accounts or remained silent.

In contrast, the Associated Press, as it had more than once that spring, showed a level of fairness. It began its story by noting that Robinson had set a precedent for spring training in the South: "It was the first time a Negro player ever participated with whites in an exhibition game for which admission was charged in the state of Florida."[25] The A.P. also distributed this description of the crowd's reaction to Robinson: "When he came to bat for the first time, the Negroes applauded. The whites, sitting back of third base, didn't engage in handclapping until [Billy Herman, the Brooklyn Dodger third baseman] had caught the foul fly. However, in his next two times at the plate, Robinson was applauded by both whites and Negroes as he took his place in the batter's box."[26]

Robinson, who as noted put just one ball in play, understandably impressed few people that afternoon. The *Journal-American* reported that Robinson "was plainly nervous in his first two trips to the plate and his lusty swings resulted in weak foul flies."[27] Burr reported that the nervous Robinson was swinging weakly at Brooklyn pitcher Ed Chandler's curve balls. "I've sure been looking at some beautiful curves. I just couldn't hit 'em at all," Robinson conceded to the press.[28] Gus Steiger of the *Daily Mirror* concurred: "At this stage he is a soft touch for such a pitch." He added ominously, "Many a rookie before him has been curved into oblivion, indicating an arduous road ahead."[29]

Sportswriters speculated that Robinson might turn out like Jim Thorpe, the great Indian athlete whose big league career never realized its potential because he could not hit curve balls. However, Robinson's timing was no doubt affected by the weight he carried on his shoulders that day. Leo Durocher, for his part, praised Robinson for his grace under pressure. "Although Robinson didn't get a hit today, he looked like a real ballplayer out there," he told the *Pittsburgh Courier*. "Don't forget he was under terrific pressure. He was cast in the middle of a situation that neither he nor the fans had ever experienced before. But he came through it like a champion. He's a ballplayer."[30]

Robinson continued to be frustrated by his hitting, or lack of it. But he was encouraged by what he saw and heard – especially after what had happened in Sanford. "I didn't get a single hit that day," he later wrote, "nor did we win the ball game; but when I got home, I felt as though I, personally, had won some kind of victory. I had a new opinion of the people in the town. I knew, of course, that everybody wasn't pulling for me to make good, but I was sure now that the whole world wasn't lined up against me. When I went to sleep, the applause was still ringing in my ears."[31]

Blacks in Daytona Beach felt the same exuberance as they sat in their homes that evening talking about the game and describing it to those who did not attend. They were all too aware that progress would require courage – and even casualties. And yet none of them had ever lived in a time that so brimmed with possibilities never imagined before. When black spectators looked out over the field and saw Robinson in a Montreal uniform, playing second base, in the middle of white men, they gained a true glimpse of what racial equality might look like.

The black press communicated the lessons of the day to its readers. Joe Johnson of the *People's Voice*, noting the historic nature of the game, observed that both races cheered Robinson.[32] When Robinson stole a base in the sixth, according to the *Chicago Defender*, the crowd in the Jim Crow section "went wild."[33] The *Washington Afro-American*, noting that Robinson was cheered before each at bat, interpreted this as a good sign that Robinson and Wright would be well received in the International League.[34] The *Norfolk Journal-Guide* also reported that though some had predicted that white southerners would boo Robinson, this had not happened. The crowd had supported him.[35]

Wendell Smith characterized the response of the white spectators as the most gratifying part of the day. He reported that not even popular Brooklyn stars like Dixie Walker, Billy Herman, or Pee Wee Reese were more warmly cheered. No insulting epithets had been hurled at Robinson from the stands. "It definitely proved that baseball fans, whether in the North or South, appreciate talent and will not hesitate to give credit where credit is due," he wrote. Smith wrote that there had been some question whether Robinson would be allowed to play, but there had been no objections to the man he called "the most talked about player in baseball today."[36]

When Smith looked out over the baseball diamond and saw Robinson he did not see only what others did; he saw the personification of progress and the dream of racial equality. In characteristic hyperbole, Smith tried to capture the moment. "Six thousand eyes were glued on the mercury-footed infielder each time he came to bat," he wrote. "His performance with the willow failed to provide any thrills, but, nevertheless, his vicious swings and air of confidence as he faced real Major League pitching for the first time won the admiration of a crowd that seemed to sense the historical significance of the occasion."[37]

When Wright made his spring-training debut the following Friday, he experienced none of the fanfare that had greeted Robinson. Pitching before a much smaller crowd, he gave up 10 hits and 8 runs in less than five innings, losing to Brooklyn 9–7. "I just didn't have it," Wright told the *Courier*. "My stuff wasn't working. I'll get another shot at them and you can bet I'll do much better." Commissioner Chandler and Rickey watched from behind home plate. When Wright walked off the field, Chandler remarked, "Oh, well, maybe he'll have better luck next time."[38]

To Smith and other black sportswriters, Chandler's buoyant personality represented a distinct contrast to his craggy-faced predecessor, Kenesaw Mountain Landis. When Chandler asked Smith how Robinson and Wright were adjusting, the sportswriter answered that there had been no difficulties. "I'm glad to hear that," Chandler responded. "Yes, sir, it's nice to know that everything is working out okay and that they're getting a fair chance. That's the way it should be. That's the American way, and baseball is American in every sense of the word."[39]

Before Wright's start, Robinson, who played earlier in the morning in an intrasquad scrimmage, was introduced to Chandler. The commissioner asked him how he was doing. "Just fine," Robinson said. "But they've got so many good players trying out for the Montreal team, I'm a little worried. I've gotta do plenty of hustling." Chandler then chuckled and said, "Don't worry about the other players. All you have to do is get in there and play hard." Robinson then thanked the commissioner and returned to his seat in the segregated bleachers.[40]

During his interview with Smith, Chandler mentioned that he had just come from a baseball conference in Cuba where he had received the Cuban league's promise that American ballplayers who signed with the Mexican League would be prohibited from playing winter ball in Cuba. When Smith asked him if he was sure the Cuban league would cooperate, Rickey replied that it would never become part of organized baseball if it used outlaw players. When Smith asked Chandler about the possibility of recognizing the Negro Leagues, which would open up organized baseball to black players, Chandler balked. The Negro Leagues were too disorganized for organized baseball; they lacked uniform player contracts, schedules, and rules, he said. "They've been advised to get their house in order," he warned. "As long as Negro baseball is operated as it is now, there isn't a chance."[41]

In an editorial, the *Chicago Defender* agreed with Chandler's criticism that the Negro Leagues was too disorganized and needed to "get their house in order." But if they did, what then? Would a reasonable number of black players then get a chance at the big leagues, or would they remain segregated in their own leagues, perpetuating Jim Crow-ism? "The ideal setup would, of course, be the elimination of all Negro teams," the paper commented. "There should be only teams composed of all nationalities selected strictly on the players' ability to play ball [regardless] of his skin color. . . . Unfortunately, however, America has not matured enough racially for such a progressive step."[42]

In the same issue as Wendell Smith's interview with Chandler, the *Courier* included a story about representatives of the Negro National League agreeing on reforms that addressed the objections of organized baseball. The article noted, for example, that the black National League had banned a player for five years for jumping to the Mexican League. The *Courier* also reported that the National Negro League rejected two new franchises, one in Montreal and the other in Brooklyn. If Montreal had a black team, fans would then have to split their support between the Royals and a Negro League team, adversely affecting attendance for both teams and robbing Robinson and Wright of support.[43]

In his interview, Smith had also asked Chandler how he thought Robinson and Wright would be treated in the International League. The commissioner hesitated, then proceeded carefully: "I think they'll be treated all right," he said. "As far as I can detect, no one seems resentful about them being on the team at this time, and I can't see why anything should crop up later on. You can never tell, but I think they'll be treated all right."[44]

Smith's writing continued to suffer from too much wishful thinking. He dreamed of blacks and whites harmoniously sharing the national pastime, and he tried to share that dream with his readers. If blacks and whites could coexist together at Kelly Field, he argued, they could do so in the big leagues, too. He cited an example from one practice, in which a ball took a bad hop and hit Robinson in the face. The team's shortstop, Stanley Breard, immediately offered his sympathy. "I know that must have hurt, Jackie. How do you feel?" he asked. Robinson, grateful for Breard's concern, said he was okay.[45]

Whether it was the Wendell Smith influence or the sensitivity of the race issue, all appeared well at Kelly Field, according to newspaper accounts. *New York Post* columnist Leonard Cohen quoted Smith, whom he described as the sports editor of one of American's leading black papers, as asserting that Robinson had been receiving the same treatment as any of the white players. Cohen said that Robinson and Wright would either make the team or not based on their merits. "We're trying to give the fans of Montreal the best possible team," he quoted general manager Mel Jones as saying. "If the colored boys can help us win, they'll make the grade. We're not trying to exploit them as gate attractions or expose them in any way to harm, embarrassment, or ridicule."[46]

When Cohen interviewed Robinson the ballplayer appeared pleased with the way he had been treated thus far. Robinson said he had come to camp hoping to accomplish two things: one was to make the team; the other was to "make it possible for other members of our race to get a tryout." When the interview was over, Robinson returned to the batting cage, where his teammates yelled their encouragement – "Come on Jackie, line it out!" Cohen declared that Robinson and Wright were being given the same opportunity as anyone else in the Montreal camp.[47] *The Sporting News* also reported that there had been no friction between the two black players and their white teammates during the early days of spring training. "Everybody has been very helpful," Robinson said. "I've been told how to play the different hitters and John here has picked up a lot of pointers on pitching."[48] The Associated Press also reported that the team was treating Robinson and Wright no differently than anyone else.[49]

Black newspapers likewise reported that integration had gone smoothly thus far. The *Atlanta Daily World* noted that there had been "absolutely no friction" between Robinson and Wright and their teammates.[50] The *People's Voice* of Harlem described the relationship between the black and white teammates "as pleasant." The ballplayers joked and talked about things such as the high laundry prices and the exorbitant living costs. The article added that the Robinsons were staying with Joe Harris, "the Negro mayor of Daytona Beach," where the "charming" Mrs. Robinson did the cooking. Johnny Wright, it noted, ate his meals at a local restaurant.[51]

Despite such sanguine reports, Robinson and Wright had little contact with their teammates on the field and none off the field. Robinson later recalled that, for the most part, his white teammates generally reacted with neither hostility nor sympathy toward him. They rarely talked with him, and he rarely spoke to them: "They didn't speak to

Wright or to me except in the line of duty, and we never tried to engage them in conversation," Robinson said. "They seemed to have little reaction to us, one way or the other."[52]

There was at least one notable exception – Lou Rochelli. He had expected to be the team's starting second baseman until he was replaced by Robinson. "When I got the assignment, it would have been only human for him to resent it," Robinson said. "And he had a right to assume that perhaps I had been assigned to second base instead of him because I was black and because Mr. Rickey had staked so much on my success."[53] Instead, however, Rochelli spent long hours tutoring Robinson on the different techniques of playing second base. "He recognized that I had more experience on the left side of the infield than the right," Robinson said. "He taught me how to pivot on a double play. Working this pivot as a shortstop, I had been accustomed to maneuvering toward first. Now it was a matter of going away from first to get the throw, stepping on the bag, and then making the complete pivot for the throw to first. It's not an easy play to make, especially when the runner coming down from first is trying to take you out of the play. . . . Rochelli taught me the tricks."[54]

Other Montreal players who befriended Robinson included Johnny "Spider" Jorgenson, Marvin Rackley, and Al Campanis. Campanis would later be forced to resign in disgrace as a Dodgers executive after making racially insensitive remarks during an interview on the ABC news program *Nightline*. Speaking on the fortieth anniversary of Robinson breaking the Major League color barrier, Campanis resorted to one stereotype after another regarding blacks' qualifications as players. He finally said that the race "may not have the necessities" to succeed as either managers or general managers. His long tenure with Brooklyn ended soon after in disgrace. Though Campanis was vilified in the press for his comments they reflected the views of the baseball establishment.

Jorgensen, who had played against blacks in California winter leagues, said he was far more worried about his chances of making the team than he was about sharing a ball field with Robinson and Wright. Jorgenson claimed that his experience had taught him lessons in race relations that his southern teammates had not shared. "You didn't go up there and hug them or kiss them or anything like that," he said.

"You just observed them, talked to them, played catch. Hell, I didn't think anything about it. But some of the southern boys were a little concerned. I didn't have time to worry about [Robinson]. I was worried enough about myself."⁵⁵

Tensions were already high because of the competition for positions, exacerbated by the return of so many veterans. Interviewed by Bill Mardo, Robinson's Montreal teammate Bob Daley said was not surprised by the racial tension during the first part of training camp: "Sure, there'll be some guys with chips on their shoulders," Daley said, "and some guys who'll gun for Robinson just because he's colored – but those things will take care of themselves as Negroes establish themselves more firmly in baseball and wear down those prejudices during the course of competition."⁵⁶

Several Montreal ballplayers, southern and otherwise, resented Robinson because they believed the team would find a spot for him, which meant one fewer spot for them. If Wright also made the team two spots were gone. "I was glad I played outfield," Dave McBride, a Montreal prospect, remembered. "I always had the impression that [Robinson] had the attitude that he was better than us. He was almost cocky. Looking back at it now I guess he had to be that way. He was all business. Maybe he had to psych himself up all the time to make it through all that. Maybe he was so quiet because he didn't want to blow it."⁵⁷

Clearly, Robinson did not win over his critics with his arm, his bat, or his personality. While warm and charming with those he was comfortable with, he could be sullen, temperamental, and remote. He was not one to make friends easily, Woody Strode, his teammate on the UCLA football team, remembered. "Jackie always seemed to have a chip on his shoulder. Maybe he was ahead of his time in his thinking with regard to the blacks' situation. I think it hurt him emotionally to see how some of his friends were treated. The result was he kept pretty much to himself; to a certain extent he was a loner."⁵⁸

Robinson had never been one of the guys. Having been to college and served as an officer in the Army, he had never been comfortable in the undisciplined Negro Leagues, for example. Other black ballplayers thought that the reserved Robinson disapproved of them for their free-wheeling lifestyle, on the field or off. And yet Robinson liked the camaraderie of talking baseball and playing cards with other players. He had, after all, always played sports and been a part of a team. But things were different during spring training 1946 in Florida. Robinson felt alone on the Montreal team. His only friend on the team was Wright, but he, like Robinson, was struggling and growing more and more impatient with being a guinea pig.[59]

After practice, Robinson's white teammates returned to the Riviera Hotel, ate together, and then perhaps went downtown. But the Robinsons, Wright, Smith, and Rowe were restricted from downtown diners and theaters. Consequently, they talked away the evenings, played cards, or went to the black theater, which played two movies a week. Sometimes they were so bored they would see a movie twice or more.[60] Moreover, contrary to the stories in the press, the Robinsons felt isolated at the Harris's. Duff Harris did not share her kitchen, for example, so the Robinsons ate most of their meals at a nearby diner.[61]

When Robinson got his first hit of the spring, the Harrises allowed Rachel to cook a meal for her husband and her small circle of friends, which included Wright, Smith, Rowe, and some people from Bethune-Cookman College. Jackie enjoyed the dinner because it enabled him to forget the weight on his shoulders and relax. Rachel had her own reason to celebrate. She had found out she was pregnant but, knowing the pressure her husband was under, did not tell him.[62]

When black sportswriters began reporting that Robinson was struggling, they knew it had profound implications. Smith told his readers that Robinson's ailing arm was causing concern in the Montreal camp and jeopardizing his future in organized baseball.[63] Joe Johnson blamed Robinson's weak hitting on nerves.[64] Lem Graves of the *Journal-Guide* said the ballplayer was obviously distracted by being switched from position to position, clearly implying that the team was sabotaging Robinson's chances.[65] This was not the case, however.

If Robinson could hit, he should make the team, Graves said; if he could not hit, he should not make the team. With questionable logic, he characterized Wright as a better prospect than Robinson: "It is the consensus of baseball oldtimers that John Wright will find it easier to stick in the big time than Jackie will," he said. "Pitchers are only expected to pitch. The oldtimers say Johnny Wright can hold his own. Infielders are expected to field, throw, run, and hit."[66]

Sam Lacy, writing in the *Afro-American*, attributed Robinson's hitting problems to racial prejudice. Pitchers were playing by a different set of rules when pitching to Robinson. They cut the ball illegally to make it curve more, and they frequently threw at Robinson. Lacy asserted that Luis Olmo, a Castilian, was "the most thrown at" player in the National League for three years because he also was the darkest. Other dark-skinned ballplayers, such as Roberto Estalella, a Cuban, and Bing Miller, who was rumored to be part black, also had been a frequent target of racial abuse during games throughout their careers.[67]

People's Voice columnist Rick Hurt wrote that Robinson's tryout had been unimpressive thus far, but encouragingly the coverage by the metropolitan newspapers had been surprisingly thorough, if not necessarily positive. The white sportswriters, Hurt wrote, had described Robinson's early spring-training performance with such phrases as "not spectacular," "rather slow," and "failed to make a clean hit."[68] The reality was the reverse, however. In truth, white sportswriters had been relatively positive, though not necessarily thorough.

Over the next week or so, the story of baseball's first integrated spring training took a few bizarre twists. In one story, Smith unleashed his wrath on two New York columnists who questioned Rickey's motives and Robinson's skills. In another, the Mexican League tried to sign Robinson. And in still another, Kenny Washington, Robinson's teammate in the UCLA backfield, signed with the Los Angeles Rams, ending the National Football League's color barrier. Finally, in a story worthy in its strangeness of this historic unfolding drama, a white ballplayer, Eddie Klep, became the reverse Jackie Robinson, signing with the Cleveland Buckeyes of the Negro Leagues. Robinson and Klep – guinea pigs in different cages – suffered many of the same indignities.

1 2 3 4 5 6 7 8 9 10

Cheap Talk, Mexican Millionaires, and Eddie Klep

I N THE MARCH 19, 1946, issue of *Look* magazine, Tim Cohane wrote a feature on the Brooklyn Dodgers' Branch Rickey that portrayed him as a complex figure: literate to the point of scholarly, smart to the point of genius, religious to the point of pious, and tight to the point of miserly. Now, according to Cohane, the longtime baseball man had become "baseball's 'great emancipator.'" Like Lincoln before him, Rickey vowed that if he ever got a chance to make the world right, he would do it. Jackie Robinson provided him with that opportunity. Rickey told Cohane that his decision to sign Robinson was not based on economics or politics; it was purely spiritual. He had signed Robinson, he said, "Because I can't help it. I cannot face my God much longer knowing that His black creatures are held separate and distinct from His white creatures in the game that has given me all I can call my own."[1]

Rickey told Cohane that he had never forgotten the bitter humiliation experienced by Charlie Thomas, the black ballplayer he had coached at Ohio Wesleyan more than four decades earlier. By appropriating the Thomas tale as his inspiration, Rickey seized the credit for integration and positioned himself as baseball's Lincoln. Because Rickey was one of baseball's grand old men, the press reported the story. To those who had been a part of the campaign to integrate baseball, Rickey's claim to be baseball's Lincoln rang hollow.

Daily Worker sportswriter Bill Mardo questioned the motives of the anticommunist Rickey. To Mardo, Rickey was a disingenuous opportunist, who had sat on the sidelines while others fought the good fight, only to integrate baseball when it became clear that integration was inevitable. "There was the pre-Robinson Rickey who stayed shamefully silent for much of his baseball life," Mardo said. And there was the other Rickey, he added, "whose extraordinary business and baseball sense helped him seize the moment, jump aboard the Freedom Train as it was getting ready to pull out of Times Square, catch social protest at its apex, and then do just about everything right once he signed Robinson."[2]

Cohane wrote that Rickey wanted to win a pennant for the long-suffering Dodger fans. To do that, he would sign the best players, regardless of race or anything else. The *Look* article recounted Rickey's long search to find a black player with the courage to break baseball's color line, which culminated in his meeting with Robinson in August 1945. While the press had largely hailed the signing of Robinson, according to Cohane, Rickey's decision to do so could ultimately hit him where he was most vulnerable: the pocketbook. "The Dodgers are now a 'black' baseball team," Cohane wrote. To some, this meant it was tainted, which he suggested could hurt the quality of Dodger teams and affect attendance – thus perpetuating baseball's much-repeated myth.[3]

Cohane quoted unnamed baseball experts – none, in all likelihood, who had ever seen Robinson play – as saying that Robinson was not good enough for the Major Leagues or even the International League, but could probably play in a lower league. However, if Robinson or another black were on the Brooklyn team that captured its elusive pennant, that achievement, Cohane said, would satisfy the spiritual man in Rickey almost as much as the clicking turnstiles would please the businessman in him. Unfortunately, Rickey did not have many friends in the New York press. "Some sportswriters roared regularly for his head to be brought in on home plate," Cohane wrote, "preferably with a baseball in his mouth as a gag in the literal sense. Others are less bloodthirsty."[4]

In reaction to the *Look* article, Jimmy Powers of the *New York Daily News* and Dan Parker of the *New York Daily Mirror* used Rickey's own words to resume their attacks on him as a miser who put his own self-interests ahead of the interests of the game. Powers sniped at the depiction of Rickey as another Abraham Lincoln who has "a heart as big as a watermelon and loves all mankind." Rickey, whom Powers called "El Cheapo," paid Brooklyn pitcher Ralph Branca "less money than a colored bus boy collects each week in the lowliest Miami hotel," Powers wrote. He added that Roland Gladu, who had played for Montreal the year before, jumped to Mexico so he could make more money. "We find it awfully hard to believe that Branch Rickey is kind, generous, and full of good will to all men," he concluded.[5]

Powers asserted that progress was being made in race relations in the South without the need for interference by liberal do-gooders like Rickey – who, in fact, was anything but liberal. Powers asked his readers to go south of the Mason-Dixon line and see for themselves how black yardmen, who once made $5 a week, were now making $5.50 to $7 a day. In this March 12 commentary on race relations, which ranged from the foolish to the wildly absurd, Powers wrote about sitting in the whites-only section at a prizefight in Miami, which apparently made him an expert on segregation. Segregation, he said, was good for baseball and society. Mixing blacks and whites, whether on the field or in the stands, inevitably led to conflict and race riots. Powers again expressed doubt that Robinson would ever play in the Major Leagues.[6]

In his column, which *The Sporting News* reprinted, Parker declared that any resemblance between Lincoln and Rickey was purely coincidental. Rickey "can't deny he is a second Lincoln, lest he be accused of taking himself too seriously," he wrote. "To admit it would be an even worse *faux pas*. The middle course is the only one left under these circumstance, and the Deacon is hewing to it like the lowest ball in a pawnbroker's sign." He said that Rickey's signing of Robinson and Wright was not baseball's Emancipation Proclamation, as Rickey portrayed it, but a publicity stunt, as Tom Spink called it.[7]

Parker wrote that Clay Hopper, the Mississippi-born Montreal manager, was treating the two black ballplayers the same as their white teammates. When the day's workouts were done, however, the white ballplayers went back to their oceanfront hotel while the blacks went to a nearby boarding house. "One gets the idea that, although there has been no unpleasantness on the surface at least, Robinson and Wright are vaguely unhappy about the whole business," Parker wrote. "But that may be one of the penalties for being a torch bearer in a cause." Parker concluded that Robinson had not been living up to expectations and that Wright now appeared to be the better prospect.[8] The *Sporting News* published Parker's column.[9]

Writing in the March 30 *Courier*, Wendell Smith responded viciously to Parker and Powers – as he had the New York baseball writers' banquet a month earlier. He characterized their columns as "smutty," "smelly," "vicious," "putrid," "wacky," and "violently prejudiced." According to Smith, the two white columnists campaigned for integration because they wanted to ingratiate themselves to black readers, not because they believed in racial equality. "They prostituted the gullible population of Harlem by publishing burning stories on the great injustice that was being done to Negro players by the majors," he said.

"They published pictures of these black baseball orphans and accused the majors of perpetuating a system that 'has no place in American life.' And, as they ranted and raved and blustered like inspired abolitionists of the underground railroads, the circulation of their respective papers soared to a new high in Harlem."[10]

Despite their apparently pro-integration attitudes, however, Smith claimed that Powers and Parker expressed their true feelings by writing "vicious, putrid, and violently prejudiced stories" about Robinson and Wright. The sportswriters were attacking Rickey because he had "apparently vexed them both by giving Negro players an opportunity in organized baseball." For Smith, Powers and Parker had no right to criticize what was happening in Daytona Beach because they had not been to the city during spring training.[11]

Smith also took issue with Parker's comment that Robinson and Wright lived in boarding houses. The truth, according to Smith, was that the two ballplayers stayed in comfortable private homes. Smith added sarcastically that he did not know where "Dashing Dan" had gotten the idea that Robinson and Wright were unhappy. "As far as I can determine," he said, "and from what they have told me, both these Negro players are satisfied and as happy as any of the white players."[12] But, in fact, neither Robinson nor Wright were happy. They felt anxious, frustrated, and isolated, and of all people Smith knew that.

Smith wrote that while New York columnists were frothing about integration, southern sportswriters thus far had been fair. If saying nothing is the same as being fair, then southern writers were indeed fair – but as Smith well knew, the words can hardly be used interchangeably. Smith asserted that Daytona Beach sports editor Bernard Kahn had written some of the best articles on Robinson. In fact, Kahn had written little about Robinson or integration for that matter, and certainly nothing that merited praise or even comment of any kind.[13]

Sportswriters in Florida said little about the Robinson story. Columnists and sportswriters, some of whom who followed other teams but came to Daytona Beach to cover games against Brooklyn, made no attempt to report the story unfolding at Kelly Field. Silence continued to be the most common way of expressing journalistic nonsupport. They seemed to sense that because racial progress required the white public's approval, one could forestall discussion of the issue by simply ignoring it. The press could, therefore, obstruct integration without overtly questioning the liberal consensus.[14] The *Daily Worker* recognized this in their pages, where they took New York dailies, in particular, to task for practicing what amounted to a blackout of the story. Black newspapers chose to ignore the subtler forms of bias and jump on what they perceived to be the more outward criticisms of integration. The *Washington Afro-American* published an unbylined account, also published in the *People's Voice*, in which the Mayor's Committee on Baseball in New York City was quoted as calling Powers's column "untrue," "vicious," and "insidious."[15] It said that "Powers' thesis that whites and colored players cannot compete against each other in sports without the danger of a race riot, is against the evidence of well-proved facts."[16]

In the *Daily Worker* sportswriter Bill Mardo ridiculed Powers for his attacks against the "liberals" and "sports poseurs" who had challenged baseball's color line. "Talk is cheap," Mardo wrote. He said that the *Daily News* columnist had spent spring training in Miami – not Daytona Beach – and therefore had no firsthand knowledge of the Robinson story. Moreover, Mardo defended Rickey's business practices, adding that the Brooklyn executive understood that the Quinn-Ives antidiscrimination law had made integration inevitable. "As a business man, Rickey knows full well that having Negro players on his team will make for bigger gate receipts. So what?"[17]

Mardo also attacked Powers for his "cheap talk," writing: "It was much cheaper of you, Mr. Powers, wasn't it, to blast Rickey and his small-salary policies, than to level against the big-bankrolled Larry MacPhail, who prefers to pay fairly good wages to his white players but not a single penny for the hiring of Negroes to the Yankee organization."[18] Yankees president Larry MacPhail was indeed one of baseball's segregationists – and the mighty Yankees would be one of the last teams to sign a black player.

Powers was right about one thing – so far, anyway. Robinson had not proved himself, and Robinson's great expectations had great implications for baseball. Many Americans, most of them black, who had never previously paid attention to baseball found themselves drawn to the drama in Daytona Beach, wondering how Robinson was faring against the past and the future. Robinson also understood that his presence on a ball field was important. In the coming days, he would increasingly find himself in the middle of a story that represented a crisis for the baseball establishment.

In early February 1946 Mexican businessman Jorge Pasquel and his brothers had begun recruiting Major Leaguers for a Mexican summer league.[19] Though they were unsuccessful in signing stars such as Ted Williams, Stan Musial, Bob Feller, and Hank Greenberg, they had enjoyed some success, signing former and present American ballplayers like Brooklyn catcher Mickey Owen and St. Louis Browns slugger Vern Stephens, who had hit 24 home runs and driven in 89 the year before. In response to the threat, Commissioner Chandler said he would punish any ballplayer who went to Mexico and then tried to return to the Major Leagues.[20]

Meanwhile, sportswriters had begun doubting whether Robinson would turn out to be the breakthrough player his supporters had hoped. On March 10, the *Daytona Beach Evening News* published a brief Associated Press account in which several big leaguers who had played against Robinson and Wright were quoted as expressing unanimity "that the less-publicized Wright is the better player."[21] If Robinson continued to struggle, he would play into the hands of his critics. But while there were indeed doubts whether Robinson would play in the Major Leagues or even the International League, the Mexican League was confident he could play in that country.

On the afternoon of Tuesday, March 19, Robinson was shagging fly balls in the outfield when a man in street clothes approached him. "How are they treating you here?" Robert Janis, a Mexican League scout, asked Robinson.

"Excellent," Robinson replied. "They couldn't be any nicer."

"We are anxious to have you play in Mexico," Janis said. "We'll pay you $6,000 and all expenses. We also will pay the expenses of your wife if you care to bring her along."

Robinson declined. "I'm not interested. There's too much at stake here," he said.[22] The *Eagle* quoted Robinson as telling Janis: "I understand you offered Ted Williams $300,000. I wouldn't be interested even at that figure."[23]

Janis's six-thousand-dollar offer far exceeded Robinson's contract with Rickey. Robinson knew that if he had accepted Janis's offer –

whatever the figure, whatever his reason – it would have undermined the effort to integrate baseball. Mardo recognized this in his *Daily Worker* column of March 21. Robinson was not like the other ballplayers being recruited by the Mexican League. His Montreal tryout was not about money. "It's not the first time Jackie's stressed that money is no object with him right now," Mardo wrote. "The first Negro player in modern organized professional baseball doesn't want anyone to make an issue of his financial status with the Dodgers – when the real issue at stake is so much more vital. This won't register in the box scores, but chalk up another hit for . . . Jackie Robinson."[24]

When Rickey learned that the scout with the Mexican League was at Kelly Field, he ordered Janis expelled. Later that day, Janis showed up at City Island Ballpark to talk to Brooklyn players. When Rickey heard about this, he ordered team officials to run him out of the park and out of town, the *New York Times* reported.[25] Rickey was not the only baseball executive concerned with what the *Times* called "the Mexican Plague." Commissioner Chandler acted quickly, declaring that any ballplayer who signed to play in the Mexican League would be suspended for five years. He demanded that the Mexican League respect players' contracts with organized baseball.[26]

Jorge Pasquel argued otherwise. "All the fans in the United States know that these players had signed contracts to play in Mexico," adding that they had "abandoned the Major Leagues because of miserable salaries."[27] The Associated Press reported that the raiding of ballplayers had caused a rift in relations between the United States and Mexico. The U.S. State Department called on Major League baseball to solve its differences with the Mexican League.[28] As a result of the Mexican League's challenge, baseball signed agreements with Caribbean leagues that formalized player movement and sanctioned winter play.[29]

The story of ballplayers leaving their American teams to play in Mexico was old news in black newspapers. Under the headline, "Major League Bigots Hit by Mexican Plague," the *Washington Afro-American* reported that Major League baseball was simply facing the same issue that the Negro Leagues had confronted for years.[30] *Amsterdam News* sports editor Dan Burley noted that black players had been leaving their teams to play in Mexico since the early 1920s. "For years, the biggest howl heard in colored baseball circles has been that of complaints voiced at players who jumped contracts" to play in Mexico, Burley said. "Now the majors are getting a heavy dose of it."[31]

In 1944, Wendell Smith had written a story about Willie Wells, arguably the best shortstop in the Negro Leagues. Wells had left America to play in Mexico because he was treated as a man there rather than the second-class citizen he was in America. "One of the main reasons I came back to Mexico is because I've found freedom and democracy here, something I never found in the United States. I was branded a Negro in the United States and had to act accordingly," he said. "Everything I did, including playing ball, was regulated by my color. They wouldn't even give me a chance in the big leagues because I was a Negro, yet they accepted every other nationality under the sun."[32]

Now that baseball's color line had been broken, the black press began reporting that football would follow. The American Negro Press Association quoted an unnamed newspaper as saying that former UCLA star Kenny Washington would soon sign with the National Football League's Los Angeles Rams, formerly the Cleveland Rams. If true, the story said, the announcement would end the league's twelve-year ban against blacks. "It's high time in the hot season to crack the ice in the football field and let some of our better players get a chance to coin a little of that fancy dough," the wire service reported.[33]

The National Negro Press called Washington the first black to sign a contract with a team in organized professional football since 1933.[34] During its formative years in the 1920s and early 1930s, the National Football League had several black players on its rosters, including Fred "Duke" Slater, Paul Robeson, Fritz Pollard, Jay "Inky" Williams, Ray Kemp, and Joe Lillard. While in college, Slater, Robeson, Pollard, and other blacks had been named to Walter Camp's All-America team. After Camp died in the mid-1920s, his successor, Grantland Rice, virtually excluded blacks from his All-America team for the next three decades.[35]

Professional football excluded blacks after the 1933 season. "It was my understanding that there was a gentlemen's agreement in the league that there couldn't be no more blacks," Kemp later recalled.[36] Black newspapers reported that Lillard, a onetime running back at the University of Oregon, had been "too good for his own good." After playing with the Chicago Cardinals in 1932 and 1933, he had been driven out of the NFL because of the "color of his skin." In 1935, Lillard's ex-coach,

Paul Schlissler, who would become Washington's coach in Los Angeles, said Lillard had been cut for own his safety. He called Lillard "a marked man, and I don't mean that just the Southern boys took it out on him either; after a while whole teams, Northern and Southern alike, would give Joe the works, and I'd have to take him out."[37]

Mainstream sportswriters spent little time fretting over issues of racial discrimination. As they did with baseball, sportswriters turned a blind eye when the football establishment created its color line. Jimmy Powers was once again one of the exceptions. After watching Kenny Washington play against the Green Bay Packers with college all-stars, Powers suggested that the owners of New York's professional football teams sign the gifted athlete. "He played on the same field with boys who are going to be scattered throughout the league. And he played against the champion Packers," he said. "There wasn't a bit of trouble anywhere."[38] Unlike Rice, Powers regularly selected blacks for his All-America squad.

When Washington, a second-team All-American, was ignored in the NFL draft, NBC sportscaster Sam Balter criticized pro football's gentlemen's agreement. He asked NFL owners why no one had signed Washington and expressed disappointment "on behalf of millions of American sport fans who believe in fair play and equal opportunity."[39] Black journalists often criticized professional football. William Brower wrote in the magazine *Opportunity* that there were "no arresting or rational excuses for professional football to follow the dubious precedent set by professional baseball."[40]

When a new professional football league – the All-America Football Conference – was created, there were hopes that it would allow blacks. This did not happen. "It's the same old story," Wendell Smith wrote, "Negroes won't be permitted to play."[41] However, both the Rams of the National Football League and the Dons of the All-America Football Conference asked the city of Los Angeles if they could play in its spacious Municipal Stadium. Journalists Halley Harding of the *Los Angeles Tribune* and Herman Hill, the *Pittsburgh Courier*'s West Coast correspondent, argued that the stadium should not be used by any organization that discriminated against blacks. Under tremendous pressure, the Rams and Dons were given permission only after they agreed they would sign blacks. The Rams made good by signing Washington.[42]

The breaking of professional football's color line marked another victory for equality in sports, and raised hopes for an end to all insidious gentlemen's agreements. Robinson was elated when he heard about his former teammate. "He's a great football player and Los Angeles will make a lot of money with him in the lineup," he said. "People will come from far and near to see him play."[43] Black newspapers celebrated the signing of Washington and predicted good things ahead for him. Washington did not have the sensitivity to racial slights that Robinson did. His friendly and nonconfrontational personality was much closer to the one the white press had fashioned for Robinson.

Norfolk Journal and Guide columnist Lem Graves Jr. called Washington one of the ten best football players of all time. He argued that there was not a better player in the league than Washington. Graves, however, could not say the same for Robinson, who was not hitting and still had not found a steady position. "Negro fans who are busy 'sweating out' Jackie Robinson and Johnny Wright in organized baseball have no such worries about whether Kenny Washington will make it in football," Graves observed.[44] As it turned out, Washington's career would be shortened by injuries and the great expectations for his football career frustrated. Meanwhile Jackie Robinson ended up in the Baseball Hall of Fame.

Graves, though disappointed by Robinson's early progress, remained hopeful – at least in print. "Most ball players have a batting slump now and then and it's a cinch that Dodger pitchers have not been serving him anything in the groove," he wrote. "We don't think they should. We want them to give him the works. If he can snap out of it and make the grade against the best the big leagues can offer, we will be happy to see him in the Montreal lineup."[45] In private, Graves, like other sportswriters, began to wonder if Robinson had been the best man for the job.

If Robinson and Wright had not come to Daytona Beach, they probably would have been at spring training with their former teams, the Kansas City Monarchs and Homestead Grays, respectively. Unlike the big leagues, where ballplayers went through a period of conditioning and coaching before beginning their preseason schedule, the Negro Leagues began playing games soon after they came to camp. Wendell Smith noted in his column that the Homestead Grays had opened spring drills in Jacksonville, Florida. Wright, who had pitched for them the year before, was only ninety miles away in the Montreal camp. "What a difference a year makes!" Smith wrote.[46]

As two black ballplayers tried out in the white leagues, a white player named Eddie Klep began his tryout in the Negro Leagues, becoming "a reverse Jackie Robinson." Unlike Robinson, however, there was no press conference announcing that Cleveland Buckeyes owner Ernie Wright had signed Klep. The news received no national publicity. Only one white newspaper, the *Erie Dispatch-Herald*, mentioned it. Black newspapers also said little. The *Cleveland Call and Post*, however, provided a detailed account under the headline, "Ernie Wright Does 'Rickey' in Reverse; Gives White Sandlot Pitcher a Tryout."[47] Ernie Wright, sounding like Rickey, explained that he had signed Klep because he thought the pitcher could contribute to the team. He also thought that signing the pitcher would further civil rights and give the team some publicity. "He said that he wanted to show that it didn't make any difference to him whether a player was white or black on the ball club," Cleveland Negro League manager Quincy Troupe remembered. When Wright told Troupe he would be managing a white player, Troupe asked: "'Can this boy play? That's all I care about.' It was hard to get a first-class white player because if a guy could really play, he would go into the Major Leagues."[48]

Klep and the Buckeyes arrived for spring training on March 18 – a day after Robinson's first game in Daytona Beach.[49] In organized professional baseball, ballplayers jogged, stretched, did calisthenics, and worked on fundamentals during the first several days of spring training. In the Negro Leagues, however, teams began playing soon after players reported to spring training. When Cleveland appeared for its first game against the Birmingham Black Barons the following Sunday at Birmingham's Rickwood Field, two police officers sought out the team's press agent, Jimmie Jones, and asked if the team had a white player. When Jones answered in the affirmative, one of the officers told Jones: "Get him out of here quick. We don't have no mixin' down here!" When Jones asked if Klep could stay in the dugout, the answer was, "No, he can't sit in the dugout or any place with you. If you want the game to go on, get him off the field and out of the ball clothes."[50] At this, Klep changed into street clothes and watched the game from the white section of the stands.

Jimmie Jones criticized the banishment of Klep in the *People's Voice*. Jim Crow was Jim Crow, he said, whether it applied to a black playing with a white team or a white playing with a black team.[51] A wire service story appeared in such black weeklies as the *Call and Post*, *Courier*, and *New Jersey Afro-American*. Fay Young also acknowledged the incident in the *Defender*. The Rebels were still in control of the South, he said. But other black columnists, such as Smith, Lacy, Hurt, Joe Bostic, Dan Burley, and Joe Johnson, said nothing. "Their silence was hypocritical," baseball historian Larry Gerlach wrote, adding that the white press unanimously ignored the story.[52]

After other cities also prohibited Klep from playing, the Cleveland team sent him back to Erie, where he could train with his former team until the Buckeyes returned to the North for the start of the season.[53] But Ernie Wright decided to confront the ban directly and headed back South with his pitcher. "If Branch Rickey and others of organized baseball can choose material of their liking to produce a winning ball club and without question of race or color, despite the Southern 'Jim crow' tradition, then why can't I do the same?" Wright asked.[54]

Klep was scheduled to pitch against the Atlanta Black Crackers on April 7. No one on the Cleveland team, including Wright, Troupe, or Klep, probably knew whether there would be a repeat of the Birmingham incident. As Klep warmed up before the game, Troupe saw a few police officers and asked them if they were going to remove the pitcher. "No," one of them said, "we don't have anything to do with that. As far as I'm concerned he's all right.'" Klep pitched three innings and won the game.[55] Despite the game's historic significance, the *Atlanta Daily World* did not mention Klep's race in the story.[56] Other newspapers said nothing.

After the game, the Cleveland team dined in the city's black section on Peachtree Street. Seeing two women who looked white in a restaurant they assumed it was desegregated and walked in. A few minutes after they sat down, one of the restaurant's employees approached their table, gestured at Klep, and said, "He can't eat here. We don't serve whites. He can go uptown and eat in any restaurant." Troupe answered, "What do you mean? What about those two ladies sitting over there?" The waiter laughed and said, "Oh, they're not white." Troupe told Klep to go uptown and find himself something to eat.[57]

Klep did not pitch again that spring, and in fact, had few opportunities to prove himself. He was released after just two regular season games, leaving the Negro Leagues as quietly as he entered them. Only one newspaper, the *Call and Post*, mentioned Klep's release.[58] The *Biographical Encyclopedia of the Negro Baseball Leagues* notes that though it was hoped that Klep would be "'a reverse Jackie Robinson,' he met with little success and his playing career was brief and undistinguished."[59]

After his tryout in the Negro Leagues, Klep returned to Erie, played a few years of semipro baseball, held a series of odd jobs, and then after a burglary conviction, spent time in prison. In the 1950s, he abandoned his family and moved to Texas and then California, where he had two children with a woman, though still legally married to his wife in Erie. After being institutionalized in a mental hospital after years of alcohol abuse, Klep died in 1981. He was buried in his hometown without an obituary to mark his odd contribution to the history of baseball.[60]

Robinson and Wright probably never heard of Klep – though they had more in common with him than anyone else that spring. All three ballplayers were prohibited from playing in games, and none could lodge nor eat with their teammates. While Robinson and Wright endured the resentment of their teammates, Klep was accepted more willingly by his. Robinson and Wright had a small support network; Klep did not. Like Robinson and Wright, Klep's playing would be confined to mostly intrasquad games. And like Wright, Klep faded quietly into baseball obscurity, becoming barely a footnote in the much bigger story of baseball's first integrated spring training.

1 2 3 4 5 6 7 **8** 9 10

Lights Out in Deland and Locked Gates in Jacksonville

B RANCH RICKEY ACHIEVED success in baseball because he was willing to take chances. He also succeeded because he left as little as possible to chance. He now found himself somewhere between the two, staking his organization's future on two black men – Jackie Robinson and Johnny Wright – in the racially divided Deep South. To win his gamble, Rickey needed luck. "Good luck is what is left over after intelligence and effort have combined at their best," he often said. "Luck is the residue of design." Rickey and his two Montreal rookies had thus far been relatively lucky; they had survived racial threats in Sanford, and nothing bad had happened in Daytona Beach.

But Montreal could not stay in Daytona Beach the rest of the spring. It had 11 road games on its spring schedule. Rickey said he would not force Jackie Robinson or Johnny Wright on any city or town. If a city insisted on enforcing its segregation ordinances, he would abide by its wishes. *New York Post* columnist Leonard Cohen wondered if Rickey really knew what he had gotten himself into. "Branch Rickey knew he was handling a hot potato when he signed Jackie Robinson and Johnny Wright," Cohen wrote before Montreal's scheduled game in Jacksonville. "But the potato is really getting hot now and fans all over the country are waiting to see how far Rickey will go to defend the presence of his colored performers."[1]

On Wednesday, March 20, the *Florida Times-Union* of Jacksonville reported that Robinson would likely be in the lineup that Sunday afternoon when the Montreal Royals played the Jersey City Giants, the New York Giants' AAA team. If Robinson played, the article said, it would be the first time a black had taken the field with whites at the city-owned Durkee Field. When a *Times-Union* sportswriter asked Montreal general manager Mel Jones if Robinson would make the trip, Jones replied, "I don't know of any reason why Robinson won't accompany our squad to Jacksonville."[2]

Noting that Robinson's first game in Daytona Beach had drawn a crowd of four thousand, the *Times-Union* indicated that a good crowd was expected for Sunday's game – although the four hundred seats in the park's segregated section probably would be inadequate. "One of the largest crowds ever to see an exhibition game in Jacksonville un-

135

doubtedly will turn out," the newspaper said.[3] In Friday's newspaper, however, a cryptic three-paragraph story stated that the game had been canceled because Durkee Field was "not available."[4]

It turned out that on Thursday George Robinson, director of Jacksonville's Parks and Public Property, had notified the Jersey City team that local laws prohibited games between blacks and whites.[5] He did not contact either Brooklyn or Montreal.[6] When New York Giants general manager Charley Stoneham was asked to confirm the game's cancellation, he did not answer. Instead, he said he would discuss the matter with Montreal.[7] Jones told the Associated Press that neither he, his manager Clay Hopper, nor Brooklyn president Branch Rickey had received word from Jacksonville. "Jersey City is a member of our league and this game will be a good test of our team's strength. For that reason particularly, I think Clay would like to use Robinson," Jones said. "However, if Jacksonville will not allow Robinson to play, I don't think Hopper will take him along."[8]

Rickey told the *New York Daily News* that he was unaware of any laws that would prohibit either Jackie Robinson or Johnny Wright from playing. "If there is," he said, "we will certainly obey the law, but I have not been notified of it as yet." The newspaper quoted unnamed sportswriters who covered the Giants as saying that even if Robinson made the trip, he would not be allowed on the field because of Jim Crow laws.[9] A more detailed account of the cancellation was widely distributed in Saturday's newspapers. George Robinson explained that there was a Jacksonville ordinance forbidding competition between blacks and whites. "Rules, regulations, and policies of the Jacksonville Playground and Recreation Board," he said, "prohibit mixed contestants in athletic events."[10]

The *Daily News* reported that Jersey City's president Steve Freel had wanted to go ahead with the game, but the four members of the city's recreational department – banker Frank Sherman; labor leader John Maxim; soft-drink dealer Ray McCarthy; and lawyer Harry Reinstein – voted to uphold the segregation ordinance.[11] Durkee Field's commissioner, Guy Simmons, however, told the *New York Times* that George Robinson had been solely responsible for the decision to cancel the game.[12] In a joint statement, Stoneham and team treasurer Edgar Feeley said that they had nothing to do with the cancellation. "We were willing to play the Montreal club even if Branch Rickey sends a team composed of nine Negroes," the statement said. "But [George] Robinson told us the game had been canceled."[13]

Rickey, while obviously displeased by the cancellation, repeated his earlier statement that he would not defy existing segregation laws. "We do not desire to disturb any community, and we shall conform with any official request not to bring the boy," he said. "But we will not accept the onus for this."[14] Leonard Cohen sensed something unnecessarily combative in Rickey's response. "That high-sounding speech of indignation," Cohen said, "helps the colored players like a bag of cement would aid a drowning man."[15]

Times sportswriter Roscoe McGowen reported that Jacksonville had become the first southern city to ban Montreal's black ballplayers.[16] The Associated Press story noted that Robinson and Wright had played in other games in Florida.[17] The National Negro Press Association also mentioned that Robinson and Wright had played in other integrated games.[18] This was misleading, however; Robinson and Wright had practiced in Daytona Beach and for two days in Sanford. Only Daytona Beach had thus far allowed Robinson and Wright to play in games. Although the *Daytona Beach Morning Journal* published the Associated Press account, other Florida newspapers said nothing.[19] Wendell Smith did not mention the cancellation in the *Pittsburgh Courier*, but the *Montreal Gazette* published McGowen's story from the *Times* and the account, respectively, on consecutive days.[20]

The *Washington Afro-American* blamed the cancellation of the game on *Times-Union* columnist Arnold Finnerock. Nearly three weeks earlier, according to the *Afro-American*, Finnerock had raised doubts about whether Robinson would be allowed to play when Montreal came to Jacksonville: "We can't help but wonder if Robinson will accompany the Montreal club when it comes here to play an exhibition with Jersey City."[21]

The *Afro-American* termed this a veiled threat and added that Branch Rickey Jr. and Clyde Sukeforth agreed. However, Finnerock's comment does not appear, on the surface anyway, to be a threat, veiled or otherwise, but rather a concern shared by others.[22] *People's Voice* sportswriter Joe Johnson wrote that officials with the Dodgers and Giants should have supported the two black ballplayers. He also provided a

137

brief critique of Robinson's progress: "He has been spending a lot of time working out his coordination before the pitching machine. His fielding continues to be good."[23]

Robinson had promised Rickey he would not fight back. He had withheld his natural tendency to be aggressive. As a result, he had no outlet to express his sense of indignation at the cancellation. He released his frustrations by snapping at his wife as well as Smith, Rowe, and Wright. Despite his public statements, Robinson felt uneasy around his teammates, in the field, and at the plate. As the March temperatures heated up, Robinson could feel every degree whenever he swung and missed or tried to throw and felt the ball float from his grip.

Wendell Smith was now predicting that Robinson would become the team's starting first baseman, where his difficulties would be less detrimental. Having initially predicted that Robinson would play shortstop and then second base, by assigning him to first he was completing a journalistic double play.[24] Rickey, too, was growing more concerned. He ordered Hopper to keep Robinson at first, where Montreal was so weak it had borrowed first basemen from Brooklyn. When asked about Robinson, Rickey hardly gave him a ringing endorsement: "I believe he can play that position. Anyone with any mental capacity can play first base."[25]

On March 23, Montreal returned to the friendly confines of City Island Ballpark for another game against Brooklyn. Robinson played errorless ball at first and went hitless in three official at bats; in addition, he had a sacrifice bunt and a walk. Harold Burr noted that the game was important for no other reason than because Daytona Beach had permitted it. "This liberal community held no objections to Jackie Robinson playing first base at City Island Park and Montreal showed its appreciation by beating the Dodgers," he said.[26]

Bernard Kahn of the *Daytona Beach Sunday News-Journal* reported that Robinson had played but said nothing more.[27] The *Daily News*, *Times Mirror*, *Times*, and other New York dailies did not even mention Robinson in their stories. As a rule, American sports fans read little about Robinson and Wright – and saw less of them. While northern newspapers did not have a formal policy banning photographs of blacks, they generally acted as if they did, which dampened public interest in the story.

138

This was not the case in Montreal, however. The *Gazette* referred to Robinson by name in the headline of its story: "Royals Top Brooks; Robinson on First." A subhead added, "Negro Infielder Fails to Get a Hit But Gains Walk, Sacrifice." The brief story was accompanied by a large International News Service photograph, which showed Robinson and Wright with several of their teammates in the dugout before the game. The caption identified the ballplayers as the first two blacks signed by a Major League team.[28]

To black weeklies, the story continued to be framed in democratic terms – a piece of history that was unfolding in Florida. For instance, the *Norfolk Journal and Guide* ran a banner headline that read, "Democracy Given Tryout in Florida as Baseball Stars Make Bid for Major League Positions." The issue included several photos – including one of Robinson and Wright with their teammates and another that showed Robinson rounding third about to score.[29] The *Courier* filled its pages on March 16 with photos of Robinson and Wright.[30] On March 23, it published photos of the Robinsons, the Harrises, Rickey, Hopper, and Bob Finch as well as one of a Montreal trainer massaging Jackie's throwing arm.[31] On March 30, it ran the International News photo of the Montreal teammates in the dugout and another of Robinson swinging at a pitch.[32]

Wendell Smith remained characteristically optimistic – though Robinson's inability to either hit or throw was beginning to wear on him. Robinson "continued to look dangerous at the plate," he wrote, "but it was evident that he hasn't quite adjusted himself to the environment at City Island Park." Smith expressed his concern about his friend's sore arm. "Jackie Robinson's future in organized baseball may very well lie in the ailing muscles of his right arm," he wrote. "Failure of the bronze infielder's flipper to respond to treatment rapidly is causing considerable concern in the Montreal camp this week."[33]

The second Montreal-Brooklyn game drew fifteen hundred spectators, less than half the crowd of his first game. Nonetheless, it was a good crowd for a spring-training game. More importantly, Robinson nor Wright had still not faced any unpleasantness. They had seen and heard the applause of blacks and whites alike. Smith wrote that two hundred blacks had taken the two-hundred-mile bus ride from West Palm Beach to watch Robinson play in Daytona Beach.[34] And this fact, to paraphrase the March 19 issue of *Look* magazine, had pleased both the spiritual and business side of Branch Rickey.

Baseball owners had long justified their decision to keep blacks out of organized baseball by saying that integration would cause race riots among the fans. Yet thus far, spring training had shown these justifications to be unfounded. Black journalists understood better than their white colleagues what this meant. The *New York Age* wrote that the 1946 spring training had silenced those "who've screamed for years that putting Negroes and Whites together on the same battlefield would be like setting a match to kerosene."[35]

The Royals' next road game was scheduled against Brooklyn's AA team, the Indianapolis Indians, in Deland, Florida, on Monday, March 25. However, that morning the Indians informed Jones that it would have to cancel the game because it had a night game the following evening. To test the lighting system, it would have to dig up the cables under the field. In other words, a day game had been canceled because of inoperative lights – or at least that was the story the city of Deland was holding to.[36] "We were playing a daytime game," Jones said. "It had nothing to do with lights."[37]

The *New York Daily Mirror*, which published a United Press account of the reason for the game's cancellation, joked in its headline, "Good Night! Watt Happens Next!"[38] This was not a laughing matter to blacks, however. They saw nothing funny in a town preventing Robinson and Wright from trying to make a living in the manner they chose. *Chicago Defender* sports editor Fay Young lashed out at the city of Deland. While Jacksonville had "come right out with the reason" it had banned the players, he said Deland had cowardly used the lights as an excuse to prevent Robinson from taking the field.[39]

A few days later, the *Deland Sun News* published the United Press account, which included the city's official reason for canceling the game. On April 9, the newspaper published a letter to the editor from nearly one hundred central Florida blacks. They expressed shock that something like this had happened in a town where people "boasted to others of the tolerance, liberalism, and unprejudiced behavior here. . . . There's a feeling of uncertainty and having been let down."[40] The letter stated that Robinson and Wright had fought in the war to defend America; they deserved more than this. It quoted Mel Jones as telling the *Daytona*

Beach Morning Journal that a second game between Montreal and Indianapolis, scheduled for April 10, had been moved from Deland to Daytona Beach. The letter appealed to the city's white citizens to bring pressure so the next game between the two teams would instead be played in Deland.[41] It had thus far been a bad week for integration – and it did not appear that things would get any better. Montreal's next game on its schedule was against Jersey City in Jacksonville on Thursday, March 28.

On Wednesday, March 27, the *Times-Union* reported that Montreal would not bring Robinson and Wright with them to Jacksonville.[42] However, the *Daytona Beach Morning Journal* quoted Jones as saying that the game would be played and both Robinson and Wright would be in the lineup. The story explained that the earlier game had been canceled because Montreal had two black players on its roster.[43] It did not mention that Montreal had said it would be willing to play with or without them. In a follow-up story the next day, the *Times-Union*, without mentioning either Robinson or Wright, reported that the International League rivals, Montreal and Jersey City, would play that day at 3 p.m.[44]

Contradicting its report from the day before, the *Morning Journal* now told its readers that the game had not been approved. The article quoted Jones as criticizing the *Times-Union* for reporting that Robinson and Wright would not join the Montreal team. In hopes of clarifying things, Jones sent a telegram to Charley Stoneham, blaming the Jacksonville newspaper for "evasive reporting" designed to pressure Montreal into leaving Robinson and Wright behind. "Must have official word in telegram from authorities there regarding stand on Robinson and Wright?" he wrote. "If not received they must come along to play as members of squad."[45]

Jones also sent the following telegram to George Robinson: "Wired you earlier in week requesting official notice in writing as to your stand on Robinson and Wright appearing with Montreal club in Jacksonville. Have received no answer. Advise quick, direct to me, or Robinson and Wright will accompany and will be available to play."[46] Jones heard nothing from either Stoneham or George Robinson.

On Thursday morning, the Montreal team headed north on Highway 1 for the ninety-mile bus ride to Jacksonville. Robinson and Wright rode separately with Smith and Rowe. When Montreal arrived at Durkee Field, they saw a large crowd outside the stadium, its gates padlocked. "What's wrong?" Hopper asked someone standing near the gates. "The game's been called off," the man said. "The Bureau of Recreation won't let the game be played because you've got colored guys on your club."[47] Robinson, Wright, Smith, and Rowe got a less genteel explanation. According to Rowe, when a man sitting outside the stadium saw the four men approaching the gate, he said: "The game has been canceled." When one of the four asked him why, he snapped: "There will be no niggers playing here!"[48]

A frustrated Jones tried to contact George Robinson but without success. He then went to the Seminole Hotel, where the Jersey City team stayed. A note left there said that the game had been canceled and included the names of players who were to report to a scrimmage in Gainesville.[49] "We went to the hotel and found out they had gone somewhere else to play a pickup game," Jones said.[50] After that, the team got back on the bus and returned to Daytona Beach, having played no game and wasted the better part of a day. As they sat in their seats and stared out at the rural, northern Florida landscape, it seems likely that the object of their discussion was Robinson and Wright.

To the two ballplayers, the cancellation meant another lost opportunity to prove themselves. But the lockout was not a total disappointment. Robinson and Wright were encouraged by the number of people they saw outside the ballpark. "That meant a lot to us. It meant that it wasn't the people of Jacksonville who objected to our playing in the park – it was the politicians," Robinson said. "Had the decision been left to those people in line, the game would have been played."[51]

Rickey, his patience worn thin, decided to change his strategy. Thus far, he had said Montreal would obey segregation laws and leave the ballplayers behind if a city insisted. Now if a city said it would allow the game if Montreal did not suit up Robinson and Wright, there would be no game. Rickey had drawn a line in the sand and stood defiantly with his black players. "We don't care if we fail to play another single exhibition game," Jones told the *Afro-American*.[52]

Wendell Smith, too, had seen enough. For the first time all spring, he openly condemned a Florida city. He left little doubt about what he thought of Jacksonville. "It is a city festering from political graft and vice," he said. "And as a result there is less progress there economically, politically and racially than any other city of a comparable size below the Mason-Dixon line." The lockout, Smith asserted, had resulted in Jacksonville receiving more bad press than any Florida city since the lynching of Jesse Payne in Madison the previous fall.[53]

In the *Chicago Defender* of April 6, Fay Young again condemned a southern city for practicing racial discrimination. He also reported that northern sportswriters were indignant over the treatment of Jackie Robinson. Young reported that one unnamed Boston sportswriter had written that the outcome of the Civil War, long thought settled, was apparently still in doubt in some areas of Florida. A triple by Robinson could well start another civil war.[54]

In an editorial in the same issue, the *Chicago Defender* praised the Montreal team for supporting its black players. "If Montreal had capitulated and left the Negro players behind, the setback would have encouraged the obstructionists to close the gates tight against any additional dark aspirants," it said. "Montreal has accepted the Negro players and is determined that they be used in all contests according to their ability to play rather than their skin color. They proved this in Jacksonville."[55]

The *Washington Afro-American* also praised Montreal for not yielding to intimidation. The newspaper published a letter of protest from the Chevy Chase Presbyterian Church in Washington DC to the Jacksonville Playground and Recreation Department that called for greater tolerance. "There was never a time in the history of the world when it was more important for people of different races and different creeds to get along together," it said. "Democracy cannot be real so long as its members discriminate against each other. We feel that you have done a great injury to democracy and to brotherhood."[56]

The April 1 *Daily Worker* acknowledged that racism was racism, regardless of where it occurred. Thus, those who supported Jacksonville and Deland supported the same sort of racism Hitler had practiced in Germany. By canceling the game, Bill Mardo wrote, Jacksonville had indeed prohibited Robinson and Wright from taking the field. However, it had also prohibited Montreal's white teammates and their white opponents from playing and thousands of white spectators from watching them.[57]

The Associated Press and United Press reported that the game had been canceled after city officials in Jacksonville learned that Montreal would bring Robinson and Wright. The United Press added that a conspiracy existed between southern cities against Montreal and its two black players. The *Deland Sun News* published the UP story, which said that "officials of Southern cities are united today in a lockout campaign against the Montreal Royals, who have been barred three times this week because Negroes Jackie Robinson and John Wright are members of their team."[58]

For its part, the *Brooklyn Eagle* attempted to provide some perspective on the developing story. Under the headline "Rhubarbs Abound in the South," columnist Tommy Holmes reported that when Montreal had gone to Jacksonville, it found the ballpark closed and locked tight, and several policemen on hand "just in case. . . . And so they climbed back on the bus and drove right back again. It must have been a rather silent journey."[59]

In the same column, Holmes included a lengthy interview with an upbeat Rickey, who said he was more encouraged than discouraged from what he had seen and heard so far. "I was told Robinson and Wright would be reviled and shunned by other ball players. They haven't been. I was told that they would be thrown at and spiked. That hasn't happened," he told Holmes. "I was told that the fans would boo them when they appeared on the field, but the crowds have treated them with no discourtesy."[60]

The mixing of blacks and whites had not brought down the bleachers after all. Rickey wanted sportswriters to report that most white spectators would accept black players, provided they had the proper skills. If this happened, Brooklyn would see a dramatic increase at its ticket windows. But sportswriters remained reluctant to believe Rickey. To Holmes, who had not yet seen Robinson play, Rickey sounded like a man determined to fight all summer and beyond for his cause. "And, from what I have observed so far and from what I have listened to in other baseball camps," Holmes said, "he'll probably have to."[61]

After the cancellations, Arch Murray of the *New York Post* interviewed Robinson inside the Harris home. Sitting on a sofa, nursing both a bruised heel and his throwing arm, Robinson was asked about the cancellations. He answered as Rickey would have wanted him to. "I can't help that," he said. "Nobody can. If those people who called off those games want to feel that way, there's nothing anybody can do about it. All you can do is forget it."[62]

Three weeks earlier, Robinson had arrived in Sanford as cameras clicked and sportswriters asked questions. Today, according to Murray, he was just another ballplayer resting after another hard day on the diamond. Robinson expressed confidence that he would make the Montreal team – even though he had not yet proven himself. "My throwing arm is coming around," he said. "And I know I'll hit him. My big trouble so far has been that I've been trying too hard, pressing up there at the plate. The pressure and the tension were very heavy on me at first. I've felt so deeply upon how much the fate of so many other colored boys depends on what I do here."[63]

Instead of taking readers into Robinson's home, most mainstream sportswriters continued to stoke the story of the Pasquel brothers and their Mexican League. The United Press, for example, distributed an extended series on the Pasquels' raids on American ballplayers. According to one article, the Pasquels had already signed seventeen present and former Major Leaguers, including Luis Olmo, Mickey Owen, Vern Stephens, Sal Maglie, George Haussmann, Danny Gardella, and Roy Zimmerman. Though Stephens would return to the Browns before opening day, when Owen tried to return Rickey turned him away. He did not play again in the majors until 1949.

As American ballplayers took jobs south of the border, they appear to have brought their racial biases with them. Fay Young reported, for example, that Vern Stephens returned to the Major Leagues because his manager in the Mexican League had been black. Rogers Hornsby, who had criticized integration six months earlier, was hired to manage in Mexico. One of the Pasquels asked him why he did not play one of the blacks on his team, Hornsby reportedly answered that he did not want to use "any niggers."[64]

Mexican League scout Robert Janis predicted that the Dodgers were fed up with Rickey's cheapness, and "there would be mutiny in the Brooklyn Dodgers camp."[65] *Daily News* columnist Jimmy Powers then seized on this opportunity to criticize Rickey for driving away ballplayers with his low salaries. Rickey and other owners were responsible for the Mexican problem, he wrote: "They had no one to blame but themselves. The competition would do baseball good."[66] Dan Parker of the *New York Daily Mirror* agreed: "It would appear that while Branch Rickey has been busy emancipating Negro ballplayers, Jorge [Pasquel], the mad Mexican, has undertaken to liberate the underpaid white players on Mr. Rickey's Brooklyn club."[67] *Journal-American* columnist Bill Corum said Rickey was getting what he deserved for treating his ballplayers miserably. In the same issue of the *Journal-American* Frank Graham also criticized Rickey for driving away stars like Owen. "Baseball has no more intriguing story than this story of Mickey Owen," Graham wrote.[68]

But the main story pulling at baseball's seams that spring had nothing to do with Mexico. Wendell Smith later stated that beat writers Dick Young of the *New York Post* and Gus Steiger of the *Mirror* were among the few who were interested in what was happening. "They were constantly querying me," Smith remembered. "Every day they'd talk to me. After all, I was living with Jackie and he was the big story."[69]

Smith considered himself part of the press corps, though it is doubtful that many mainstream sportswriters regarded him as such. Being black, Smith was denied a press card, which kept him off the field and out of the locker rooms though he was allowed in the press box at City Island. Jim Crow laws also prohibited him from socializing with the other writers away from the field. "If they wanted me to go to dinner with them, it was against the law," he said. "I'm sure they would have liked me to join them. They didn't ask because they knew it was impossible."[70]

Smith may have been right. Perhaps Jim Crow provided a convenient excuse for sportswriters to remain comfortably on one side of their own profession's color line. White sportswriters, for the most part, kept their racial attitudes to themselves, or at least out of print. Once, however, according to a Billy Rowe column, when Smith entered the press box at City Island, a sportswriter with the *Eagle* said, "'This was a good job until Mexicans, Cubans, and Negroes started cluttering up the diamond.' His statement wasn't that mild, but this is a family paper. Don't write your senator, write the Brooklyn *Eagle*."[71] If Rowe's information was correct, the comment came either from Tommy Holmes or Harold Burr.

Rickey's decision to integrate baseball was driven, in part, by economics: he could obtain talented black players at little cost. A better team meant more spectators at Ebbets Field, which translated into a better bottom line for Rickey and the Dodgers. Rickey negotiated a favorable contract for the Dodgers to have them train in Daytona Beach. That city's officials hoped that having the Dodgers' training camp would be a boon to its tourism industry. According to sports editor Bernard Kahn, the New York press portrayed Daytona Beach as more tolerant than other Florida cities. This, according to Kahn, would lure New Yorkers to vacation in the resort city. This potentially meant big business: Kahn estimated that the combined daily circulation of the newspapers that sent sportswriters to cover the Dodgers was more than nine million.[72]

Throughout the spring, city officials and local businessmen tried to sign the Brooklyn organization to a long-term spring-training contract, even buying a two-page advertisement in the *Daytona Beach Evening News* to make their case. The newspaper quoted Rickey as saying he wanted to come back next year. "I'd like to return to Daytona Beach," he said. "I want to come back without embarrassment to you all."[73] The article did not explain what Rickey meant by "without embarrassment," but, according to Burr, he was referring to the "Negro question."[74]

Burr doubted whether the Dodgers would return to Daytona Beach because of the climate – racial and otherwise. The weather had been so cold and rainy that a number of games had been canceled and others had to be played in miserable conditions. In addition, team executives, ballplayers, and sportswriters had complained about the high cost of meals and hotel rooms.[75] There also were logistical problems. Brooklyn manager Leo Durocher said he did not like having players scattered throughout the city. "I like to keep an eye on my players at night," he said. "They're down here to train and it's my business to see that they behave themselves and stay in shape. That's difficult when the players are scattered around."[76]

Other Florida cities were aware of the lucrative crowd in Daytona Beach. Newspaper stories reported that cities such as Fort Lauderdale, West Palm Beach, and Deland were interested in becoming Brooklyn's spring-training site in 1947. The mere rumor that the Dodger organization might train in Deland produced a front-page story in the *Sun*

News under the headline, "Rickey May Bring Dodgers Here."[77] The newspaper quoted Rickey as saying he was "very much interested" in relocating to Deland after hearing that the city wanted to modify its naval air station into a training complex. If it did so, Brooklyn and its massive farm system could all train at one site. Before committing to Deland, however, Rickey needed to be convinced that the city could make the appropriate renovations.[78]

Having flunked Rickey's test for color blindness, however, it is doubtful that Rickey would have made any kind of agreement with Deland. As it turned out, Rickey moved his spring-training base from Florida to Cuba the next year. After playing his first season in the minor leagues in Canada, therefore, Robinson went to spring training the following February in Havana. "It could be reasonably expected that the racist atmosphere I had had to face in Florida and other parts in the United States," Robinson said, "would not exist in another country of non-whites."[79]

1 2 3 4 5 6 7 8 **9** 10

Integration Stands Its Ground against Southern Intolerance

THROUGHOUT HIS ATHLETIC career what set Jackie Robinson apart from others was his speed. He had always been faster than anyone else. He demonstrated this time and time again on football fields and in track meets. In baseball, however, one cannot outrun a curve ball or hope to field a ground ball and run to first base before the runner. But as the 1946 spring training neared its final two weeks, Robinson turned to his speed to begin manufacturing hits. As he had done in the Negro Leagues, he bunted or chopped at pitches and then outran the infielder's throw to first. Once on base, his speed could affect the outcome of a game, as he accelerated, then stopped, and accelerated again, unnerving pitchers. Meanwhile his arm had grown stronger, and he had become more confident on defense, becoming the team's regular second baseman.

On Thursday, March 28, Robinson had a hit in four at bats as Montreal beat the Daytona Beach Islanders, Brooklyn's single-A team, 9-2.[1] Three days later, Robinson had a bunt single as Montreal lost, 3-1, to St. Paul. The *Daytona Beach Evening News* reported that "Montreal's Negro infield prospect, who has been on short rations at the plate, got himself a single in the game when he laid down a 'neat bunt.'"[2] Wendell Smith wrote that Robinson played flawlessly at second base and then in the seventh inning, "dropped a perfect bunt down the third base line and beat it out with a burst of blazing speed." After the game, Branch Rickey told Smith: "He'll hit. The only question is his arm. I only hope it comes around."[3]

On April 2, Robinson had 2 more hits, walked once, and stole a base as Montreal defeated Brooklyn, 6-1, at City Island. During the game, according to Smith, Brooklyn's pugnacious Eddie Stankey collided "unnecessarily" with Robinson when Jackie was covering a play at first base.[4] Mel Jones, too, remembered that Stankey went "out of his way to spike Robinson."[5] In his biography of Branch Rickey, Murray Polmer gave a different account. Robinson, Polmer said, tagged Stankey hard in the testicles, prompting a warning from Rickey: "Control yourself, Jackie. You know what I told you." Robinson replied: "Don't worry, Mr. Rickey, I will."[6]

The Polmer account came from Rickey. It bears Rickey's self-righteous signature, which he often inserted in place of the actual order of events. Of the two accounts, the former has the clearest ring of authenticity, as it demonstrates Robinson's restraint in the face of physical abuse. During that spring, Robinson learned to practice nonviolence. Restricted by his promise to Rickey, he withheld his temper and carried on, ignoring racist taunts and attacks. The Stankey incident provides a metaphor for Robinson's first few years in professional baseball.

Wendell Smith liked what he was seeing in Robinson, but he continued to jump to his own conclusions. He reported, for example, that Rickey refused to either confirm or deny a rumor that Robinson and Wright would be promoted to the Major Leagues by midseason. "It is," Smith wrote, "the consensus of sportswriters covering the Brooklyn and Montreal camps here that the Negro players are expected to grace the fertile turf of Ebbets Field some time between now and September."[7] The *Norfolk Journal and Guide* also reported that Robinson had begun "to click, both at bat and in the field." It published a photo of Robinson with the caption, "Snaps Out of Batting Slump."[8]

The *Washington Afro-American* concurred that Robinson "broke the ice here Tuesday." The article added that the ballplayer, "who had experienced untold difficulty connecting safely in previous games," singled in his first and third at bats.[9] The *People's Voice* reported that Robinson had begun to relax and had become the team's starting second baseman. His early-season difficulties, it said, "can be traced to the terrific pressures he bore upon his shoulders as 'the first Negro to crash [Jim Crow] in big-league baseball.'"[10]

The *Montreal Daily Star* also noted that Robinson – the "much publicized Negro infielder" – was shedding his early-spring nervousness and improving every day.[11] In the *Brooklyn Eagle*, Harold Burr quoted Rickey as saying that Robinson "looked like 'a big league prospect.'" Rickey, however, was less optimistic about the future of Johnny Wright, who had not yet established himself as an International League–caliber pitcher. "He's 28 years old and the Royals have 12 pitchers," he said. "If Wright can't make the Montreal staff he will be released."[12]

Under a headline that said "Robinson Plays First Good Game," the *Eagle*'s Tommy Holmes also wrote that it appeared Robinson had made the Montreal roster. He added, however, that Robinson still looked nervous at the plate, waving "his bat around a great deal more than is necessary," though this was Robinson's batting style. Holmes reported that black fans reacted enthusiastically to Robinson. One of his hits sent the fans in the segregated wing of the bleachers "into a spasm of hysteria," for example. There was little reaction to Robinson from white fans. After a long Robinson foul ball down the left-field line was caught, a young white woman screamed: "Goody! Goody!" That, according to the *Eagle* columnist, was the extent of the anti-Robinson sentiment.[13]

After the game, Robinson told reporters that he felt more comfortable than he had at the beginning of spring training. "In my early days down here, I was conscious, or thought I was, of a feeling of resentment among a few players but that has worn off," he said. He said that during the first few weeks of training camp Wright and he had received little support from their teammates. "All the fellows seem to be pulling for us," Robinson said. "And if we don't make the team it will be because we were unable to do as well as the other members of the club."[14]

The *Washington Afro-American* agreed that Montreal's white players had warmed up to Robinson and Wright. An unnamed white ballplayer who had earlier refused to have his photo taken with Robinson or Wright was now giving them playing tips.[15] Not all the ballplayers had accepted their black teammates, however. When *Courier* photographer Billy Rowe asked one white player to stand next to Robinson for a photo, the player refused. "This is a white man's game," he told Rowe. When Rowe tried to explain that the addition of blacks to baseball would bring more fans to ball games, which would translate into higher salaries, the ballplayer abruptly walked away.[16]

Black sportswriters implied that white players were conspiring against Robinson and Wright, either by running over or throwing at Robinson or ignoring Wright's signals on the mound. These suspicions apparently were justified. One story asserted that white players had considered going on strike to protest the signing of blacks. In another story, Brooklyn outfielder Augie Galan claimed that his teammate Hugh Casey, of Georgia, once threw at Robinson on four consecutive pitches. When asked about the incident later, one Dodger player said he could not remember. Another said: "I wouldn't even touch that."[17]

According to sportswriter Bill Roeder, manager Clay Hopper asked Indianapolis pitcher Paul Derringer, a former star pitcher who had won

223 games but was now at the end of his career, to try to provoke Robinson out of his hitting slump. "Tell you what I'm going to do, Clay," said Derringer, a Kentuckian. "I'm going to knock this colored boy down a couple of times and see what makes him tick."[18] When Robinson came to bat for the first time, Derringer knocked him down. Robinson responded by lining a single to right field. When Robinson came up to bat again, Derringer threw at his head. On the next pitch, Derringer threw a curve ball that Robinson hit to left center for a triple. The Indianapolis pitcher then turned to Hopper in the Montreal dugout and shouted, "Clay, he will do!" There is at least some evidence that this incident happened. Robinson had 2 hits, a single and a triple, and 2 stolen bases against Derringer and Indianapolis at City Island on April 5.[19] The *Montreal Gazette* reported the Derringer story a month later.[20]

People's Voice sportswriter Joe Johnson praised Robinson's performance on the base paths in the Indianapolis game. However, in calling him "another Ty Cobb," Johnson chose a description that both Robinson and the racist Cobb would find objectionable. Johnson noted that Robinson was playing like he had a year earlier when he tore up the Negro Leagues: "With the pressure that goes with being the first Negro in modern organized baseball apparently wearing off," Johnson wrote, "Jackie is beginning to hit his stride. He is commencing to lace out the horsehide, and his fielding is on a high, impressive level."[21]

In his next game, Robinson went hitless against St. Paul but played error-free ball at second base.[22] Pitching the seventh, eighth, and ninth innings, Wright gave up 3 runs and got the loss. "Wright was fast but a trifle wild," the *Evening News* reported.[23] Wright had suffered control problems most of the spring, and he was running out of opportunities to prove he belonged on the Montreal team. In one game, after walking four and hitting another in just one inning, Smith described Wright as "wilder than an Egyptian Zebra."[24]

On April 7, Montreal traveled to Sanford Municipal Athletic Field for another game with St. Paul. Robinson and Wright had not been in Sanford since they had been run out of town a month earlier, and were not anxious to return. Montreal expected to hear that the game was canceled, but no word came. Montreal put Robinson in the lineup, and the game started without incident. In the top of the first inning, Smith later reported, Robinson singled, stole second, and then scored on another single, beating the throw with a slide. A police officer then appeared on the scene to assist Robinson off the field. "Now you git off'n this heah field now," he drawled. "Eff'n ya don't, ah'm puttin' ya' in the jail house right now. So hep me eff ah don't!"

Robinson quoted Smith's account in his biography *My Own Story*. It continued:

> As the police officer escorted Robinson away from home plate, Hopper came out of the dugout to protest. "He didn't do anything wrong, did he?" the Montreal manager asked.
>
> "Yes, he did," the cop snapped back.
>
> "What?" Hopper asked meekly.
>
> "We told y'all to leave them Nigra players home," the officer said. "We ain't having Nigras and white boys playing on the same field in this town. It's agin the law and ah'm heah to tell ya."
>
> As Robinson sat in the dugout, he said he felt sorry for Hopper, who obviously didn't know what to do. He didn't want to tell Robinson to leave the dugout but also knew that he didn't have much of a choice.
>
> "Git him off'en thet there bench," the cop demanded, waving a club at Robinson. "He can't sit there. They's white boys a-setin' there. That's agin the law, too. They cain't set togetha on no baseball benches, either . . ."
>
> Hopper started walking toward the bench. I guess he had decided he'd have to tell me, although I could see he didn't want to. The cop was walking a few feet behind him, waving his stick and getting more boisterous. "Tell him ah said to git!"
>
> Hopper was within a few feet of me now. "Jackie . . . ah . . . the cop says . . . ." But before he could say anything else, I threw up my hand to save him the embarrassment. "Okay, Skipper," I said, using my best imitation of a Southern drawl, "tell him that ah'm a-gittin." And I headed for the shower room with Johnny Wright on my heels."[25]

The incident in all probability did not happen precisely as Smith told it in Robinson's autobiography. Never one to let the facts get in the way of a story, Smith tossed in the dialect for effect. There were other errors in *My Own Story*'s account of the incident: the game was played in Sanford, not Deland; Robinson led off the second inning, not the first; and he was ordered off the field after the top of the second inning, not after the top of the first.

However, Smith, though he witnessed the incident, did not write about in his *Courier* column. To read about it, you had to live in Montreal or at least read the *Montreal Gazette*. In an unbylined article, the newspaper stated that Robinson had left after being ordered off the field by the Sanford police chief. "It was the first time," the article said, "the Montreal club had been officially notified that their two colored players, Robinson and Wright, would not be allowed to play here."[26] For Robinson and Wright, their second visit to Sanford was as humiliating as their first. Their exit left them dispirited.

The *Sanford Herald* reported nothing of the incident in its edition. Years later, its sports editor, Julian Stenstrom, remembered a far different version of events. His account – softened by decades of denial and wishful thinking – included a number of errors. According to Stenstrom, Robinson had played his first game of the spring against Brooklyn during February in Sanford. No objection was made to Robinson, he claimed, until Robinson went out to his position at the bottom of the first inning. At that point, a fan left the ballpark and called police chief Roy Williams, demanding that he enforce the city's Jim Crow ordinance. Williams then escorted Robinson off the field.[27]

After the Sanford game, Stenstrom continued, Williams, Hopper, and Rickey reached a gentlemen's agreement, whereby Robinson would play no more than three innings of any game. There were no problems after that, Stenstrom said.[28] One black living in Sanford at the time recalled that Williams was an easygoing sheriff. "He was the kind of fellow who would usually tell you to 'keep on moving' . . . he wouldn't go out trying to bully anyone," he said. "The chief, himself, wasn't all that bad . . . he did what those above him told him to do."[29]

Until his death, Stenstrom told readers that baseball's color line was broken in Sanford – not in Daytona Beach. His account, while a stretch, is not entirely incorrect. Robinson practiced his first two days in Sanford and later played two innings of the April 7 game there.

Years later, Stenstrom bristled after reading an article that said Robinson had played all his games in Daytona Beach because he was banned in Jacksonville, Deland, and Sanford. "That may have occurred in Jacksonville and Deland," he wrote. "But it did not happen in Sanford." According to Stenstrom, Sanford paved "the way for professional baseball's color line to be broken," and Stenstrom's newspaper, the *Herald*, was behind Robinson and Wright from the beginning.[30] During a phone conversation with Sanford native "Red" Barber, Stenstrom mentioned that Robinson had broken baseball's color line in Sanford. Barber corrected him that the city "had run Robinson out of town." Stenstrom objected and criticized Barber's version in a newspaper column. On February 23, 1997, however, the *Herald* corrected its longtime sports editor's version in a story on Robinson's brief stay in Sanford. Barber, the paper said, had never forgiven his hometown for its treatment of Robinson and White.[31]

Two months later, on April 20, 1997 – fifty years after Robinson broke the Major League color barrier – Sanford mayor Larry Dale signed a proclamation honoring Jackie Robinson. In it, Dale apologized for the city's "regrettable actions in 1946," when the city had forced Robinson off Municipal Athletic Field. The proclamation did not sit well with all townspeople, however. Many believed that the city had let Robinson play and therefore had no reason to apologize. Others, cloaking themselves in the denial that prevented so many from taking responsibility for generations of discrimination, saw no reason to dredge up the sins of the past.

As the press had predicted, Rickey did not stop with Robinson and Wright. On April 4, 1946, a month after Robinson and Wright first stepped on the practice field in Sanford, Rickey announced that catcher Roy Campanella and pitcher Don Newcombe had been assigned to Brooklyn's AA team in Nashua, New Hampshire, in the New England League.[32] Already an established star at twenty-four, Campanella had hit .365 and led the league in RBIS for the Baltimore Elite Giants in 1945. Newcombe, then nineteen, had posted an 8–3 record for the Newark Bears in 1945.

In an in-depth account of the story, the Associated Press provided personal background on the two ballplayers and explained how Robinson had broken the color line the previous fall. It also quoted Fred Dobens, president of the New England League, who said that the Brooklyn club "is carrying on its plan to give deserving Negro players a chance to make good in organized baseball down through its farm clubs."[33] In striking contrast, *The Sporting News* published a curt three-paragraph story on the Campanella and Newcombe signing, hiding it at the bottom of page six.[34]

For the black and communist press, the signing of Campanella and Newcombe meant another victory against Jim Crowism. It also meant further progress in black America's domestic war against discrimination. In the *Daily Worker*, Bill Mardo called the news "another body-blow ripped into the heart of jim crow in America's national pastime."[35] Sam Lacy of the *Baltimore Afro-American* again praised Rickey for his efforts to eradicate prejudice in baseball. He also reported that Rickey had long been interested in Campanella.[36] The previous October Campanella had been the catcher on an all-black team that played a 5-game series against the Dodgers. Rickey asked to see him after one game and secretly signed the catcher to a contract.[37] The *Courier* reported that Campanella had signed with the Brooklyn organization before leaving for winter ball, but the news had been "smothered" until the April announcement. The newspaper noted that the two black ballplayers were first assigned to Danville, then moved to Nashua in the New England League "for some unknown reason."[38]

Under the headline "Is Rickey Still Kidding?" Rick Hurt of the *People's Voice* wrote that the April 4 news silenced those who had questioned Rickey's sincerity after he signed Robinson.[39] A week later, Hurt wrote that Campanella and Newcombe had both been offered contracts in the Mexican League but had rejected them. He too reported that Campanella had secretly signed a contract with Rickey in the fall, but the organization had postponed the announcement, as it had done with Robinson.[40]

In his autobiography, *It's Good to Be Alive*, the catcher remembered a meeting with Rickey on October 17, 1945. Without explaining why, Rickey had asked Campanella not to sign a contract with anyone until he was contacted again. Campanella assumed Rickey wanted to sign him for his black team, the Brown Dodgers. A few days later, the Elite Giants were playing against Robinson's Kansas City Monarchs. During a game of gin rummy after the game, Robinson said, "I hear you went to see Mr. Rickey."

"How did you know?" Campanella asked.

"I was over there myself," Robinson answered.

Robinson then asked Campanella if he had signed a contract with Rickey. Campanella said he had not, but agreed that he would not sign with anyone until he had again heard from Rickey. Robinson then told Campanella that he had signed with Brooklyn's AAA team, the Montreal Royals. "It's a secret," he said. "Mr. Rickey told me to keep it quiet, so you got to promise me not to tell anyone." A couple days later, Montreal announced it had signed Robinson.[41] After the 1945 baseball season ended, both Robinson and Campanella had played winter ball in Venezuela. As Robinson talked anxiously about the following spring, Campanella waited to hear from Rickey, but no word came. Finally, on March 1, he received a telegram asking him to report to Daytona Beach on March 10. Meeting with Bob Finch, Campanella signed a contract and finalized the details of his minor league assignment.

Campanella thought he would be joining Montreal. But Finch told him that Rickey had rejected that idea after Robinson and Wright had been pressured to leave Sanford. "Mr. Rickey says you can't go to Sanford right now," Finch said. "There's been . . . uh . . . some unpleasantness regarding Robinson in Sanford. Mr. Rickey feels it would not be wise to have you join the Montreal team at this time." Rickey instructed Finch that he wanted Campanella to go to Danville, a AA team in Illinois. When Finch called Danville, however, the team said it did not want the catcher. Finch then called Nashua.[42]

The signing of Campanella and Newcombe again caught Negro League owners in the dilemma of wanting to support integration while trying to hold on to their best players. Bill Mardo quoted Newark owner Effa Manley as saying that most of her ballplayers were potential big leaguers. The newspaper said that Manley had been a long supporter of integrating baseball. "One of the best sports in the world to break down prejudice is in baseball," she said, "and that's why I've always supported the fight to end jim crow in the majors."[43]

Manley, however, opposed Rickey's method of raiding ballplayers from the Negro Leagues without compensating the teams. She also knew that if she protested, she would be vilified by men like Wendell Smith and Sam Lacy – as Kansas City owners Thomas Baird and J. L. Wilkinson had been when they protested Montreal's signing of Robinson. As a result, she said nothing publicly, but pleaded privately with Rickey to compensate her for Newcombe. Rickey ignored her. Later, when Manley bumped into Rickey at a Negro League game, she told him that if he signed any more of her players, she would make trouble for him. When word of this leaked out, however, black sportswriters convinced her to do nothing.[44]

On March 26, 1946, Grays' owner Cumberland "Cum" Posey, one of the Negro League's leading figures, died. It is ironic – even symbolic – that Posey's death came when it did, as integration spelled the beginning of the end for the Negro Leagues. He knew that the world he had helped create was fading. Beginning as a player, Posey had become a manager, booking agent, business manager, an owner of the Homestead Grays, and one of the pillars of black baseball. He initiated night games before the Major Leagues, was executive secretary of the Negro National League, and wrote a regular column for the *Pittsburgh Courier*.[45]

Posey's death was honored with fanfare befitting a head of state. Eulogies filled the sports columns of black weeklies such as the *Courier*. "Surrounded by a sea of flowers," Ches Washington wrote, "a fragrant tribute to the sagacious sportsman who made the Homestead Grays as magic a name in the baseball world as Joe Louis in the fistic firmament and incidentally put the steel town of Homestead on the athletic map, Cum Posey lay in state here Sunday as thousands of friends of both races paused in a final salute to a brilliant athlete, a peerless magnate and an outstanding civic leader."[46]

In his *Courier* column, Smith presented a poem titled "Game Called," which concluded: "There'll be no cheering in the stands today, / The Captain of the team has passed away. / Put down the ball; that's the end of the game, / Baseball has lost its greatest name – Cum Posey."[47] Fay Young also paid tribute in the *Defender*: "He had a way of making his enemies respect him and sometimes winning them over as friend. As for his friends, he could rely on their loyalty. He had a forceful way of making you agree with him. That was Cum Posey. And now he is no more."[48]

In the same issue of the *Courier* as the Posey obituary, Smith provided yet another encouraging note on Robinson and Wright. Although it was not yet official, the two ballplayers, he said, would go north with Montreal at the end of the spring. Smith again hinted that Robinson would be promoted to the Major Leagues by season's end. In another article, Smith said that Robinson's throwing arm had fully healed. Indeed, Coach Clyde Sukeforth said that Robinson's arm was now "good enough for any team in any league."[49]

In an April 13 interview with Lacy, Rickey addressed the obstacles that integration was facing in Florida. The Brooklyn president continued to emphasize that the cause was bigger than a few lockouts. "We are having our troubles, but we see no reason why we should not see this thing through," he said. "The colored player is entitled to the same chance given other fellows. He has five fingers, five toes and his eyes are in the same place. There is absolutely no difference in him and his brothers of other racial groups . . . only color, and I don't look at that."[50]

But about this time, several newspapers began referring to a conspiracy among southern cities to thwart integration. On April 6 Montreal general manager Mel Jones announced that the games on April 9 in Jacksonville, April 12 and 14 in Savannah, and April 15 in Richmond had been canceled after officials in those cities said they would not allow black players to share their ball fields with white players. In addition, Jones said, the April 10 game in Deland had been transferred to Daytona Beach.[51] According to Wendell Smith, Rickey stood up defiantly to the bigoted towns by declaring: "Without Robinson and Wright, there will be no games!"[52]

Norfolk Journal and Guide columnist Lem Graves Jr. also praised Montreal for its support of Robinson and Wright and urged black fans to patronize Montreal's games during the International League season.[53] When the newspaper asked Richmond Colts owner Eddie Mooers to comment on the cancellation of his game against Montreal, he refused. He did not want to offend black spectators who patronized his ballpark, he said. The *Journal and Guide* published a letter from a Richmond baseball fan who said he would never again attend a game at Mooers Field. It also published an editorial cartoon that showed Mooers Field with a Confederate flag flying high above, with the caption, "Richmond Still Capital of Confederacy."

When the *Daily Worker* asked Mooers why he had refused to let Robinson and Wright take the field, he replied that he wanted to save them from the embarrassment of verbal abuse. When pressed further, he said that he "didn't want a race riot." The *Worker* reporter then asked if Mooers had ever seen a race riot at the stadium. Mooers replied that the

161

black players would be "insulted if they played in Richmond." According to the *Worker*, Mooers then adopted the Deland story: his field would not be ready for a night game because the floodlights had not yet been replaced.[54]

Montreal finished its spring season in Daytona Beach with games against other Dodger organization teams on April 8, 9, 10, 11, and 12. New York sportswriters said nothing about the end of Montreal's spring training; its writers had already headed north with the big league teams. For its part, *The Sporting News* had not mentioned Robinson since Dan Parker's column attacking Rickey three weeks earlier. In that column, Parker had written that Robinson "hadn't been living up to his advance billing."[55]

A lot had changed since then. But for most of the sportswriters, nothing had changed. Most registered their disapproval of – or lack of interest in – integration by paying it little mind. The *Brooklyn Eagle* and the *New York Post* did do some primary reporting; so did the *Worker* and a number of black newspapers. But the majority of sportswriters and columnists who came to Florida for newspapers in New York City and elsewhere never came close enough to Robinson to report anything about him.

The *Daytona Beach Morning Journal* did not mention Robinson in any of its final stories on the spring season. The *Evening News* also left his name out of a preview of Montreal's upcoming season.[56] The *Montreal Daily Star* briefly mentioned Robinson in its preview of the upcoming season. "The dark Jack Robinson has been pretty steady around second base," it said.[57] In another story the next day, it again called Robinson "dark" though the skin color of none of the other players was mentioned.[58] Later, when Robinson played for Brooklyn, he complained that New York City sportswriters continually referred to him as a "Negro" player, though the various nationalities of his Brooklyn teammates went unremarked.[59]

Daily Worker columnist Bill Mardo had followed Robinson's progress since the paper had sent him to cover baseball's first integrated spring training in March. To Mardo, integration was not a fad that would go away at the end of the spring, and on April 11, he wrote that his newspaper would not stop pressuring baseball until other teams had signed black players. "Yes," he wrote. "Something has been added to the great game of baseball. And this is only the beginning."[60]

The story resonated deeply with blacks, in part because they had themselves suffered the abuses of discrimination and in part because they had read about the campaign to integrate baseball for years and now felt intimately involved in it. As racial discrimination increased, so had the influence of the black press. "Whether they were fighting for the end of slavery, integration into the political system, or equal opportunity," author Lauren Kessler wrote, "black editors informed, inspired, unified and mobilized their readers. They not only offered information . . . the journals undoubtedly helped blacks understand, and then realize, their political potential."[61] As the spring of 1946 had progressed, Robinson's and Wright's names had passed from newspaper to newspaper and person to person, making them heroes to millions of blacks. When black Americans talked about Robinson or Wright, they talked about their own dreams. In reaching out to touch them, blacks felt they could touch their own dreams. If Robinson and Wright could succeed, so, too, could they.

Toward the end of spring training, Robinson and Wright drove together to Jacksonville to see a Negro League exhibition game between the Newark Bears and Jacksonville Eagles. Spike Washington of the *Atlanta Daily World* reported that the other spectators received the ballplayers as heroes, throwing them a postgame celebration. The ballplayers on Jacksonville and Newark wanted to know everything Robinson and Wright had experienced and seen, and asked them whether other blacks would follow them and when. Neither Robinson nor Wright, however, appeared anxious to talk about the discrimination they had endured. Washington wrote that both were playing for more than themselves and praised them for making history and for making other things seem possible. "All Negroes," Washington wrote, "are pulling hard for them."[62]

More than anyone else, this had been Wendell Smith's story. And when Montreal announced that Robinson and Wright had made the team, Smith captured the end of baseball's first integrated spring training with uncharacteristic understatement: "After six weeks of tedious training, Jackie Robinson and Johnny Wright have won berths on the Montreal Royals baseball club. They are now officially a part of Orga-

163

nized Baseball – a distinction no Negro player has had since way back in the eighties."[63]

Smith, too, understood that this was only the beginning of integration, and that the hardest part of the struggle lay ahead. He also recognized that neither Robinson nor Wright could succeed by themselves. He lectured his readers on their responsibilities. "Never in history have two ballplayers had so many people pulling for them to make good," he said. "But at the same time, never in history have two ball players been so dependent upon these same fans who are pulling for them, for they could very easily make or break Montreal's Robinson and Wright."[64]

Smith warned fans to control themselves in the stands lest they put too much pressure on the ballplayers – or even embarrass them. He even cautioned readers against taking off their shirts and behaving boisterously. Smith referred specifically to the spectator who "stands up in the stands and rants and raves, yells and screams before they even so much as picked up a ball."[65] If they really wanted to support Robinson and Wright fans should act appropriately.

Robinson later said he drew strength from black fans during spring training – though he admitted their enthusiasm put additional pressure on him. Sometimes, he said, he tried so hard to please his supporters that it affected his playing. "I could hear them shouting in the stands," Robinson said, "and I wanted to produce so much that I was tense and over-anxious. I found myself swinging hard enough to break my back. I started swinging at bad balls and doing a lot of things I wouldn't have done under ordinary circumstances. I wanted to get a hit for them because they were pulling so hard for me."[66]

Nobody outside Robinson's inner circle could fathom what he endured that spring. Rachel remembered the evenings in the Harrises' upstairs apartment when the two, alone and married only a few weeks, reflected back on their day. Some nights Jackie was so angry at what was happening around him or so frustrated with his inability to adjust to it that he wanted to quit, and some nights she would cry for him. "Each evening we would huddle together in our room to recover from the pressures of the day," she said. "Jackie would tell me everything that went on on the field and I would tell him everything that happened in the stands."[67]

And the next morning, Robinson would put on his uniform at the Harrises and walk with Johnny Wright to Kelly Field a few blocks away, often passed by his Montreal teammates riding in their bus. When the practice ended for the day, the white players would get back on the bus and leave Robinson and Wright behind in the town's black neighborhood. Their white teammates would then spend the evening talking baseball, playing cards, or hanging out at a downtown bar or establishment that treated them with basic decency and respect. They would sometimes gripe about the special treatment afforded Robinson and Wright – treatment that, in fact, exacted a heavy toll on both men, who put far more than their talent on the line that spring.

To Billy Rowe, Jackie Robinson understood that he would have to sacrifice a piece of himself for the good of black Americans, and he did this at great risk to himself. "I will never forget his magnificent courage," Rowe said. "He realized that this was an experiment and for it to work out, there were certain things he had to accept. . . . He stood up for what it meant to be an American and he changed the attitudes of both races."[68] In one of his *Courier* columns, Wendell Smith reported that a white man once walked up to Robinson in Daytona Beach and said, "I want you to know I'm pulling for you to make good. In fact, everyone here feels the same way I do. We believe a man deserves a fair chance if he has the goods."[69]

Baseball's road to integration did not just pass through Daytona Beach. The city provided a safe passage for both Robinson and Wright, an asylum from the bigotry of other southern towns, where blacks were shot just for being. Instead of being denied opportunity, Daytona Beach gave the two ballplayers an opportunity to succeed. Rachel Robinson later wrote: "Compared to the adjacent towns, Daytona Beach stood out as a kind of political oasis. We moved freely in downtown Daytona Beach."[70] Billy Rowe noted that neither he nor anyone else in the Robinson circle was given so much as a parking ticket in Daytona Beach.[71]

In 1990, Daytona Beach recognized Robinson's contributions by erecting a statue of the ballplayer outside City Island Ballpark, which is now called Jackie Robinson Ball Park. The ballpark and the statue serve as constant reminders of the spring of 1946. To Ed Charles, who was in

Daytona Beach, no statues are needed to prompt his memories. "I remember when Jackie came through town," he said.

> Everybody in our part of town wanted to see him. Old people and small children, invalids and town drunks all walked through the streets. Some were on crutches, and some people clutched the arms of friends, walking slowly on parade to the ball park to sit in the segregated section.
>
> We watched him play that day and finally believed what we had read in the papers, that one of us was out there on the ball field. When [spring training] was over, we kids followed Jackie as he walked with his teammates to the train station, and when the train pulled out, we ran down the tracks listening for the sounds as far as we could. And when we finally couldn't hear it any longer, we ran some more and finally stopped and put our ears to the tracks so we could feel the vibrations of that train carrying Jackie Robinson. We wanted to be a part of him as long as we could.[72]

PART

1234

1 2 3 4 5 6 7 8 9 **10**

Robinson Wins the Day during His First Game in Montreal

O
N APRIL 18, the sun shone brilliantly at Roosevelt Stadium in Jersey City, New Jersey, for the opening day of the 1946 International League season. Mayor Frank Hague required city workers to buy tickets to the game and canceled school so children could attend. As marching bands played, the ebullient Hague then reveled in the pregame parades and watched spectators fill the stadium beyond its twenty-five-thousand-seat capacity. The crowd included a large number of blacks, who had come from as far away as Baltimore and Philadelphia, to see Jackie Robinson take the field for the first time in a Montreal uniform during an official game.[1]

"I remember the parades, the brass band's playing of this 'day of destiny' for me," Robinson later remembered.

Nothing else mattered now – not even the people who, I now know, had ordered me out of Sanford, not even the insults and humiliations, the days and nights of strain. None of this would show up in the records of the years to come – only the hits, runs and errors of this day. As they played "The Star Spangled Banner" and Old Glory rolled slowly toward that azure blue sky, I stood on the base line with a lump in my throat and my heart beating rapidly, my stomach feeling as if it were full of feverish fireflies with claws on their feet.[2]

At 3:04 that afternoon, Robinson came to bat in the top of the first inning, feeling weak in his knees and stomach.[3] Swinging with a full count, he dribbled a weak grounder to the shortstop who threw him out easily. When he batted again with two on and none out in the third inning, Jersey City expected him to bunt. Instead, he swung away at a fastball and sent it into the left-field stands for a home run. As Robinson passed third base, manager Clay Hopper patted him on the back, and his teammate George Shuba, who was batting next, gave him a congratulatory handshake at home plate. Watching from the dugout, Johnny Wright laughed loudly. And in the press box, Wendell Smith looked at Joe Bostic and chuckled with delight. "Our hearts beat just a little faster," Smith said, "and the thrill ran through us like champagne bubbles."[4]

In the fifth inning, Robinson dropped a bunt single, then stole second, and went to third on a ground out. When Jersey City brought in a new pitcher, Robinson unnerved him by sprinting up and down the third base line, forcing a balk that sent Robinson home with another run. Robinson had 4 hits at 5 at bats, scored 4 runs, and stole 2 bases as Montreal won, 14–1. "The cold figures of the box score do not tell the whole story," reported the *New York Times*, which reported that Robinson had converted "his opportunity into a brilliant triumph."[5]

When the game ended, Robinson was immediately surrounded by a mob of kids. According to Smith, they "came swarming out of the bleachers and stands . . . like a great ocean wave," wanting to touch their hero and begging Robinson for autographs. Finally, one of his teammates had to escort him into the Montreal dressing room, where reporters, photographers, and his teammates awaited him. "As he left the park and walked out onto the street, the once-brilliant sun was fading slowly in the distant western skies," Smith wrote. Rachel greeted him. "You've had quite a day, little man," she said sweetly. "Yes," he replied softly. "God has been good to us today."[6]

Bostic, who had left the *People's Voice* to become sports editor of the *Amsterdam News*, wrote: "The most significant sports story of the century was written into the record books as baseball took up the cudgel for democracy and an unassuming but superlative Negro boy ascended the heights of excellence to prove the rightness of the experiment. And prove it in the only correct crucible for such an experiment – the crucible of white hot competition."[7] Bill Mardo wrote in the *Daily Worker* that the day "belonged to Jackie Robinson . . . and all the progressive forces who fought so tirelessly to drive a wedge into baseball's jim crow ban."[8]

Johnny Wright, who had shared the strain of spring training with Robinson, could now share with him the joy of Robinson's opening-day triumph. Soon after the beginning of the season, however, Montreal released Wright, who had withered under the intense glare of social progress and never found his control. He continued playing until the mid-1950s and finished his career with the Homestead Grays in the familiarity of the Negro Leagues. He died in Jackson, Mississippi, in 1990, his role in baseball history largely forgotten.[9]

Montreal finished the 1946 season with 100 victories, the most in team history, and won the pennant by eighteen and a half games. Robinson led the league in hitting with a .349 batting average and runs scored with 113. He finished second in stolen bases with 40 and also had the highest fielding percentage among second basemen. After the team won the league's world series, Robinson left the dressing room in his street clothes. A crowd of French-Canadian fans ran to him, hugged and kissed him, and serenaded him with "*Il a gagne ses epaulettes*" ("he has earned his stripes"). They later chased him as he ran away from the stadium. "It was probably the only day in history," *Pittsburgh Courier* sportswriter Sam Maltin wrote, "that a black man ran from a white mob with love instead of lynching on its mind."[10]

Before Robinson left the dressing room that day, Clay Hopper – who had once wondered if Robinson was human – sought him out and shook his hand. "You're a great ballplayer and a fine gentlemen," Hopper said. "It's been wonderful having you on the team."[11] There had been no reluctance on Hopper's part; the easiness of his handshake showed how the racial sensibilities of the Mississippi cotton broker had shifted since spring training. As the season progressed, the Montreal players, too, came to see Robinson not as a black ballplayer but as a productive teammate who could win them games.

A lot had changed since the early spring for Robinson, who had had to endure so much to finally triumph. In doing so, he had demonstrated that he belonged, vindicating all those who had believed for so long that blacks belonged in organized baseball. Robinson's tryout in organized baseball was different than that of the thousands of other ballplayers who came to Florida that spring. He carried the weight of millions of blacks on his shoulders. From the day Montreal announced it had signed him, Robinson acknowledged that he was playing for his fellow blacks. If he succeeded they, too, could succeed; if he could be given equal opportunity in baseball, they could be given equal opportunity in housing, education, and employment.

What began as an experiment in Sanford, Florida, was played out during the summer in many International League cities, including those with southern sensibilities such as Baltimore and Louisville – where fans showered Robinson with racial abuse. Wherever Montreal went that summer, crowds of blacks and crowds of whites came together to watch Robinson play. There were no race riots in the stands, as the white baseball establishment had predicted. Indeed, Robinson answered every baseball owner's objections that summer. By the end of the season, all that owners had left to justify segregation were their own prejudices.

Baseball's arguments for maintaining segregation were as entrenched as society's arguments for discriminating against blacks. They were based not on reasonableness or fairness or democracy but on biases, fears, and suspicions, none of which died in 1946 but would persist as long as American eyes remained shut and sensibilities undisturbed. As long as southerners believed that segregation was the natural order of things and northerners remained indifferent, blacks, their dreams deferred, would continue to live as second-class citizens.

As blacks demanded greater civil liberties in the months after World War II, violence against them increased. At least two dozen blacks were lynched in the South in 1946, and many others were beaten or shot on city streets by white law-enforcement officers sworn to uphold the law. Many of the dead or injured were either active or recently discharged servicemen.

In the South, the violence against blacks coincided with an increase in Ku Klux Klan membership. In Georgia, the Klan intimidated blacks from voting by posting signs that said: "The first Negro to vote will never vote again." On July 20 a war veteran named Macio Snipes was one of the few blacks who attempted to vote. He was later dragged from his home and shot. His killers went free. A few days later, four blacks were lynched by twenty to thirty white men near Monroe, Georgia, after one of the blacks had quarreled with his landlord. Under pressure from NAACP secretary Walter White, the federal government investigated but nobody was arrested.[12]

In early August, a veteran named John Jones was arrested on trumped-up charges near Minden, Louisiana. On August 8 he was released from jail and immediately abducted by a mob of Klansmen. He was lynched, and his bloated body turned up a week later in a nearby lake. Upon his discharge from the army, Jones had filed suit to recover the oil-producing land owned by his grandfather and leased to an oil company. Jones's family received one dollar a month for the land, which produced thousands of barrels of oil each month. All the suspects in the lynching went free.

During a meeting of the Ku Klux Klan in Atlanta in May 1946, members were warned to be more careful after some Klansmen had murdered a black cab driver but failed to wipe their fingerprints off the taxi's steering wheel. A Klansman on the police force had wiped the fingerprints off the wheel to protect his fellow members. Rather than report that the cab driver had been murdered an Atlanta newspaper reported that he had died in an automobile accident. A report on the Klan meeting was given to the Georgia Department of Law and the Federal Bureau of Investigation but nothing came of it.[13]

Black newspapers published details of such murders and other acts of random violence on their front pages. They warned their readers of the rise in Klan membership in the South and of Klan burnings in Florida, Tennessee, Georgia, and Alabama. A story in the *Chicago Defender* of March 30, 1946, reported that the FBI had shown little interest in investigating the Klan, thus providing aid and comfort to the racist organization. "Apprehension grows in the South that resurrection of the Klan may be a prelude to race riots and bloodshed," the *Defender* warned.[14]

Southern politicians used their clout to resist an attempt to create a permanent Fair Employment Practice Commission (FEPC). In February, Southerners in the U. S. Senate defeated a bill to prevent discrimination in employment on account of race, religion, or color by conducting a twenty-four-day filibuster. "The real sufferers were not alone the minorities who could not defend themselves in this unrestricted and unbridled marathon attack," one journalist wrote. "The demonstration was in itself a dark warning for the nation, not so much on the status and fate of minorities, but on the status and fate of the American democratic process."[15]

In reporting the death of the Fair Employment Practices bill, the *Defender* characterized it as the most decisive measure ever taken on civil rights. The newspaper vowed that blacks would not forget the southern Democrats and northern Republicans who had supported the filibuster that put the issue to rest.[16] "Like the anti-lynching and anti-poll tax bills before it," the *Courier* reported, "the measure for a permanent FEPC was sentenced to die in the Senate death house."[17]

In an editorial, the *Courier* asserted that, despite the defeat, there were reasons to be optimistic about future efforts to bring about racial equality. For instance, the well-organized pro-FEPC coalition had put a scare into the opposition, which only won the day by resorting to a last-ditch filibuster. Second, the publicity surrounding the measure had brought the issue of job discrimination to the attention of millions of Americans. The *Courier* called on its readers to continue the fight.[18]

On February 28, between fifteen and twenty thousand people attended a pro-FEPC rally at Madison Square Garden in New York City. The speakers, who included Eleanor Roosevelt; Roy Wilkins of the NAACP; and A. Philip Randolph, chairman of the National Council for a Permanent FEPC, told the crowd that the measure was not dead because it was right and therefore had to prevail. "It is sheer hypocrisy to hurl our anathemas at Bulgaria, Yugoslavia, Rumania, and other countries in Europe for their sins against democracy when our house is not in order," Randolph said.[19]

Seventeen years later, in August 1963, Randolph would be in the nation's capital for the March on Washington. There Martin Luther King Jr. and tens of thousands of blacks and whites insisted before the nation that blacks be given the rights guaranteed them in the U.S. Constitution. A year earlier, on July 20, 1962, King had paid tribute to Jackie Robinson before nearly a thousand people. "Back in the days when integration wasn't fashionable," King said of Robinson, "he underwent the trauma and the humiliation and the loneliness which comes with being a pilgrim walking the lonesome byways toward the high road of Freedom. He was a sit-inner before sit-ins, a freedom rider before freedom rides."[20]

On that late February day in 1946 when thousands met at Madison Square Garden to demonstrate for racial equality, Robinson and his wife had boarded a plane in Los Angeles to begin their long journey to Daytona Beach, Florida, with the hopes of millions of black Americans in his suitcase. Having signed a contract that ended professional baseball's color line, Robinson immediately emerged as a force for greater civil rights for all blacks. His ability to embrace his opportunity made it possible for others to rest their hopes on him. Robinson's capacity to rise above his difficulties made it possible for others to strive to achieve dreams that had previously been unimaginable. His restraint in the face of southern Jim Crowism provided a living and breathing demonstration of nonviolent resistance.

During the spring training of 1946, the inequalities and prejudices of baseball converged with the inequalities and prejudices of the Jim Crow South. These six weeks thus serve as a metaphor to illustrate that racial progress – and in a sense the survival of blacks – depended on the self-sacrifice of a relative few. Robinson understood before he left Los Angeles that he would have to sacrifice a part of himself for the sake of something bigger. "He accepted it," Billy Rowe said. "He realized how things were and that there were certain things he had to accept for it to work. He was part of the agenda to change baseball, to truly make it America's game."[21]

Once in the South, Robinson, as a black man, was forced to forfeit his personal freedoms. He could not eat in the same restaurant as his teammates or stay in the same hotels. He had to ignore ugly racial taunts and walk away from fastballs that plucked him in the ribs. If someone told him he could not play, he did not play. One city after another drew a line in the dirt, depriving Robinson of his place on the field. Only in Daytona Beach could he take the field with whites. But all Robinson needed to make his point was one city that was willing to give him a chance.

Just because Robinson had to tolerate discrimination, of course, did not mean he had to like it. Within his inner circle of Wright, Wendell Smith, Billy Rowe, and his wife, Rachel, he raged privately. He had to restrain himself time and time again. Rachel calmed him at night, massaging both his sore arm and his sense of righteous indignation. Never before or since has one ballplayer faced such hostile conditions. Robinson's career truly began during the spring training of 1946. Fortunately for so many ballplayers and spectators who drew strength from him, it did not end in Florida in 1946.

Given the racial climate of postwar Florida, so many things could have gone terribly wrong. As it happened, a lot did go wrong, but none of it had tragic consequences. Amid the tumult and the turmoil, Robinson struggled but did not fail. He confronted Jim Crow on his own turf and did not merely survive but endured, thereby providing blacks and those who supported them not just with a measure of victory but cause for optimism.

We do not give this story justice if we limit it to baseball, however. It transcends the national pastime, and provides us with a glimpse into what lay ahead for those who demanded that America live up to its promise as the land of opportunity. "Aided and abetted by sympathetic whites," Jules Tygiel wrote, "a handful of individual blacks shouldered the physical risks inherent in a policy of direct confrontation with the institutions of Jim Crow. In face of opposition from local public officials, baseball's integration coalition refused to retreat."[22]

For his part, Branch Rickey worked carefully, skillfully, and secretly to bring blacks into the game. For reasons that were not entirely noble, he accomplished something that was purely noble. He promised Robinson an opportunity to be the equal of anyone in the game. He supported Robinson in his opportunity, amid the howls of protest from journalists, ballplayers, and owners. He refused to capitulate when southern cities canceled games against Montreal. During a meeting of team owners in 1946, only Rickey of the sixteen Major League owners had voted to integrate baseball. One of the lessons of the civil rights movement was that black Americans could not change society by themselves; they needed the support of influential whites.

To his discredit, Rickey neither compensated Negro League teams for the players he signed nor shared the credit for integrating baseball. According to Rickey, he had integrated the game because he could never forget Charlie Thomas trying to rub off his black skin. As a Christian, Rickey said that if he were ever given the opportunity to do something for all of God's creatures, he would do it – and signing Robinson became his mission. Rickey repeated this story often to sportswriters working for mainstream newspapers, and because they did not question it it was accepted as the sole truth.

To black and communist journalists, however, the campaign to integrate baseball did not begin with Rickey. It began with them – more than a decade before. The unabridged story of the integration of baseball in America – like the story of civil rights in America – cannot be found in the mainstream press but in the alternative press. Men like Wendell Smith, Sam Lacy, Bill Mardo, and Lester Rodney fought the good fight when mainstream sportswriters remained silent. Smith, who had recommended Robinson to Branch Rickey, became an adviser to Rickey and a confidant of Robinson, and wrote the inside story of baseball's first integrated spring training.

When Robinson joined the Dodgers, Smith continued to cover the so-called Jackie Robinson beat, but by then it had grown beyond his grasp. In 1948, Smith co-wrote Robinson's first autobiography: *Jackie Robinson: My Own Story*. Then, the friendship between the two men cooled. Robinson was upset by a number of errors in the book, and Smith was hurt because Robinson had not given him sufficient credit for his role in integration. And when Robinson criticized the Negro Leagues, as Smith himself had done repeatedly, Smith and other black sportswriters attacked the ballplayer for his ingratitude. Smith sniped that Robinson owed everything he had to the black press.[23]

In 1948, Wendell Smith left his job with the *Courier* to join the *Chicago American*, making him one of the first black sportswriters to work for a mainstream daily. Now that he was working for a daily newspaper, he qualified for membership in the Baseball Writers Association, where he received his long-sought press card. Smith, who began his career as a crusader for racial equality, never quit crusading. After winning his long campaign to integrate baseball, he called for the integration of spring-training camps and once again saw his hard work come to fruition. On November 9, 1961, he told his readers that the Chicago White Sox had announced that they would integrate their training camp in Florida.[24]

After leaving the *American*, Smith moved to television, where he worked for wbbm and wgn in Chicago. He also wrote a weekly column for the *Sun-Times*. When he died at age fifty-eight in 1972, he was president of the Chicago Press Club. His death followed by just a month and two days that of his old friend Robinson, with whom he had shared so much. Ten years before, in 1962, Robinson had been elected to the Baseball Hall of Fame.

During the 1962 ceremonies the Baseball Writers Association inducted J. G. Taylor Spink into the hall, the first journalist so honored. Since then, the Baseball Writers Association has presented the J. G. Taylor Spink Award to selected sportswriters for their "meritorious contributions to baseball writing." In 1993, Smith became the first black sportswriter inducted into the Spink writer's wing of the hall. Five years later, Sam Lacy was also honored with the Spink award for his efforts to integrate baseball. Ironically, Spink had done more than any other journalist to delay integration, and the same Baseball Writers Association that voted Smith and Lacy into the hall had once barred them from membership.

Until his death in 2003, Lacy, approaching his one-hundredth birthday, remained at his desk at the *Baltimore Afro-American*, inextricably linked to the story of the integration of baseball and the spring training of 1946. He could still recall his own feelings of uneasiness as a black man in Florida and his anxiety as Robinson struggled during the early days of spring training. And he remembered how he had recognized the special burden of responsibility that Robinson bore on his shoulders. As Lacy sat and watched Robinson in Sanford, he knew he was covering a story that would have profound implications. "Wendell and I, for us, we knew that it would have great impact on the social consciousness and racial attitudes," he said, "that it was going to shake up the social structure."

Sportswriters working for mainstream newspapers, however, treated the integration of baseball "as a passing event," Lacy recalled.[25] He and Smith had approached sympathetic white sportswriters to enlist their cooperation. Their pleas were ignored. The *Daily Worker*'s Bill Mardo recalled some sportswriters who were sympathetic to integration. However, "they didn't think they had the freedom, working for newspapers that reflected the culture of a white society," or "they simply reflected the status quo of most whites." However, the majority of sportswriters, Mardo added, were pessimistic or simply indifferent toward racism. "'You guys are wasting your time,' they told me. 'This country wasn't going to change. . . . Those club owners will never give in. The hatred against blacks is so ingrained.'"[26]

While a few writers reported the story of baseball's first integrated spring training, most gave it little more than an obligatory nod. Some today say it is not right to judge these sportswriters critically because they merely reflected the biases and attitudes of their day. According to Grantland Rice's biographer, their writing "represented mainstream America and mainstream journalism."[27] Writers do need to be judged in the context of their times but not excused for failing to acknowledge those times' injustices.

Sportswriters and all journalists need to be held accountable for perpetuating society's sins. Sportswriters bear culpability for prolonging baseball's "gentlemen's agreement" – just as the baseball establishment has been condemned for its role in keeping the national pastime segregated. Sportswriters were indeed quasi members of the baseball establishment. They reflected the views of baseball's management and served as its apologists. They saw for themselves that talented black athletes were capable of playing in the big leagues, yet remained silent, thereby serving as conspirators in the greatest offense that baseball exacted upon any group.

A deeper understanding of the story of baseball's first integrated spring training can help us understand the problems facing a society struggling with the complexities of integration as well as the role of the press in that drama. In the mainstream press, the reporting was limited, both in content and context, by a mindset that kept white sportswriters, their newspapers, and their readers from appreciating the story's historical significance.[28] "Racism was culturally acceptable at the time. People felt comfortable in a racist society," Lester Rodney recalled. "The sheer ignorance of the details of racism kept people from understanding it."[29]

An examination of the press and its role in the integration of baseball underscores the conclusions of the 1947 Hutchins Report, which heavily criticized the media of the day for failing to provide a flow of information and interpretation that would help its readers understand the day's events.[30] If we are to give the journalists and particularly the sportswriters of the 1930s and 1940s a free pass on their coverage of race, at what point – if ever – do we make them accountable?

When Robinson entered the Major Leagues, the mainstream press began perpetuating a myth that the color line had been destroyed once and for all. Yet for the next several years, most of the blacks in the game would play for a relatively small number of teams. Throughout the 1950s and into the 1960s, black ballplayers had to be better than their white counterparts to play alongside them. And there would be no black managers until the mid-1970s.

When Los Angeles Dodgers executive Al Campanis said that blacks did not have the intelligence for front-office positions, baseball writers reacted with appropriate indignation. But nothing changed. When Cincinnati Reds owner Marge Schott and later Atlanta Braves pitcher John Rocker were punished for uttering racist slurs, the baseball writers turned them into punch lines, laughing sanctimoniously at the grossness of such offenses. And yet, more than fifty years after Robinson integrated professional baseball, there is little or no outrage in the mainstream press about the fact that baseball can claim only one black general manager and no black teams owners. Those who cover the game still represent mainstream America and mainstream journalism. Is their silence still defensible?

Monte Irvin, who followed Jackie Robinson into the Major Leagues in 1949, once said that "Baseball has done more to move America in the right direction than all the professional patriots with all their cheap words."[31] Irvin's remark is more accurate for baseball in 1946 than for baseball today. As one looks back at the 1946 spring training in light of what followed in later decades, one recognizes that a few men – and not the sport as a whole – dragged baseball ahead of society. Even today baseball continues to be criticized for not doing enough to level the playing field for blacks and other minorities. And the mainstream press continues to do too little to pressure the baseball establishment into doing more.

In their campaign to integrate baseball half a century ago, black sportswriters and their newspapers recognized a critical juncture in the story of baseball and the fight for civil rights and shared the story with their readers. They framed the story in terms of democracy and equal opportunity. It was not just a baseball story but a civil rights story. Black newspapers reported that southern communities, with the acquiescence and involvement of law-enforcement officers, committed acts of willful violence in places like Columbia, Tennessee. These newspapers reported lynchings and other murders against blacks in both the South and the North. And they reported how southern reactionaries in Congress had denied passage of civil rights legislation.

In the midst of this gloomy prospect, Jackie Robinson went to Florida and integrated professional baseball. His story provided something both substantial and tangible for black America. As black newspapers were widely distributed, black America found in Robinson a hero who stood for better days ahead, an America moving toward the civil rights movement. As is often the case with the stories that mean the most to society, they appear in the alternative press long before they do in the mainstream press. In the final result, the United States Communist Party would, however ironically, be a part of a campaign that would make the national pastime more democratic. For more than a decade, the *Daily Worker*, with Lester Rodney and Bill Mardo as sports editors, refused to accept the status quo in baseball and clamored loudly and clearly above the din of prejudice that protected segregation.[32] Because of the sheer number of the columns and articles they published, one can find in the pages of the *Worker* the most comprehensive treatment of the campaign to integrate baseball. The Communists had hoped that by ending segregation in baseball they could make a revolutionary change in society, and become a political force in America. When asked to assess the impact that the *Daily Worker* had had in ending baseball's color line, Mardo answered, "I think we had a major effect."[33]

Rodney was more specific – though perhaps more hyperbolic. "I'm not silly enough to think it wasn't going to happen," he said. "I think we probably speeded up the process by a few years."[34] The *Worker* and communism generally would be left in tatters after the Red Scare of the 1950s. Rodney left the Communist Party in 1957 in protest its failure to condemn the atrocities of Josef Stalin in the Soviet Union. He remained, however, an "unrepentant liberal," condemning baseball's miserable record on hiring blacks for front-office jobs.[35]

During the 1947 spring training, Branch Rickey moved his Brooklyn organization from segregated Florida to Havana, Cuba. That year, Montreal would have four blacks on its roster: Robinson, Roy Campanella, Don Newcombe, and Roy Partlow. As spring training progressed, rumors spread that Rickey would promote Robinson to the Dodgers. On March 29, Wendell Smith broke the story that Brooklyn would sign Robinson on April 10. *New York Times* columnist Arthur Daley also knew in advance, but he withheld the story on Rickey's insistence. "My boy," Rickey told Daley, "I must hold you to your solemn word of honor. This is the most important thing I ever did in my life and a premature leak could destroy it."[36]

By the second week of April, the Brooklyn organization had left Cuba and returned to finish its preseason at Ebbets Field. On the morning of April 10 Rickey told Robinson that the day's game between Brooklyn and Montreal would be his last as a Royal. During the sixth inning of the game, Rickey's assistant Arthur Mann walked through the press box and handed a sheet of paper to reporters that read: "The Brooklyn Dodgers today purchased the contract of Jackie Roosevelt Robinson from the Montreal Royals. He will report immediately."[37]

Mardo and Rodney were in the press box when another sportswriter tapped Mardo on the shoulder and said, "Robinson's a Dodger." Soon the news became official. Mardo stared at his typewriter but could not write anything. In his column the next day Mardo recalled when Robinson signed his contract with Montreal in October 1945 and began his first spring training in Sanford the following March. Mardo remembered the way Robinson handled the questions from reporters and how he took his first swings in the batting cage, knocking the third pitch into a pasture, nearly hitting a cow.[38] And, finally, Mardo remembered Robinson's first game of his International League season. He knew life would not be easy for Robinson, that racism awaited him in the big leagues just as it had in the minors. On this day, however, none of that mattered. "There's time tomorrow to remember that the good fight goes on. But, for today, let's just sit back and feel easy and warm. As that fellow in the press box said, 'Robinson's a Dodger' – and it's a great day, isn't it?"[39]

Notes

CHAPTER 1. *Fried Chicken and Hard-Boiled Eggs*

1. Rampersad, *Jackie Robinson*, 136.
2. Rowan and Robinson, *Wait Till Next Year*, 130–31.
3. Robinson, *Jackie Robinson*, 46.
4. Rowan and Robinson, *Wait Till Next Year*, 130–31.
5. Robinson, *Jackie Robinson*, 46.
6. Tygiel, *Baseball's Great Experiment*, 8.
7. Logan, "The Negro and the Post-War World," 5:540–49.
8. White, "A Rising Wind," in Aptheker, ed., *Documentary History of the Negro People*, 5:60.
9. Branch, *Parting the Waters*, 13.
10. Myrdal, *An American Dilemma*, 41.
11. Roark, "How Dixie Newspapers Handle the Negro," 34–35.
12. Lamb and Bleske, "Democracy on the Field," 58.
13. Tygiel, *Baseball's Great Experiment*, 9.
14. Frommer, *Rickey and Robinson*, 11–13.
15. *New York Times*, October 24, 1945.
16. Rampersad, *Jackie Robinson*, 136.
17. "The Pogrom at Columbia, Tennessee," in Aptheker, ed., *Documentary History of the Negro People*, 5:116. Also see Shapiro, *White Violence and Black Response*, 362–65.
18. Williams, *Thurgood Marshall*, 133.
19. "The Pogrom at Columbia, Tennessee," 5:116.
20. Williams, *Thurgood Marshall*, 133–34; and Brooks, *Walls Come Tumbling Down*, 56.
21. Williams, *Thurgood Marshall*, 133–34; and Brooks, *Walls Come Tumbling Down*, 56.
22. *Daily Worker*, March 9, 1946.
23. *Daily Worker*, March 9, 1946.
24. "The Pogrom at Columbia, Tennessee," 5:119.
25. Williams, *Thurgood Marshall*, 135.

26. *Chicago Defender*, March 9, 1946.

27. Williams, *Thurgood Marshall*, 134–35.

28. Brooks, *Walls Come Tumbling Down*, 57.

29. Williams, *Thurgood Marshall*, 135; and Brooks, *Walls Come Tumbling Down*, 57.

30. Williams, *Thurgood Marshall*, 138–41.

31. Robinson and Smith, *Jackie Robinson*, 65.

32. Robinson, *Jackie Robinson*, 40–43

33. Rowan and Robinson, *Wait Till Next Year*, 131.

34. Rampersad, *Jackie Robinson*, 111–12.

35. Robinson, *Jackie Robinson*, 46.

36. Rowan and Robinson, *Wait Till Next Year*, 132; Robinson and Duckett, *I Never Had It Made*, 40.

37. Rowan and Robinson, *Wait Till Next Year*, 132; Robinson and Duckett, *I Never Had It Made*, 40.

38. Rowan, *Wait Till Next Year*, 132; Robinson and Duckett, *I Never Had It Made*, 40.

39. Rowan, *Wait Till Next Year*, p, 133. See *Chicago Defender*, February 23, 1946.

40. Robinson and Duckett, *I Never Had It Made*, 41.

41. Rowan, *Wait Till Next Year*, 133.

42. *Chicago Defender*, February 23, 1946.

43. *Pittsburgh Courier*, March 9, 1946.

44. *Chicago Defender*, March 9, 1946.

45. *New York Times*, March 3, 1946.

46. *New York Daily News*, March 1, 1946, and *Montreal Gazette*, March 2, 1946.

47. *New York Daily News*, March 3, 1946.

48. *Chicago Defender*, March 9, 1946.

49. *Pittsburgh Courier*, April 13, 1946.

50. Robinson and Duckett, *I Never Had It Made*, 40–41.

51. Rowan and Robinson, *Wait Till Next Year*, 134; Billy Rowe, telephone interview with author, March 10, 1993.

52. Robinson and Duckett, *I Never Had It Made*, 42.

53. Rowan and Robinson, *Wait Till Next Year*, 134–35; Golenbock, *Bums*, 137.

54. Rowan and Robinson, *Wait Till Next Year*, 134–35.

55. Robinson and Duckett, *I Never Had It Made*, 42.

56. Rowan and Robinson, *Wait Till Next Year*, 136.

57. *Chicago Defender*, 16 March 1946.

58. *Chicago Defender*, 30 March 1946.

59. Wendell Smith, untitled article, Wendell Smith personal papers.

60. Wendell Smith, personal papers.

61. Wendell Smith, personal papers.

62. Branch Rickey to Wendell Smith, January 8, 1946, Wendell Smith personal papers.

63. Wendell Smith to Branch Rickey, January 14, 1946, Wendell Smith personal papers.

64. Billy Rowe, interview, March 10, 1993.

65. *Pittsburgh Courier*, March 9, 1946.

66. *Daytona Beach Sunday News-Journal*, November 13, 1988.

67. *Pittsburgh Courier*, March 9, 1946.

68. Faulkner, *Great Time Coming*, 128.

69. Faulkner, *Great Time Coming*, 128.

70. Billy Rowe, interview, March 10, 1993.

71. Billy Rowe, interview, March 10, 1993.

CHAPTER 2. *Jim Crow Baseball Must End*

1. *New York Times*, February 6, 1933.

2. *Sporting News*, February 16, 1933.

3. Quoted in *New York Daily News*, February 8, 1933.

4. *New York Daily News*, February 8, 1933.

5. *New York Daily News*, February 8, 1933.

6. *New York Daily News*, February 8, 1933.

7. Peterson, *Only the Ball Was White*, 57.

8. Rader, *Baseball*, 52.

9. *New York Daily News*, February 8, 1933.

10. *New York Daily News*, February 8, 1933.

11. *Pittsburgh Courier*, February 11, 1933.

12. *Pittsburgh Courier*, February 11, 1933.

13. *Pittsburgh Courier*, February 18, 1933.

14. *Pittsburgh Courier*, February 25, 1933.

15. *Pittsburgh Courier*, February 25, 1933.

16. *Pittsburgh Courier*, March 18, 1933.

17. *Pittsburgh Courier*, March 18, 1933.

18. Wiggins, "Wendell Smith," 6.

19. Wilson, "They Could Make the Big Leagues," 4:113–15.

20. *Philadelphia Tribune*, August 6, 1936. Quoted in Reisler, *Black Writers/Black Baseball*, 150–51.

21. *Chicago Defender*, August 6, 1938.

22. *Chicago Defender*, August 6, 1946.

23. *Norfolk Virginian-Pilot*, July 31, 1938.

24. *Sporting News*, August 4, 1938.

25. *Chicago Daily News*, July 30, 1938.

26. *Sporting News*, August 4, 1938.

27. *New York Herald Tribune* (Paris edition), July 31, 1938.

28. *New York Times*, July 30, 1938.

29. *Washington Post*, July 31, 1938.

30. *Washington Post*, August 1, 1938.

31. *Dayton Daily News*, November 6, 1948.

32. *Chicago Defender*, August 6, 1938.

33. *Chicago Defender*, August 20, 1938.

34. *Chicago Defender*, August 6, 1938.

35. *Amsterdam News*, August 13, 1938.

36. *Chicago Defender*, August 6, 1938; *New York Age*, August 13, 1938.

37. *Philadelphia Afro-American*, September 3, 1938.

38. *Philadelphia Tribune*, August 4, 1938.

39. Crepeau, "The Jake Powell Incident," 36.

40. *Chicago Defender*, August 27, 1933.

41. See Rusinack, "Baseball on the Radical Agenda." Also see Rusinack and Lamb, "Demand the End of Jim Crow in Baseball!"

42. Rusinack and Lamb, "Demand the End of Jim Crow in Baseball!" 3.

43. Lester Rodney, telephone interview with author, November 11, 1997.

44. Lester Rodney, interview, November 11, 1997.

45. *Sunday Worker*, August 16, 1936.

46. *Sunday Worker*, August 23, 1936.

47. Rusinack, "Baseball on the Radical Agenda," 31, 57.

48. Rampersad, *Jackie Robinson*, 55.

49. Pietrusza, *Judge and Jury*, 417.

50. Stout and Johnson, *Jackie Robinson*, 33.

51. Pietrusza, *Judge and Jury*, 418.

52. *Daily Worker*, July 17, 1942.

53. Bill Mardo, telephone interview with author, November 18, 1997.

54. Lester Rodney, interview, November 11, 1997.

55. Pietrusza, *Judge and Jury*, 418.

56. Campanella, *It's Good to Be Alive*, 95; Tygiel, *Baseball's Great Experiment*, 40.

57. Lester Rodney, interview, November 11, 1997.

58. Pietrusza, *Judge and Jury*, 418.

59. *Sporting News*, August 6, 1942.

60. Tygiel, *Baseball's Great Experiment*, 39.

61. Peterson, *Only the Ball Was White*, 169.

62. Tygiel, *Baseball's Great Experiment*, 39.

63. Quoted in Tygiel, *Baseball's Great Experiment*, 46.

64. Shirley Povich, telephone interview with author, July 8, 1996.

65. Kelley, "Jackie Robinson and the Press," 138.

66. *Sporting News*, April 11, 1941.

67. Crepeau, *Baseball: America's Diamond Mind*, 166.

68. *Sporting News*, August 6, 1942.

69. Peterson, *Only the Ball Was White*, 181.

70. Earl Brown, "The Detroit Race Riot of 1943," 4:449.

71. *Sunday Worker*, February 3, 1943. Quoted in Rusinack, "Baseball on the Radical Agenda," 171.

72. Duberman, *Paul Robeson*, 282.

73. Lacy and Newton, *Fighting for Fairness*, 42.

74. Lacy and Newton, *Fighting for Fairness*, 47.

75. Tygiel, *Baseball's Great Experiment*, 42.

76. *People's Voice*, April 14, 1945. Quoted in Reisler, *Black Writers/ Black Baseball*, 87.

77. *People's Voice*, April 14, 1945. Quoted in Reisler, *Black Writers/ Black Baseball*, 88.

78. Roeder, *Jackie Robinson*, 10.

79. Tygiel, *Baseball's Great Experiment*, 46.

80. Tygiel, *Baseball's Great Experiment*, 44.

81. *Pittsburgh Courier*, April 21, 1945.

82. Tygiel, *Baseball's Great Experiment*, 44.

83. Wendell Smith, untitled article, Wendell Smith personal papers.

84. Roeder, *Jackie Robinson*, 14.

85. Wendell Smith, untitled article, Wendell Smith personal papers.

86. Rowan and Robinson, *Wait Till Next Year*, 104; Rampersad, *Jackie Robinson*, 123; and Tygiel, *Baseball's Great Experiment*, 47.

87. Polmer, *Branch Rickey*, 161.

88. Rowan and Robinson, *Wait Till Next Year*, 104.

89. Rampersad, *Jackie Robinson*, 123.

90. Frommer, *Rickey and Robinson*, 103.

91. Wendell Smith, untitled article, Wendell Smith personal papers.

92. *Negro Baseball*, April 1945. Quoted in Tygiel, *Baseball's Great Experiment*, 64.

93. Wendell Smith, personal papers.

94. Frommer, *Rickey and Robinson*, 104–6; Tygiel, *Baseball's Great Experiment*, 59.

95. Lamb and Bleske, "Democracy on the Field," 53.

CHAPTER 3. *Rickey and Robinson Challenge Segregated Baseball*

1. *Montreal Daily Star*, October 23, 1945.

2. *Detroit Times*, October 24, 1945.

3. *New York Times*, October 24, 1945.

4. *Sporting News*, November 1, 1945.

5. *Philadelphia Inquirer*, October 24, 1945.

6. *New York Times*, October 24, 1945.

7. *Brooklyn Eagle*, October 24, 1945.

8. *New York World-Telegram*, October 24, 1945; *Detroit Times*, October 25, 1945; and *Chicago Defender*, October 27, 1945.

9. *New York World-Telegram*, October 24, 1945; *Detroit Times*, October 25, 1945; and *Chicago Defender*, October 27, 1945.

10. *Sporting News*, November 1, 1945.

11. *Chicago Defender*, November 10, 1945.

12. *Baltimore Afro-American*, November 10, 1945.

13. *Daily Worker*, October 26, 1945.

14. *Sporting News*, November 1, 1945; *Chicago Defender*, November 3, 1945; and Tygiel, *Baseball's Great Experiment*, 80.

15. *Sporting News*, November 1, 1945; *Chicago Defender*, November 3, 1945; and Tygiel, *Baseball's Great Experiment*, 80.

16. *Charleston News and Courier*, November 25, 1945.

17. *Miami Herald*, October 24, 1945.

18. Kelley, "Jackie Robinson and the Press," 139.

19. *Amsterdam News*, November 3, 1945. See Weaver, "The Black Press," 305–6.

20. *New York Herald-Tribune*, October 25, 1945.

21. *Chicago Defender*, November 10, 1945.

22. *Chicago Defender*, November 3, 1945.

23. *New York Age*, November 3, 1945.

24. *Sporting News*, November 1, 1945.

25. *Sporting News*, November 1, 1945.

26. *Pittsburgh Courier*, November 3, 1945.

27. *Pittsburgh Courier*, November 3, 1945.

28. *Baltimore Afro-American*, November 3, 1945.

29. *Baltimore Afro-American*, November 3, 1945.

30. *Baltimore Afro-American*, November 10, 1945.

31. Jackie Robinson to Wendell Smith, October 31, 1945, Wendell Smith personal papers.

32. *Daily Worker*, October 26, 1945.

33. *Daily Worker*, October 25, 1945.

34. *Daily Worker*, October 26, 1945.

35. *Daily Worker*, October 26, 1945.

36. *New York Times*, October 24, 1945.

37. *New York Times*, October 25, 1945.

38. *Sporting News*, November 1, 1945.

39. *New York Herald-Tribune*, October 24, 1945; *New York World-Telegram*, October 24, 1945; *New York Daily News*, October 24, 1945; and *New York Post*, October 24, 1945.

40. *New York World-Telegram*, October 26, 1946.

41. Sam Lacy, telephone interview, May 20, 1999.

42. *Pittsburgh Courier*, November 3, 1945.

43. *Daily Worker*, October 26, 1945.

44. *New York Herald Tribune*, October 25, 1945.

45. Quoted by Winterich, "Playing Ball," 12.

46. *Time*, November 5, 1946, 77; *Newsweek*, November 5, 1945,

63–64; *Saturday Review*, November 24, 1945, 12; *Life*, November 26, 1945, 77; *Opportunity*, January 1946, 41; and *Look*, November 27, 1945, 68.

47. Winterich, "Playing Ball," 12.

48. *Sporting News*, November 1, 1945.

49. *Sporting News*, November 1, 1945.

50. *New York World-Telegram*, October 26, 1946.

51. *Sporting News*, November 1, 1945.

52. *Sporting News*, November 1, 1945.

53. *Brooklyn Eagle*, October 24, 1945.

54. Tygiel, *Baseball's Great Experiment*, 88.

55. *Philadelphia Inquirer*, October 25, 1945.

56. *Pittsburgh Courier*, November 3, 1945.

57. Feller and Gilbert, *Now Pitching Bob Feller*, 140–41.

58. Tygiel, *Baseball's Great Experiment*, 76.

59. *Pittsburgh Courier*, November 10, 1945.

60. Tygiel, *Baseball's Great Experiment*, 78–79.

61. *Negro Digest*, March 1946, 41–43.

62. *Brooklyn Eagle*, October 24, 1945.

63. *Daytona Beach Evening News*, October 24, 1945.

64. *Deland Sun-News*, October 24, 1945.

65. *Chicago Defender*, November 3, 1945.

66. *Miami Herald*, October 24, 1945.

67. *Louisville Courier-Journal*, October 25, 1945.

68. *Charlotte Observer*, October 25, 1945.

69. *Atlanta Journal*, October 24, 1945.

70. *Detroit News*, October 26, 1946.

71. *Washington Post*, October 27, 1945.

72. *Washington Post*, October 27, 1945.

73. *Montreal Gazette*, October 25, 1945.

74. *New York Times*, October 24, 1945.

75. *Montreal Daily Star*, October 24, 1945.

76. *Pittsburgh Courier*, November 3, 1945.

77. *Montreal Gazette*, October 24, 1945.

78. *Montreal Gazette*, October 25, 1945.

79. *Washington Post*, October 28, 1945.

CHAPTER 4. *Robinson and Wright Take Their Game to Sanford*

1. *Chicago Defender*, February 23, 1946.
2. *Chicago Defender*, February 23, 1946.
3. *Pittsburgh Courier*, November 17, 1945.
4. Patterson, "We Charge Genocide," 5:34.
5. Patterson, "We Charge Genocide," 5:110–11.
6. Patterson, "We Charge Genocide," 5:34–36.
7. Woodward, *Strange Career of Jim Crow*, 120.
8. *Deland Sun-News*, October 24, 1945.
9. *Deland Sun-News*, October 24, 1945.
10. *Pittsburgh Courier*, March 9, 1946, 1, 16.
11. *Daytona Beach Evening News*, October 25, 1946.
12. Lamb and Bleske, "Democracy on the Field," 3.
13. *Daytona Beach Evening News*, October 30, 1946.
14. *Pittsburgh Courier*, November 3, 1945.
15. *Pittsburgh Courier*, 9 March 1946.
16. Mel Jones, telephone interview with author, July 16, 1996.
17. Tygiel, *Baseball's Great Experiment*, 103–4.
18. Rowan and Robinson, *Wait Till Next Year*, 39.
19. *Baltimore Afro-American*, March 16, 1946.
20. Barber and Creamer, *Rhubarb in the Catbird Seat*, 274.
21. Allen, *Jackie Robinson*, 77.
22. Rowan and Robinson, *Wait Till Next Year*, 139, 145.
23. Mann, *Jackie Robinson Story*, 142.
24. Lipman, *Mr. Baseball*, 142.
25. Mann, *Branch Rickey*, 230, 231.
26. Mann, *Branch Rickey*, 230, 231; Polmer, *Branch Rickey*, 177–78.
27. Mann, *Branch Rickey*, 230–32.
28. Rampersad, *Jackie Robinson*, 133.
29. Wendell Smith to Branch Rickey, December 19, 1946, Wendell Smith personal papers.
30. Branch Rickey to Wendell Smith, January 8, 1946, Wendell Smith personal papers.
31. Wendell Smith to Branch Rickey, January 14, 1946, Wendell Smith personal papers.
32. Wendell Smith, untitled article, Wendell Smith personal papers.

33. *Daily Worker*, January 30, 1946.

34. *Daily Worker*, January 30, 1946.

35. *Baltimore Afro-American*, March 16, 1946.

36. Tygiel, *Baseball's Great Experiment*, 103.

37. *Baltimore Afro-American*, February 9, 1946.

38. *Sporting News*, February, 7, 1946.

39. Ruck, "Baseball in the Caribbean," 606; Turner, *When the Boys Came Back*, 60–61.

40. Turner, *When the Boys Came Back*, 60–61.

41. *Sporting News*, February 28, 1946.

42. Mel Jones, interview, July 16, 1996.

43. Julian Stenstrom, interview (typed transcript), July 14, 1989. Sanford Museum, Sanford FL.

44. Julian Stenstrom, interview, July 14, 1989.

45. *New York Times*, February 6, 1933.

46. *Sporting News*, February 14, 1946.

47. *New York Times*, February 4, 1946.

48. *New York Times*, February 4, 1946.

49. *New York Times*, February 4, 1946.

50. Polmer, *Branch Rickey*, 186.

51. *Pittsburgh Courier*, February 23, 1946.

52. *Twentieth-Century American Sportswriters*, 270.

53. Fountain, *Sportswriter*, 247–48.

54. Williams, *Joe Williams Reader*, 203.

55. Fountain, *Sportswriter*, 247–48.

56. *New York World-Telegram*, February 19, 1946.

57. Mann, *Branch Rickey*, 234; Lipman, *Mr. Baseball*, 144.

58. *Sanford Herald*, February 8, 1946.

59. *Sanford Herald*, March 1, 1946.

60. Wendell Smith, untitled article, Wendell Smith personal papers.

61. Wendell Smith, untitled article, Wendell Smith personal papers.

62. *Pittsburgh Courier*, March 9, 1946.

63. *Washington Afro-American*, March 9, 1946.

64. *Pittsburgh Courier*, March 2, 1946.

65. *Daily Worker*, March 5, 1946.

66. *Sanford Herald*, February 23, 1997.

67. Sam Lacy, telephone interview with author, June 24, 1996.

68. *New York World-Telegram*, February 19, 1946.

69. *Montreal Gazette*, March 1, 1946; *New York Daily News*, March 1, 1946.

70. *New York Times*, March 1, 1946.

71. *Pittsburgh Courier*, March 9, 1946.

72. *Daytona Beach News-Journal*, June 28, 1987; Rust, *Get That Nigger Off the Field*, 68.

73. *Brooklyn Eagle*, March 1, 1946.

74. *Brooklyn Eagle*, March 1, 1946.

75. *Daytona Beach Evening News*, March 1, 1946.

76. *Chicago Defender*, March 9, 1946.

77. *Pittsburgh Courier*, March 2, 1946.

78. *Washington Afro-American*, March 9, 1946.

79. *Pittsburgh Courier*, March 2, 1946.

CHAPTER 5. *Robinson and Wright Flee Sanford by Sundown*

1. Rowan and Robinson, *Wait Till Next Year*, 137–38.

2. Robinson and Smith, *My Own Story*, 68.

3. *Brooklyn Eagle*, March 5, 1946.

4. *New York Herald Tribune*, March 5, 1946.

5. *Brooklyn Eagle*, March 5, 1946.

6. *Washington Afro-American*, March 9, 1946.

7. *Norfolk Journal and Guide*, March 9, 1946.

8. *Daytona Beach Morning Journal*, March 5, 1946.

9. Bill Mardo, interview, November 18, 1997.

10. *Daily Worker*, March 8, 1946.

11. *Daytona Beach Morning Journal*, March 5, 1946, and *Evening News*, March 5, 1946.

12. *Deland Sun News*, March 5, 1946.

13. *New York Times*, March 5, 1946.

14. *New York Daily News*, March 1, 1946.

15. *Brooklyn Eagle*, March 1, 1946.

16. Bob Daley's name has also been spelled "Daily," "Bailey," and "Daly" in different news stories. See *New York Times*, March 5, 1946; *Brooklyn Eagle*, March 5, 1946; and *New York Age*, March 16, 1946.

17. *New York Herald Tribune*, March 5, 1946.

18. *Daily Worker*, March 5, 1946.

19. *Washington Afro-American*, March 9, 1946.

20. *Brooklyn Eagle*, March 5, 1946.

21. *Sporting News*, March 7, 1946.

22. Robinson and Smith, *My Own Story*, 70.

23. *New York Times*, March 5, 1946.

24. *New York Herald Tribune*, March 5, 1946.

25. *New York Post*, March 5, 1946.

26. *Washington Afro-American*, March 9, 1946.

27. *New York Daily News*, March 5, 1946.

28. Robinson and Duckett, *I Never Had It Made*, 43.

29. Robinson and Duckett, *I Never Had It Made*, 43.

30. *Brooklyn Eagle*, March 1, 1946.

31. *Sporting News*, March 7, 1946.

32. *Pittsburgh Courier*, March 2, 1946.

33. Billy Rowe, interview, March 10, 1993.

34. Wendell Smith, untitled article, Wendell Smith personal papers.

35. Robinson and Smith, *My Own Story*, 72–73.

36. Robinson and Smith, *My Own Story*, 78; Robinson and Rowan, *Wait Till Next Year*, 142.

37. Robinson and Rowan, *Wait Till Next Year*, 142.

38. Shuba, informal presentation, 1996.

39. *Pittsburgh Courier*, April 13, 1946. See Lamb and Bleske, "Democracy on the Field," 55.

40. *Sanford Herald*, March 7, 1946.

41. Marshall, *Baseball's Pivotal Era*, 133.

42. *Sanford Herald*, February 23, 1997.

43. *Pittsburgh Courier*, March 9, 1946.

44. *Pittsburgh Courier*, March 9, 1946.

45. *Pittsburgh Courier*, March 9, 1946.

46. *Atlanta Daily World*, March 12, 1946.

47. Kirby, "The Roosevelt Administration and Blacks," 281.

48. Bethune, "My Secret Talks with FDR," 62.

49. Bethune, "Let the Voices Thunder," 5:151.

50. Charles, informal presentation, 1996.

51. Billy Rowe, interview, March 10, 1993.

52. *Daytona Beach News-Journal*, October 21, 1991.

53. Charles, informal presentation, 1996.

54. Charles, informal presentation, 1996.

55. *Daytona Beach Morning Journal*, March 7, 1946; *New York Times*, March 7, 1946.

56. *Baltimore Afro-American*, March 12, 1946; *Washington Afro-American*, March 23, 1946.

57. *Sporting News*, March 14, 1946.

58. *Pittsburgh Courier*, March 16, 1946.

59. Robinson and Smith, *My Own Story*, 76; Rowan and Robinson, *Wait Till Next Year*, 142–43.

60. *New York Daily News*, March 8, 1946.

61. Robinson and Smith, *My Own Story*, 76; Rowan and Robinson, *Wait Till Next Year*, 143.

62. Rowan and Robinson, *Wait Till Next Year*, 142.

63. Robinson and Smith, *My Own Story*, 77.

64. *Pittsburgh Courier*, March 16, 1946.

65. Robinson and Smith, *My Own Story*, 77.

66. *Pittsburgh Courier*, March 30, 1946; Rowan and Robinson, *Wait Till Next Year*, 144.

67. Robinson and Duckett, *I Never Made it Made*, 45.

68. Rowan and Robinson, *Wait Till Next Year*, 144.

69. Tygiel, *Baseball's Great Experiment*, 107.

70. Rampersad, *Jackie Robinson*, 145.

71. *Baltimore Afro-American*, March 11, 1946.

72. *Washington Afro-American*, March 11, 1946.

73. Sam Lacy, interview with author, May 22, 1995.

74. Sam Lacy, interview, May 20, 1999.

75. Reisler, *Black Writers/Black Baseball*, 12, 99; Sam Lacy, interview, May 20, 1999.

76. Sam Lacy, interview, May 20, 1999.

77. Sam Lacy, interview, May 20, 1999; Lacy and Newton, *Fighting for Fairness*, 45; and Pietrusza, *Judge and Jury*, 425.

78. Pietrusza, *Judge and Jury*, 426.

79. Lacy and Newton, *Fighting for Fairness*, 45

80. Lacy and Newton, *Fighting for Fairness*, 46.

81. Pietrusza, *Judge and Jury*, 426.

82. Lacy and Newton, *Fighting for Fairness*, 47–48.

83. Tygiel, *Baseball's Great Experiment*, 42.

84. Tygiel, *Baseball's Great Experiment*, 42.

85. Holway, *Voices from the Great Black Baseball Leagues*, 14; and Pietrusza, *Judge and Jury*, 417.

86. *Sporting News*, March 14, 1946.

87. *Atlanta Daily World*, March 16, 1946, and *Norfolk Journal and Guide*, March 23, 1946.

88. *Atlanta Daily World*, March 16, 1946.

89. *Brooklyn Eagle*, March 13, 1946.

90. *Sporting News*, March 21, 1946.

91. Tygiel, *Baseball's Great Experiment*, 109.

92. Berkow, *Red*, 109.

93. Berkow, *Red*, 108–9.

CHAPTER 6. *Robinson Takes the Field*

1. *Brooklyn Eagle*, March 17, 1946.

2. *New York Times*, March 17, 1946.

3. Robinson and Smith, *My Own Story*, 77.

4. *Brooklyn Eagle*, March 17, 1946.

5. *Daytona Beach Sunday News-Journal*, March 17, 1946.

6. Robinson and Smith, *My Own Story*, 78.

7. Robinson and Smith, *My Own Story*, 78.

8. Robinson and Duckett, *I Never Had It Made*, 46.

9. Allen, *Jackie Robinson*, 4.

10. *Daytona Beach Sunday News-Journal*, August 19, 1984.

11. *Daytona Beach Morning Journal*, August 19, 1984.

12. *New York Times*, March 17, 1946.

13. Billy Rowe, interview, March 10, 1993.

14. *New York Times*, March 17, 1946.

15. *New York Times*, March 18, 1946.

16. Robinson and Smith, *My Own Story*, 78.

17. *Daytona Beach Evening News*, March 18, 1946.

18. *New York Daily News*, March 18, 1946.

19. *New York Daily Mirror*, March 18, 1946.

20. *New York Times*, March 18, 1946.

21. Quoted in the *Daily Worker*, March 19, 1946.

22. *Brooklyn Eagle*, March 18, 1946.

23. *Sporting News*, March 21, 1946.

24. *Daytona Beach Evening News*, March 18, 1946.

25. The story appeared in many newspapers, including the *Florida Times-Union*, March 18, 1946; the *Tampa Tribune*, March 18, 1946; and the *Montreal Gazette*, March 18, 1946.

26. *Florida Times-Union*, March 18, 1946.

27. *New York Journal-American*, March 18, 1946.

28. *Brooklyn Eagle*, March 18, 1946.

29. *New York Daily Mirror*, March 18, 1946.

30. *Pittsburgh Courier*, March 23, 1946.

31. Robinson and Smith, *My Own Story*, 79.

32. *People's Voice*, March 23, 1946.

33. *Chicago Defender*, March 23, 1946.

34. *Washington Afro-American*, March 23, 1946.

35. *Norfolk Journal and Guide*, March 23, 1946.

36. *Pittsburgh Courier*, March 23, 1946.

37. *Pittsburgh Courier*, March 23, 1946.

38. *Pittsburgh Courier*, March 23, 1946.

39. *Pittsburgh Courier*, March 23, 1946.

40. *Pittsburgh Courier*, March 23, 1946.

41. *Pittsburgh Courier*, March 23, 1946.

42. *Chicago Defender*, March 9, 1946.

43. *Pittsburgh Courier*, March 23, 1946.

44. *Pittsburgh Courier*, March 23, 1946.

45. *Pittsburgh Courier*, March 16, 1946.

46. *New York Post*, March 22, 1946.

47. *New York Post*, March 22, 1946.

48. *Sporting News*, March 20, 1946.

49. *Daytona Beach Sunday News-Journal*, March 10, 1946.

50. *Atlanta Daily World*, March 17, 1946.

51. *People's Voice*, March 23, 1946.

52. Robinson and Duckett, *I Never Had It Made*, 44.

53. Robinson and Duckett, *I Never Had It Made*, 45.

54. Robinson and Duckett, *I Never Had It Made*, 45.

55. Golenbock, *Bums*, 137.

56. *Daily Worker*, March 9, 1946.

57. *Daytona Beach News-Journal*, June 29, 1987.

58. Strode, *Goal Dust*, 89.

59. Robinson and Rowan, *Wait Till Next Year*, 146.

60. Robinson and Smith, *My Own Story*, 74.

61. Robinson and Duckett, *I Never Had It Made*, 47; Rampersad, *Jackie Robinson*, 143.

62. Rampersad, *Jackie Robinson*, 144, 146.

63. *Pittsburgh Courier*, March 30, 1946.

64. *People's Voice*, March 23, 1946.

65. *Norfolk Journal and Guide*, March 23, 1946.

66. *Norfolk Journal and Guide*, March 23, 1946.

67. *Washington Afro-American*, March 23, 1946.

68. *People's Voice*, March 16, 1946.

CHAPTER 7. *Cheap Talk, Mexican Millionaires, and Eddie Klep*

1. Tim Cohane, "A Branch Grows in Brooklyn," *Look*, March 19, 1946, 72.

2. Mardo, "Robeson – Robinson," 102–3.

3. Cohane, "A Branch Grows in Brooklyn," 72.

4. Cohane, "A Branch Grows in Brooklyn," 70, 75.

5. *New York Daily News*, March 12, 1946.

6. *New York Daily News*, March 12, 1946.

7. *New York Daily Mirror*, March 20, 1946.

8. *New York Daily Mirror*, March 20, 1946.

9. *Sporting News*, March 28, 1946.

10. *Pittsburgh Courier*, March 30, 1946.

11. *Pittsburgh Courier*, March 30, 1946.

12. *Pittsburgh Courier*, March 30, 1946.

13. *Pittsburgh Courier*, March 30, 1946.

14. Simons, "Jackie Robinson and the American Zeitgeist," 80–81.

15. *People's Voice*, March 23, 1946.

16. *Washington Afro-American*, March 23, 1946.

17. *Daily Worker*, March 19, 1946.

18. *Daily Worker*, March 19, 1946.

19. Ruck, "Baseball in the Caribbean," 606.

20. Turner, *When the Boys Came Back*, 60–61.

21. *Daytona Beach Evening News*, March 10, 1946.

22. *Brooklyn Eagle*, March 20, 1946.

23. *Brooklyn Eagle*, March 20, 1946.

24. *Daily Worker*, March 21, 1946.

25. *New York Times*, March 20, 1946.

26. Turner, *When the Boys Came Back*, 61–62.

27. *New York Times*, April 10, 1946.

28. *Daytona Beach Evening News*, April 4, 1946.

29. Ruck, "Baseball in the Caribbean," 606.

30. *Washington Afro-American*, April 13, 1946.

31. *Amsterdam News*, April 6, 1946.

32. *Pittsburgh Courier*, May 6, 1944.

33. *Atlanta Daily World*, March 26, 1946; *People's Weekly*, March 30, 1946.

34. *Atlanta Daily World*, March 26, 1946.

35. Ashe, *Hard Road to Glory*, 93–95.

36. Barnett, "Ray Kemp Blazed Important Trail," 256.

37. *Chicago Defender*, September 29, 1934, and November 23, 1935. Quoted in Smith, "Outside the Pale," 257.

38. Smith, "Outside the Pale," 268–69.

39. Smith, "Outside the Pale," 268.

40. Brower, "Has Professional Football Closed the Door?" 272–74.

41. *Pittsburgh Courier*, January 12, 1946. Quoted in Smith, "Outside the Pale," 276.

42. Smith, "Outside the Pale," 277.

43. *Pittsburgh Courier*, March 30, 1946.

44. *Norfolk Journal and Guide*, March 30, 1946.

45. *Norfolk Journal and Guide*, March 30, 1946.

46. *Pittsburgh Courier*, March 18, 1946.

47. *Cleveland Call and Post*, March 23, 1946. For a detailed account on Eddie Klep, see Gerlach, "Baseball's Other 'Great Experiment.'"

48. Feldman, "He Was Out of His League," 89.

49. See Gerlach, "Baseball's Other 'Great Experiment.'"

50. *People's Voice*, April 6, 1946.

51. *Pittsburgh Courier*, April 13, 1946.

52. See Gerlach, "Baseball's Other 'Great Experiment.'"

53. *People's Voice*, April 6, 1946.

54. *Pittsburgh Courier*, April 13, 1946.

55. Feldman, "He Was Out of His League," 90; Gerlach, "Baseball's Other 'Great Experiment.'"

56. *Atlanta Daily World*, April 16, 1946.

57. Gerlach, "Baseball's Other 'Great Experiment.'"

58. Gerlach, "Baseball's Other 'Great Experiment.'"

59. Riley, *Biographical Encyclopedia*, 466.

60. Gerlach, "Baseball's Other 'Great Experiment.'"

CHAPTER 8. *Lights Out in Deland and Locked Gates in Jacksonville*

1. *New York Post*, March 22, 1946.

2. *Florida Times-Union*, March 20, 1946.

3. *Florida Times-Union*, March 20, 1946.

4. *Florida Times-Union*, March 23, 1946.

5. *New York Daily News*, March 21, 1946.

6. *New York Times*, March 22, 1946.

7. *New York Daily News*, March 22, 1946.

8. *Daytona Beach Evening News*, March 22, 1946.

9. *New York Daily News*, March 22, 1946.

10. *Montreal Gazette*, March 23, 1946; *Montreal Daily Star*, March 23, 1946; and *New York Times*, March 23, 1946.

11. *New York Daily News*, March 23, 1946.

12. *New York Times*, March 23, 1946.

13. *Daytona Beach Evening News*, March 23, 1946.

14. *New York Times*, March 23, 1946.

15. *New York Post*, March 22, 1946.

16. *New York Times*, March 22, 1946.

17. *Montreal Gazette* and *Montreal Daily Star*, March 23, 1946.

18. *Norfolk Journal and Guide*, March 30, 1946.

19. *Daytona Beach Morning Journal*, March 23, 1946.

20. *Montreal Gazette*, March 22, 1946, and March 23, 1946.

21. *Washington Afro-American*, March 23, 1946.

22. *Washington Afro-American*, March 23, 1946.

23. *People's Voice*, March 30, 1946.

24. *Pittsburgh Courier*, March 30, 1946.

25. *Pittsburgh Courier*, March 30, 1946.

26. *Brooklyn Eagle*, March 24, 1946.

27. *Daytona Beach Sunday News-Journal*, March 24, 1946.

28. *Montreal Gazette*, March 24, 1946.

29. *Norfolk Journal and Guide*, March 30, 1946.

30. *Pittsburgh Courier*, March 16, 1946.

31. *Pittsburgh Courier*, March 23, 1946.

32. *Pittsburgh Courier*, March 30, 1946.

33. *Pittsburgh Courier*, March 30, 1946.

34. *Pittsburgh Courier*, April 6, 1946.

35. *New York Age*, March 16, 1946.

36. *Daytona Beach Evening News*, March 23, 1946.

37. Mel Jones, interview, July 16, 1996.

38. *New York Daily Mirror*, March 26, 1946.

39. *Chicago Defender*, April 6, 1946.

40. *Deland Sun News*, April 9, 1946.

41. *Deland Sun News*, April 9, 1946.

42. *Florida Times-Union*, March 27, 1946

43. *Daytona Beach Morning Journal*, March 27, 1946.

44. *Florida Times-Union*, March 28, 1946.

45. *Daytona Beach Morning Journal*, March 28, 1946.

46. *Daytona Beach Morning Journal*, March 28, 1946.

47. Robinson and Smith, *My Own Story*, 79–80; Mel Jones, interview, July 16, 1996; Billy Rowe, interview, March 10, 1993.

48. Billy Rowe, interview, March 10, 1993.

49. *Daytona Beach Morning Journal*, March 29, 1946.

50. Mel Jones, interview, July 16, 1996.

51. Robinson and Smith, *My Own Story*, 80.

52. *Washington Afro-American*, April 6, 1946.

53. *Pittsburgh Courier*, April 6, 1946.

54. *Chicago Defender*, April 6, 1946.

55. *Chicago Defender*, April 6, 1946.

56. *Washington Afro-American*, March 30, 1946.

57. *Daily Worker*, April 1, 1946.

58. *Deland Sun-News*, March 29, 1946.

59. *Brooklyn Eagle*, March 29, 1946.

60. *Brooklyn Eagle*, March 29, 1946.

61. *Brooklyn Eagle*, March 29, 1946.

62. *New York Post*, March 26, 1946.

63. *New York Post*, March 26, 1946.

64. *Chicago Defender*, April 20, 1946.

65. *Daytona Beach Evening News*, April 4, 1946.

66. *New York Daily News*, April 7, 1946.

67. *New York Daily Mirror*, April 5, 1946.

68. *New York Journal-American*, April 13, 1946.

69. Wendell Smith personal papers.

70. Wendell Smith personal papers.

71. *Pittsburgh Courier*, April 13, 1946.

72. Tygiel, *Baseball's Great Experiment*, 110–11.

73. *Daytona Beach Evening News*, April 1, 1946.

74. *Brooklyn Eagle*, April 1, 1946.

75. *Daytona Beach Evening News*, April 4, 1946.

76. *Daytona Beach Evening News*, April 4, 1946.

77. *Deland Sun-News*, April 4, 1946.

78. *Deland Sun-News*, April 4, 1946.

79. Robinson and Duckett, *I Never Had It Made*, 55–56.

CHAPTER 9. *Integration Stands Its Ground against Southern Intolerance*

1. *Daytona Beach Morning Journal*, March 29, 1946.

2. *Daytona Beach Evening News*, April 1, 1946.

3. *Pittsburgh Courier*, April 6, 1946.

4. *Pittsburgh Courier*, April 6, 1946.

5. Mel Jones, interview, July 16, 1996.

6. Polmer, *Branch Rickey*, 178.

7. *Pittsburgh Courier*, April 6, 1946.

8. *Norfolk Journal and Guide*, April 13, 1946;

9. *Washington Afro-American*, April 6, 1946.

10. *People's Voice*, April 20, 1946.

11. *Montreal Daily Star*, April 9, 1946.

12. *Brooklyn Eagle*, April 7, 1946.

13. *Brooklyn Eagle*, April 3, 1946.

14. *Washington Afro-American*, April 6, 1946.

15. *Washington Afro-American*, April 6, 1946.

16. Billy Rowe, interview, March 10, 1993.

17. Turner, *When the Boys Came Back*, 49.

18. Roeder, *Jackie Robinson*, 81–82.

19. *Daytona Beach Morning Journal*, April 6, 1946.

20. *Montreal Gazette*, April 20, 1946. Quoted in Tygiel, *Baseball's Great Experiment*, 116.

21. *People's Voice*, April 13, 1946.

22. *People's Voice*, April 13, 1946.

23. *Daytona Beach Evening News*, April 7, 1946.

24. *Pittsburgh Courier*, April 13, 1946.

25. Robinson and Smith, *My Own Story*, 97–98.

26. *Montreal Gazette*, April 8, 1946.

27. *Sanford Herald*, January 13, 1991.

28. *Sanford Herald*, January 13, 1991.

29. *Sanford Herald*, February 23, 1997.

30. *Sanford Herald*, January 13, 1991.

31. *Sanford Herald*, January 6, 1991.

32. *New York Times*, April 5, 1946.

33. *New York Times*, April 5, 1946.

34. *Sporting News*, April 11, 1946, 6.

35. *Daily Worker*, April 6, 1946.

36. *Washington Afro-American*, April 13, 1946.

37. Riley, *Biographical Encyclopedia*, 147.

38. *Pittsburgh Courier*, April 13, 1946.

39. *People's Voice*, April 13, 1946.

40. *People's Voice*, April 20, 1946.

41. Campanella, *It's Good to Be Alive*, 109–11.

42. Campanella, *It's Good To Be Alive*, 114–16.

43. *Daily Worker*, April 6, 1946.

44. Ribowsky, *Complete History*, 285.

45. Riley, *Biographical Encyclopedia*, 638.

46. *Pittsburgh Courier*, April 6, 1946.

47. *Pittsburgh Courier*, April 13, 1946.

48. *Chicago Defender*, April 13, 1946.

49. *Pittsburgh Courier*, April 13, 1946.

50. *Washington Afro-American*, April 13, 1946.

51. *Daytona Beach Morning Journal*, April 6, 1946.

52. *Pittsburgh Courier*, April 13, 1946.

53. *Norfolk Journal and Guide,* April 13, 1946.

54. *Daily Worker,* April 11, 1946.

55. *Sporting News,* March 28, 1946.

56. *Daytona Beach Evening News,* April 8, 1946.

57. *Montreal Daily Star,* April 15, 1946.

58. *Montreal Daily Star,* April 16, 1946.

59. Williams, *Joe Williams Baseball Reader,* 203.

60. *Daily Worker,* April 11, 1946.

61. Kessler, *Dissident Press,* 40–42.

62. *Atlanta Daily World,* April 16, 1946.

63. *Pittsburgh Courier,* April 20, 1946.

64. *Pittsburgh Courier,* April 20, 1946.

65. *Pittsburgh Courier,* April 20, 1946.

66. *Pittsburgh Courier,* April 20, 1946.

67. *Daytona Beach Morning Journal,* September 15, 1990.

68. Billy Rowe, interview, March 10, 1993.

69. *Pittsburgh Courier,* April 6, 1946.

70. Robinson, *Jackie Robinson,* 51–52.

71. Billy Rowe, interview, March 10, 1993.

72. Allen, *Jackie Robinson,* 4.

CHAPTER 10. *Robinson Wins the Day during His First Game in Montreal*

1. Tygiel, *Baseball's Great Experiment,* 3–4; Rampersad, *Jackie Robinson,* 148.

2. Rowan and Robinson, *Wait Till Next Year,* 149.

3. Rampersad, *Jackie Robinson,* 149.

4. *Pittsburgh Courier,* April 27, 1946.

5. *New York Times,* April 19, 1946.

6. *Pittsburgh Courier,* April 27, 1946.

7. *Amsterdam News,* April 27, 1946.

8. *Daily Worker,* April 19, 1946.

9. Riley, *Biographical Encyclopedia,* 883–84.

10. *Pittsburgh Courier,* October 12, 1946. Quoted in Tygiel, *Baseball's Great Experiment,* 143.

11. Rampersad, *Jackie Robinson,* 157.

12. Patterson, "We Charge Genocide," 34–35.

13. Patterson, "We Charge Genocide," 37.

14. *Chicago Defender*, March 30, 1946.

15. "Filibustering Fair Employment," 5:101.

16. *Chicago Defender*, February 16, 1946.

17. *Pittsburgh Courier*, February 16, 1946.

18. *Pittsburgh Courier*, February 16, 1946.

19. *Pittsburgh Courier*, March 9, 1946.

20. Rampersad, *Jackie Robinson*, 7.

21. Billy Rowe, interview, March 10, 1993.

22. Tygiel, *Baseball's Great Experiment*, 119.

23. Rampersad, *Jackie Robinson*, 206–7.

24. *Chicago American*, November 9, 1961.

25. Sam Lacy, interview, June 24, 1996.

26. Bill Mardo, interview, November 18, 1997.

27. Fountain, *Sportswriter*, 247–48.

28. Lamb and Bleske, "Democracy on the Field," 58.

29. Lester Rodney, interview, November 11, 1997.

30. See *Free and Responsible Press*.

31. Thorn, *Baseball*, 25.

32. Rusinack and Lamb, "Demand the End of Jim Crow in Baseball!" 9.

33. Bill Mardo, interview, November 18, 1997.

34. Lester Rodney, interview, November 11, 1997.

35. Duffy, "Red Rodney," 22.

36. Rampersad, *Jackie Robinson*, 167.

37. Rampersad, *Jackie Robinson*, 167.

38. *Daily Worker*, April 11, 1947.

39. *Daily Worker*, April 11, 1947.

Bibliography

UNPUBLISHED SOURCES

Smith, Wendell. Personal Papers in National Baseball
  Hall of Fame Library and Museum, Cooperstown NY,
  and City of Sanford Museum, Sanford FL.

NEWSPAPERS AND MAGAZINES

Amsterdam (NY) News
Atlanta Daily World
Atlanta Journal
Augusta (GA) Chronicle
Baltimore Afro-American
Baton Rouge State Times
Birmingham (AL) News
Brooklyn (NY) Eagle
California Eagle
Charleston (SC) News and Courier
Charlotte (NC) Observer
Chicago American
Chicago Daily News
Chicago Defender
Chicago Daily Tribune
Daily Worker (NY)
Dayton (OH) Daily News
Dayton (OH) Forum
Dayton (OH) Journal
Daytona Beach (FL) Evening News
Daytona Beach (FL) Morning Journal
Deland (FL) Sun-News
Detroit News
Detroit Times

Bibliography

Greensboro (NC) Daily News
Jacksonville Florida Times-Union
Life
Look
Los Angeles Examiner
Los Angeles Times
Louisville (KY) Courier-Journal
Miami Herald
Michigan Chronicle
Montgomery (AL) Advertiser
Montreal (Canada) Daily Star
Montreal (Canada) Gazette
Negro Digest
New Jersey Afro-American
New Orleans Times-Picayune
Newsweek
New York Age
New York A. M.
New York Daily Mirror
New York Daily News
New York Herald Tribune
New York People's Weekly
New York Post
New York Sun
New York Times
New York World-Telegram
Norfolk (VA) Journal and Guide
Norfolk (VA) Virginian-Pilot
Opportunity
Orlando (FL) Morning Sentinel
Philadelphia Afro-American
Philadelphia Inquirer
Pittsburgh Courier
Portsmouth (OH) Times
Raleigh (NC) News and Observer
Sanford (FL) Herald Saturday Review
Savannah (GA) Morning News

Sporting News
Sports Illustrated
Tampa (FL) Tribune
The Crisis
The (Columbia SC) State
Time
Washington Afro-American
Washington Post

BOOKS AND JOURNALS

Allen, Murray. *Jackie Robinson: A Life Remembered*. New York: Franklin
Watts, 1987.
Aptheker, Herbert, ed. *A Documentary History of the Negro People of the
United States*, vols. 3–5. New York: Citadel, 1973–1974, 1993.
Ashe, Arthur. *A Hard Road to Glory: A History of the African-American
Athlete, 1919–1945*. New York: Amistad, 1988.
Barber, Red, with Robert Creamer, *Rhubarb in the Catbird Seat*. Garden
City NJ: Doubleday, 1968.
Barnett, Bob. "Ray Kemp Blazed Important Trail," *Coffin* Corner 5
(December 1983). Quoted in Thomas Smith, "Outside the Pale: The
Exclusion of Blacks from the National Football League, 1934–1946,"
Journal of Sport History 15 (Winter 1988).
Berkow, Ira, *Red*. New York: *New York Times*, 1986.
Bernstein, Barton J., and Allen J. Matusow, eds. *Twentieth-Century
America: Recent Interpretations*. New York: Harcourt, Brace,
Jovanovich, 1972.
Bethune, Mary McLeod. "My Secret Talks with FDR." In *The Negro
in Depression and War*, ed. Bernard Sternsher. Chicago: Quadrangle,
1969.
———. "Let the Voices Thunder Forth with Power." In *A Documentary
History of the Negro People in the United States*, ed. Herbert Aptheker,
vol. 5 (New York: Citadel, 1993).
Branch, Taylor. *Parting the Waters: America in the King Years, 1954–1963*.
New York: Simon and Schuster, 1988.
Brooks, Thomas. *Walls Come Tumbling Down: A History of the Civil Rights
Movement, 1940–1970*. Englewood Cliffs NJ: Prentice-Hall, 1974.

Brower, William. "Has Professional Football Closed the Door?" *Opportunity* 17 (September 1939): 375–77

Brown, Earl. "The Detroit Race Riot of 1943." In *A Documentary History of the Negro People of the United States*, ed. Herbert Aptheker, vol. 4. New York: Citadel, 1974.

Campanella, Roy. *It's Good to Be Alive*. New York: Signet, 1974.

Charles, Ed. Informal presentation, conference on fiftieth anniversary of Jackie Robinson's first spring training in baseball, Daytona Beach, Florida, March 17, 1996.

Commission on Freedom of the Press. *A Free and Responsible Press: A General Report on Mass Commission*. Chicago: University of Chicago Press, 1947.

Crepeau, Richard C. *Baseball's Diamond Mind*. Orlando: University of Central Florida, 1980.

———. "The Jake Powell Incident and the Press: A Study in Black and White," *Baseball History* (Summer 1986): 32–46.

Dorinson, Joseph, and Joram Warmund, eds. *Jackie Robinson: Race, Sports and the American Dream*. Armonk NY: M. E. Sharpe, 1998.

Duberman, Martin Bauml. *Paul Robeson*. London: Pan, 1991.

Duffy, Peter. "Red Rodney: The American Communist," *Village Voice*, June 10, 1997.

Faulkner, David. *Great Time Coming: The Life of Jackie Robinson, from Baseball to Birmingham*. New York: Simon and Schuster, 1995.

Feldman, Jay. "He Was Out of His League," *Sports Illustrated*, June 8, 1987, 89.

Feller, Bob, and Bill Gilbert. *Now Pitching, Bob Feller*. New York: Harper Collins, 1990.

"Filibustering Fair Employment (1946)." In *A Documentary History of the Negro People in the United States, 1945–1951*, ed. Herbert Aptheker, vol. 5 (New York: Citadel, 1993).

Fountain, Charles. *Sportswriter: The Life and Times of Grantland Rice*. New York: Oxford University Press, 1993.

Frommer, Harvey. *Rickey and Robinson: The Men Who Broke Baseball's Color Barrier*. New York: Macmillan, 1980.

Gerlach, Larry. "Baseball's Other 'Great Experiment': Eddie Klep and the Integration of the Negro Leagues." Paper presented at conference on fiftieth anniversary of Jackie Robinson's first spring training in baseball, Daytona Beach, Florida, March 17, 1996.

Golenbock, Peter. *Bums: An Oral History of the Brooklyn Dodgers.*
New York: G. P. Putnam's Sons, 1984.

Holway, John. *Voices from the Great Negro Baseball Leagues.* New York:
Dodd, Mead, 1975.

Kelley, William. "Jackie Robinson and the Press," *Journalism Quarterly* 53
(Spring 1976): 137–39.

Kessler, Lauren. *The Dissident Press.* Beverly Hills CA: Sage, 1984.

Kirby, John. "The Roosevelt Administration and Blacks: An Ambivalent
Legacy." In *Twentieth-Century America: Recent Interpretations*, ed.
Barton J. Bernstein and Allen J. Matusow. New York: Harcourt, Brace,
Jovanovich, 1972.

Lacy, Sam, and Moses J. Newton. *Fighting for Fairness: The Story of Hall
of Fame Sportswriter Sam Lacy.* Centreville MD: Tidewater, 1998.

Lamb, Chris. "'A Conspiracy of Silence': Mainstream Sportswriters
Provide Aid and Comfort to Professional Baseball's Color Line."
Paper presented at the Association for Education in Journalism and
Mass Communication annual conference, History Division,
Washington DC, August 2001.

———. "I Never Want to Take Another Trip Like This One," *Journal
of Sport History* 24 (Summer 1997): 177–91.

———. "Jackie Robinson Plays His First Game for the Montreal Royals,"
National Pastime: A Review of Baseball History 19 (1999): 20–23.

———. "L'affaire Jake Powell: The Minority Press Goes to Bat Against
Segregated Baseball," *Journalism and Mass Communication Quarterly* 76
(Spring 1999): 21–34.

——— "Making a Pitch for Equality: Wendell Smith and His Crusade to
Integrate Baseball." Paper presented at the Association for Education
in Journalism and Mass Communication annual conference, History
Division, New Orleans, Louisiana, August 1999.

——— "'What's Wrong With Baseball': The *Pittsburgh Courier* and the
Beginning of Its Campaign to Integrate Baseball," *Western Journal of
Black Studies* 26 (Winter 2002): 189–92.

Lamb, Chris, and Glen Bleske. "Democracy on the Field: The Black Press
Takes on White Baseball," *Journalism History* 24 (Summer 1998): 51–
59.

———. "The Road to October 23, 1945: The Press and the Integration of
Baseball," *Nine: A Journal of Baseball History and Social Policy Perspectives*
6 (Fall 1997): 48–68.

Lipman, David. *Mr. Baseball: The Story of Branch Rickey*. New York: G. P. Putnam's Sons, 1966.

Logan, Rayford. "The Negro and the Post-War World." In *A Documentary History of the Negro People of the United States*, ed. Herbert Aptheker, vol. 5. New York: Citadel, 1974.

Mann, Arthur. *The Jackie Robinson Story*. New York: Grosset and Dunlap, 1951.

———. *Branch Rickey: American in Action*. Boston: Houghton Mifflin, 1957.

Mardo, Bill. "Robeson – Robinson." In *Jackie Robinson: Race, Sports, and the American Dream*, ed. Joseph Dorinson and Joram Warmund. Armonk NY: M. E. Sharpe, 1998.

Marshall, William. *Baseball's Pivotal Era, 1945–1951*. Lexington: University of Kentucky Press, 1999.

Myrdal, Gunnar. *An American Dilemma: The Negro Problem and Modern Democracy*. New York: Harper and Row, 1962.

Orodenker, Richard, ed. *Twentieth-Century Sportswriters*. Detroit: Gale Research, 1993.

Patterson, William L. "We Charge Genocide." In *A Documentary History of the Negro People in the United States*, ed. by Herbert Aptheker, vol. 5. New York: Citadel, 1993.

Peterson, Robert. *Only the Ball Was White*. Englewood Cliffs NJ: Prentice Hall, 1970.

Pietrusza, David. *Judge and Jury: The Life and Times of Judge Kenesaw Mountain Landis*. South Bend IN: Diamond, 1998.

Polmer, Murray. *Branch Rickey, A Biography*. New York: Signet, 1982.

Rader, Benjamin. *Baseball: A History of America's Game*. Champaign: University of Illinois Press, 1992.

Rampersad, Arnold. *Jackie Robinson*. New York: Alfred Knopf, 1997.

Reisler, Jim. *Black Writers/Black Baseball*. Jefferson NC: MacFarland, 1995.

Ribowsky, Mark. *A Complete History of the Negro Leagues, 1884–1955*. New York: Birch Lane, 1995.

Riley, James. *The Biographical Encyclopedia of the Negro Baseball Leagues*. New York: Carroll and Graf, 1994.

Roark, Eldon. "How Dixie Newspapers Handle the Negro," *Negro Digest* (June 1946): 34–35.

Robinson, Jackie, and Alfred Duckett. *I Never Had It Made*. New York: Fawcett, Crest, 1974.

Robinson, Jackie, and Wendell Smith. *Jackie Robinson: My Own Story*. New York: Greenberg, 1948.

Robinson, Rachel. *Jackie Robinson: An Intimate Portrait*. New York: Harry Abrams, 1996.

Roeder, Bill. *Jackie Robinson*. New York: A. S. Barnes, 1950.

Rogosin, William Donn. "Black Baseball: Life in the Negro Leagues." Ph.D. diss., University of Texas, Austin, 1981.

Rowan, Carl T., with Jackie Robinson. *Wait Till Next Year*. New York: Random House, 1960.

Ruck, Rob. "Baseball in the Caribbean." In *Total Baseball*, ed. John Thorn and Pete Palmer. New York: Warner, 1989.

Rusinack, Kelly. "Baseball on the Radical Agenda: The Daily and Sunday Worker on the Desegregation of Major League Baseball, 1933 to 1947." Master's thesis, Clemson University, Clemson, South Carolina, 1995.

Rusinack, Kelly, and Chris Lamb. "'Demand the End of Jim Crow in Baseball!' The Communist Daily Worker's Crusade Against the National Pastime." In *Cultural Logic: An Electronic Journal of Marxist Theory and Practice* 2 (Fall 2000).

Rust, Art. *Get That Nigger Off the Field*. New York: Delacorte, 1992.

Rutkoff, Peter, ed. *The Cooperstown Symposium on Baseball and American Culture*. Jefferson NC: MacFarland, 2000.

Shapiro, Herbert. *White Violence and Black Response*. Amherst: University of Massachusetts Press, 1988.

Shuba, George. Informal presentation, conference on fiftieth anniversary of Jackie Robinson's first spring training in baseball, Daytona Beach, Florida, March 17, 1996.

Simons, William. "Jackie Robinson and the American Mind: Journalistic Perceptions of the Reintegration of Baseball." *Journal of Sport History* 12 (Spring 1985): 39–64.

———. "Jackie Robinson and the American Zeitgeist." In *The Cooperstown Symposium on Baseball and American Culture*, ed. Peter Rutkoff. Jefferson NC: McFarland, 2000.

Smith, Thomas. "Outside the Pale: The Exclusion of Blacks from the National Football League, 1934–1946," *Journal of Sport History* 15 (Winter 1988).

Smith, Wendell. Articles in *Pittsburgh Courier*, 1946.

Sternsher, Bernard, ed. *The Negro in the Depression*. Chicago: Quadrangle, 1969.

Stout, Glenn, and Dick Johnson. *Jackie Robinson: Between the Baselines*. San Francisco: Woodford, 1997.

Strode, Woody. *Goal Dust*. New York: Madison, 1990.

Thorn, John. *Baseball: Our Game*. New York: Penguin, 1955.

Thorn, John, and Pete Palmer, eds. *Total Baseball*. New York: Warner, 1989.

Turner, Frederick. *When the Boys Came Back*. New York: Henry Holt, 1995.

Tygiel, Jules. *Baseball's Great Experiment*. New York: Oxford University Press, 1997.

Washburn, Patrick. "New York Newspapers and Jackie Robinson's First Season," *Journalism Quarterly* 58 (Winter 1981): 640–44.

Weaver, Bill L. "The Black Press and the Assault on Professional Baseball's 'Color Line,' October 1945–April 1947," *Phylon* 40, no.2 (Winter 1979): 303–17.

White, Walter. "A Rising Wind." In Aptheker, *Documentary History*, vol. 5.

Wiggins, David K. "Wendell Smith, The *Pittsburgh Courier-Journal* and the Campaign to Include Blacks in Organized Baseball," *Journal of Sport History* 10 (Summer 1983): 5–29.

Williams, Juan. *Thurgood Marshall: An American Revolutionary*. New York: Random House, 1998.

Williams, Peter. *The Joe Williams Reader*. Chapel Hill NC: Algonquin, 1989.

Wilson, W. Rollo. "They Could Make the Big Leagues." In *A Documentary History of the Negro People in the United States*, ed. Herbert Aptheker, vol. 4. New York: Citadel, 1974.

Winterich, J. T. "Playing Ball: Negroes in Organized Baseball," *Saturday Review*, November 24, 1945, 12.

Woodward, C. Vann. *The Strange Career of Jim Crow*. New York: Oxford University Press, 1974.

Index